NINE CRISES

NINE CRISES

FIFTY YEARS OF COVERING
THE BRITISH ECONOMY FROM
DEVALUATION TO BREXIT

WILLIAM KEEGAN

Biteback Publishing

First published in Great Britain in 2019 by
Biteback Publishing Ltd
Westminster Tower
3 Albert Embankment
London SE1 7SP
Copyright © William Keegan 2019

ISBN 978-1-78590-304-5

10 9 8 7 6 5 4 3 2 1

A CIP catalogue record for this book is available from the British Library.

Set in Adobe Caslon Pro

Printed and bound in Great Britain by
CPI Group (UK) Ltd, Croydon CR0 4YY

MIX
Paper from
responsible sources
FSC® C020471

To my wife, Hilary Stonefrost, and my children

CONTENTS

INTRODUCTION

My interest in the economy was aroused partly by a desire to understand the political debate and partly by a distaste for translating Greek and Latin texts. The time was the 1950s. The newspapers were full of news of Britain's economic problems – *plus ça change* – and I wanted to understand what I read in the papers – or, at least, to understand more.

The connection with Greek and Latin texts was this: I had been a member of the Classical Sixth at my grammar school, Wimbledon College, and had been accepted to read the Classical Tripos at Trinity College, Cambridge. But, while I have been ever grateful to those Jesuits at Wimbledon for introducing me to – or foisting upon me – classical literature, and although I appreciated the prose and the poetry, I struggled with translation. In particular, composing Greek and Latin verse – which one was required to do in those days – was definitely not for me. Moreover, I knew in my heart of hearts that what had got me into Cambridge was not my Greek or Latin, but ancient history.

Indeed, history is my favourite subject. It embraces everything – which philosophy did in Ancient Greece. But just as I did not wish to ruin my love of English literature by reading it as a discipline, I felt that I could study history for the rest of my life, whereas, if I did not have a go at economics, I probably never would.

In those far-off days of the 1950s, the male youth of the nation, if pronounced medically fit, were required to do two years' National Service, in the army, navy or air force. While I was doing my basic training at Catterick Camp, Yorkshire, in the 5th Royal Tank Regiment, I attended an evening course of lectures on economics given by an economist from Hull University. I duly took notes, but by the evening, a day of intense drill on the parade ground had taken its toll, and I fear that not much of what I heard sank in. I became aware of this with a vengeance many years later, when I came across my notebook for that course. This was well after I had left Cambridge. It was clear that the lectures by the academic from Hull had been first rate. But sink in they had not. An embarrassing illustration of my economic ignorance at the time – and, it has to be said, of everybody else present on the occasion – was provided during a casual discussion in the officers' mess at HQ Northern Ireland Command, where I was posted in 1958–59.

A certain captain opined, 'If the economy is in such a state, why don't they just print more money?' 'Yes,' we all seemed to think, 'just give us more money and we won't feel so broke.'

Now, little did those present know it, but we had stumbled upon one of the burning issues of macroeconomic policy, which was being debated at a high level at the time and has been furiously debated ever since.

Money has to be backed by real goods and services. One of the favourite questions asked of fresh students of economics is: what would happen if you doubled the money supply? (Or, more strictly, the stock of money.) The short answer is that unless this were to be accompanied by a doubling of output of goods and services, there would be a doubling of the price level – 'too much money chasing too few goods'.

Nevertheless, those officers in HQ Northern Ireland Command may have had a naive view of the economic problem – I know I certainly did – but what successive governments and Treasury and Bank of England officials were struggling with then, and have been struggling with ever since, is the question of how to conduct economic policy so as to achieve an optimal balance between movements in output, employment and inflation.

The officers' mess 'just print more money' school does not seem so naive if the economy is heavily depressed and machines, service equipment and – above all – people are lying idle when there is latent demand for the goods and services they are potentially able to produce. More money, via increases in government spending, tax cuts or lower interest rates, is just what is required in such circumstances, as was vividly demonstrated during the Great Recession of 2008–09, which was induced primarily by the world financial crisis.

Nevertheless, steering the economy is not that simple, as I was to discover from my economics supervisors and lecturers at Cambridge, and during my subsequent career in financial journalism.

I confess that there are many aspects of economics that do not appeal to me. My interest has always been in 'political economy', the relationship between economics and politics, and the discussions and battles that go on in public and private between economists and policymakers. This involves a close study of the relationships between the most senior people responsible for economic policy decisions – namely, the Prime Minister (who is also, after all, the First Lord of the Treasury), the Chancellor and the Governor of the Bank of England, and their advisers.

These men or women may be ultimately responsible for the big economic policy decisions in our democracy – with the approval, if they deign to seek it, of Parliament – but they are only 'in charge' up to a point. They are, as former Prime Minister Harold Macmillan once said, at the mercy of 'events'. Macmillan, when asked what he feared most, replied: 'The opposition of events.' This subsequently became 'The opposition of events, dear boy, events.' The 'dear boy' was apparently not actually said by Macmillan, but it did sound like him. Such great remarks become clichés for a good reason. They strike a chord. His comment was also a dig at the weakness of the opposition.

'Events' can include the impact of wars or other military operations – Suez in 1956; the Falklands in 1982 – and what economists call 'shocks': the two oil crises of the 1970s; the unexpected financial crash of 2007–09; and, more recently, Brexit.

The Queen, not known for her views on economic policy, became celebrated in November 2008 for her observation about the unanticipated nature of the crash. 'Why', she asked, when opening a new wing of the London School of Economics, 'did nobody notice it?'

This gave me a golden opportunity when, shortly afterwards, I was awarded the CBE and found myself in front of the monarch, who looked at me and said, 'And what do *you* do?'

'I write about the economy for *The Observer* newspaper,' I replied. There was a brief silence. Then I added, 'I was one of the people who didn't warn you.'

PART I

CAMBRIDGE, FLEET STREET AND THE BANK OF ENGLAND

CAMBRIDGE

Before I embarked on economics, I had a brief brush with the law. I read part of a book by a distinguished academic lawyer, Glanville Williams, but could rustle up little enthusiasm for the subject. My memory, probably distorted, is that at some stage close to page 90 the author suggests that if by now the reader is bored, he should certainly not contemplate reading law.

This was during the year I spent teaching, between the end of my National Service in 1959 and going up to Cambridge in October 1960. It was during a spell teaching English in La Tour-de-Peilz, near Vevey, Switzerland, that I met another prospective Cambridge undergraduate, David Simons, who was working as a *stageur* at the Nestlé headquarters there.

David told me that the American (strictly, Canadian) economist J. K. Galbraith had come down from the Swiss mountains to give a lecture, and how impressive he was. Not only was Galbraith 6ft 8in. tall; he had written a book, *The Affluent Society*, which was seriously critical of the conventional economics that I was about to study.

There was no shortage of affluence in the Vevey region at the time. Among the local residents we were to see at the expats' favourite café (Les Trois Rois, long since transformed into a bank) were Charlie Chaplin, Peter Ustinov and Van Johnson. Vladimir Nabokov lived in Montreux. But the 'affluent society' Galbraith was writing about was the USA, about which he made his celebrated criticism of the contrast between 'private opulence' and 'public squalor'.

This was also the book in which Galbraith coined the term, and berated, the 'conventional wisdom'. Galbraith was a Keynesian who believed in the power of governments to intervene beneficently in the economy, to influence the level of output and employment. He had it in for the classical economists, who believed in the automatic steadying influence of market forces. He reserved especial contempt for the adherents of 'Say's Law' – the belief, after the nineteenth-century French economist Jean-Baptiste Say, that 'supply creates its own demand'. Galbraith's tirade did not make him popular with many of his fellow economists.

I read *The Affluent Society* while in Switzerland, and it was under Galbraith's influence that I arrived in Cambridge. Years later, one of my former supervisors, Amartya Sen, by this time Master of Trinity (and winner of the Swedish Riksbank/Nobel Prize for Economics – a prize instituted by the Swedish central bank and in a different category from the other Nobel Prizes), invited me to toast the health of the college at a commemorative feast. This was a great honour, and I was doubly touched when Professor Sen introduced me by saying, 'I always felt that

William Keegan was a pupil who was suspicious of economics.' Yes, indeed.

There was not a great gulf between the Keynesian economics taught in Cambridge at the time and what I had picked up from Galbraith. Keynes himself had dominated Cambridge, and Galbraith had been there briefly in the 1930s, in Keynes's heyday. (The veteran British politician Roy Hattersley told me that he was once dining with Galbraith and his wife Kitty, and the great man said meeting Keynes had been the greatest day of his life. To which his wife rejoined, 'Today is our 50th wedding anniversary.') But there was an awful lot of basic economics – demand curves, supply curves, the economics of 'the firm' (not the Mafia) – which was pretty dry stuff to me. It was the macro picture that interested me most and, heretically for most economists, I preferred words to charts and diagrams.

Words? Yes. From the age of about seven I had wanted to be a journalist. I helped to produce a class newspaper at my primary school – on the classroom wall – and circulated an 'underground' newspaper (handwritten) at Wimbledon College, entitled *The Weekly Wail*.

But my great juvenile breakthrough was having a series of short essays printed in the *Cork Weekly Examiner* when I was eleven and in my first year at Wimbledon College. My mother had been born in Cork City, and maintained strong links. The publication of these essays – or 'compositions', as we used to call them at my primary school – was a significant event in shaping my ambition to be a journalist. For my younger brother Victor and me, there was a certain glamour in newspapers. We got to know the news vendors outside Raynes Park Station – there were three, in the days when London boasted three evening newspapers, the *News*, *Star* and *Standard*, with multiple editions. We used to help the news vendors by going up to the platforms and collecting the bunches – 'quires' – of newspapers dumped on the platform by the guard. We just loved newspapers, subsequently graduating to paper rounds.

In those days, most boys wanted to grow up to be footballers or engine drivers, but I felt newspapers were already in my blood. The sense of achievement about those essays in the *Cork Weekly Examiner* was only slightly diminished when my mother told me that one of her cousins was a sub-editor on the paper. He might just have had a hand in their publication. At Cambridge, in the hope of eventually attracting the attention of Fleet Street, I wrote for various undergraduate publications. I ventured to write to the editor of the old *Daily Herald* suggesting he should start a satirical column, and offered him a sample. Back came the most courteous of rejection letters, encouraging words and a postal order for ten pounds.

My obsession with words was not necessarily shared by economists. I found that most economists seemed to have a natural inclination to produce the words only after they had constructed the diagrams and compiled the tables. They just loved charts. And economics was becoming increasingly mathematical. I was greatly relieved by the story told by a friend of mine, the late Sir Dennis Proctor, who had been a friend of Keynes. Proctor, a classicist, had asked Keynes, a mathematician, 'Maynard, does one have to be a mathematician to understand economics?'

'No, Dennis,' came the reply, 'but one does need a sense of proportion.'

When I arrived at Trinity in October 1960, an early port of call were the rooms of Alan Ker, the Classics don, who was also my 'moral tutor'. Moral tutors, in addition to teaching, kept an avuncular eye on the behaviour and well-being of their charges.

Looking up from a sheaf of papers, Ker peered over his half-moon spectacles and said, in a puzzled tone, 'Keegan, I see you completed your National Service in 1959. Why did you not come up last year? You should have got in touch with us.' But those were deferential days: I had not dared to do so. They had offered me a place for 1960! And, in any case, I rather enjoyed that year of teaching. I then told Mr Ker that I wished to switch from his subject to economics, and he could hardly have been more understanding.

Despite my suspicions about many areas of economics, it was a fantastic time to be at Cambridge. In addition to the renowned Amartya Sen, among my supervisors was Maurice Dobb, an unrepentant communist who was the great expert on all those Soviet five-year plans. Dobb was a kindly gentleman in tweeds. He gave excellent one-to-one supervisions (as we call tutorials in Cambridge) in his comfortable rooms in Trinity's Nevile's Court, with a glass of sherry often included. It was a shock to be told later that he had almost certainly been a recruiter of Soviet spies. But this intelligence fitted all too well with the fact that three of the notorious 'Cambridge Five' – Blunt, Burgess and Philby – had been Trinity men. This presented me with an opening line when I toasted the health of Trinity at that commemoration feast: 'Well, here we are again, back at Spy College.'

Frank Hahn, a mathematical economist who was very under-standing towards those of us less interested in abstract theory, also taught me. The seemingly most theoretical economists, like Hahn, were very good at descending to lower levels and having heated discussions about the kind of practical macroeconomic problems that most interested the likes of me.

Many of the great names associated with Keynes were still there – not least legendary figures such as Richard Kahn, who made a valuable contribution to Keynes's work via the theory of the 'multiplier', which demonstrated how initial increases in public spending or reductions in taxation could have a greater impact than the nominal cost implied, via 'multiplier' ripples through the rest of the economy. (During what I regarded as the mistaken policies of austerity adopted after 2010, one saw the 'reverse' or negative multiplier at work.)

Another future Nobel Prize-winner was the gentle and un-assuming James Meade, who had worked in Whitehall during the war and was an expert on international trade. I got to know him years later but was somewhat disappointed by his lectures because he had just been advising the government of Mauritius, and the subject of the Mauritian economy and its dependence on sugar had become an obsession with him. When he won the Nobel Prize in 1977, Donald Trelford, my editor at *The Observer*, asked me to see if Meade would write an article for us. Although Professor Meade was only too keen to offer newspaper articles in due course, on this occasion he politely declined, saying he had received over 450 letters from around the world, to all of which he was replying by hand.

In subsequent years, when he had completed his Herculean letter-writing task, I was honoured but slightly shocked when the great man invited me to lunch at Cambridge and told me that he had been advised to contact economic journalists such as Sir Samuel Brittan and myself to get his ideas across.

Back to Professor Kahn, whose lectures were fascinating. He would use them to attack the 1957–58 chancellorship of Peter Thorneycroft, who had fallen out with his Prime Minister, Harold Macmillan, over the latter's refusal to cut public spending and had resigned along with two Treasury ministerial colleagues.

Kahn would fulminate against Thorneycroft as if he were some kind of monster. Decades later, it turned out that when the newly ennobled Lord Thorneycroft was chairman of the Conservative Party under Mrs Thatcher, he proved to be one of the so-called wets who harboured doubts about her approach.

It seems incredible now, when unemployment was so recently in the 7 to 8 per cent range for a prolonged period following the onset of the financial crisis, that Kahn and others used to attack Professor Frank Paish of the London School of Economics for arguing that an unemployment rate of 2 to 2.5 per cent was necessary in order to keep inflation under control.

One of the towering figures of Cambridge economics at the time was Professor Nicholas (Nicky) Kaldor – later a Labour life peer – who subsequently incurred much opprobrium in the largely Conservative (and xenophobic) British press as one of the two 'Hungarians' who were brought in from academia to advise the 1964–70 Wilson governments. The other was Thomas Balogh; Denis Healey, then Defence Secretary, used to refer to them as Buda and Pest.

After the post-1945 reconstruction had taken place, when wartime controls had been abandoned and (virtually) full employment achieved, the big macroeconomic obsession in the UK became the rate of economic growth and how to boost it. Kaldor produced various growth models and I vividly recall an evening lecture in Mill Lane, Cambridge, in the early 1960s when the veteran economist Sir Dennis Robertson made fun of 'Kaldor Mark I' and 'Kaldor Mark II' in front of an audience of the great and the good which included Kaldor himself in the front row.

The Cambridge Economics Faculty was riven with personal feuds. It was Henry Kissinger, when asked why academic disputes were so fierce, who liked to say, 'Because the stakes are so low.' Galbraith knew Kissinger at Harvard and was a vehement opponent of Kissinger over the Vietnam War. Many years later, Galbraith was asked why Kissinger had such a strong Teutonic accent when his elder brother had no trace of a German accent. 'It's quite simple,' said Galbraith. 'Henry never listens.'

Anyway, from my point of view, suspicious of economics or not, I was happily immersed at Cambridge in the Keynesian tradition. After the Depression and the protectionism of the interwar years, it was considered the duty of governments and central banks to intervene in the economy to maximise output and employment, and Keynes and Cambridge had furnished governments with the theory and policy tools with which to do so.

Given my long-nurtured ambition to go into journalism, and my interest in political economy, it was a natural step to attempt economic or financial journalism. Early in 1963, I wrote to Richard Fry, the financial editor of *The Guardian*, whose commentaries I admired.

Fry was a naturalised Austrian, with a very high reputation. His office fixed an appointment for 3 p.m., and I knew I was being introduced to the world of journalism when his secretary said, on my arrival on the appointed day, 'Oh, please wait here. Mr Fry is not back from lunch yet.'

When the great man arrived, he was in a genial mood. After a few formalities, he asked me whether I had ever read Gibbon. I gave an 'up to a point' answer and he said, 'You must read Gibbon. I have just been having lunch with Oliver Lyttelton, and we agreed how good Gibbon is for one's prose style.'

Lyttelton, a distinguished public figure (later Lord Chandos), was a prominent Conservative at the time. Lunch with such important people? This sounded like the life.

FLEET STREET

After a most enjoyable talk – a very soft interview – Fry said he would like to offer me a job but had no vacancies at the moment. He suggested that I should write to Gordon Newton, editor of the *Financial Times* (*FT*) and Patrick Sergeant, City editor of the *Daily Mail*.

I duly did so and was offered interviews by both. The first was with Newton, at the red-brick Bracken House, diagonally opposite St Paul's Cathedral. This was the building occupied by the *FT* for many decades before its headquarters crossed over the Thames to One Southwark Bridge, but to which it is now due to return. It was designed by the architect Albert Richardson and, like most modern architecture, was the subject of great controversy at the time. But the beauty of it was that it was not all that modern. It proved an agreeable place in which to work – in my case for ten years.

My interview with Gordon Newton took place in his first-floor office, with a pleasant view of St Paul's. I was asked to bring examples of my undergraduate journalism. Newton had a great air of authority – indeed, frightened a lot of people. He was of medium height, bespectacled and with a permanently suntanned, rather wizened face. After greeting me, he got behind his desk and went through my cuttings. There were two interruptions: first, when someone rang him and he said, with great gravity, 'The shares of C. A. Parsons may be worth looking at.' This was clearly meant to impress me, and it did for a brief time, until I told the story later that day to an old school friend, Alastair Macdonald, who said, 'The Lex column tipped C. A. Parsons this morning.'

The second interruption was the arrival of Michael Shanks,

a celebrated *FT* journalist of the time, who had written a best-selling Penguin entitled *The Stagnant Society*. The mere presence of Shanks impressed me, and it was clear that Newton loved treating him nonchalantly as a typical member of his staff, not a celebrity.

When Shanks had gone, Newton carefully put one group of my cuttings on the left side of his desk, and the other on the right. 'I liked these,' he sniffed. 'But I don't like those.' 'Those' were my favourites. He went on, pointing to an article that I by no means regarded as the pick of the bunch. '*This* could easily be an *FT* feature.' It was an article about the early days of 'fashion models', in which I had written, 'Not all male models are model males.'

It was left that I should be hearing from him.

A few weeks later, I was summoned back. When I entered his office – it was a large one – he surprised me by saying, 'Just walk up and down, will you?' I did, and, after a pause, the editor of the *Financial Times* said, 'That'll do. I just wanted to take another look at you.' There was another pause and he went on, 'I think we can offer you a job,' adding ominously, 'There's just one other person.'

My third summons was to meet the managing director, Lord Drogheda. Drogheda had an effete, rather languid manner. The first I knew that I had got the job was when Drogheda said, 'One problem you will find here is that it's a long way from the West End. You can't just wander out at lunchtime and buy a picture.'

Well, I never did go to the West End to buy a picture, but I went there often for lunch. It was drummed into me that lunch with politicians, officials, businessmen and City figures was an important part of the job. In effect, I was told to go out and spend the company's money cultivating contacts.

The offer of a job at the *FT* was good in one sense but bad in another. Many of my fellow undergraduates were working hard in order to get the best qualifications to impress future employers. But my offer, which I immediately accepted, came in the springtime of my final year, and I fear that I subsequently became rather less diligent in my studies.

But there was another offer. Richard Fry's advice had been amazing. I went to see Patrick Sergeant at the City offices of the *Daily Mail* – a Dickensian office in Angel Court. Sergeant, too, offered me a job. When I said that I had accepted one at the *FT*, he offered me a summer relief job during July and August, to deputise for staff who went away. I snapped this up, because even in those far-off pre-top-up-fees days, students usually ran up debts.

But there was yet another offer. I joined the *FT* in the first week of October 1963, during the same week as Reginald Dale, who became a senior *FT* foreign correspondent, and Andreas Whittam Smith, who, many years later, co-founded *The Independent* newspaper. Patrick Sergeant had asked me whether I wanted to stay on at what was then called the *Daily Mail and News Chronicle*, but quite understood when I declined. He thought very highly of the *FT*.

When I joined the *FT*, the Conservatives were coming to the end of their long period in office, lasting from 1951 to 1964. Reginald Maudling was Chancellor, and the brakes were off the economy. His aim was to win the next election. The years 1963–64 saw the 'Maudling boom', which did not win the election for the Conservatives, and whose consequences caused prolonged trouble for the Wilson governments of 1964–70.

The seeds were being sown for the first of the nine crises covered in this memoir: the 1967 devaluation of the pound.

THE *DAILY MAIL AND NEWS CHRONICLE*, 1964–67

When Gordon Newton had said, 'There is another person,' I assumed that I was meant to conclude that I had not yet got the job. The job was in the *FT*'s Features Department, as a trainee. But when Reggie Dale turned up, it was clear that we had both got jobs. (Andreas Whittam Smith was in the separate Company Comments section.)

The first article I had to write proved to be a harbinger of what was in store for much of British industry. The brief was 'The British motorcycle industry'. The features editor told me the name of a good contact at BSA – then supposed to be the giant of the industry. I forget his name, but it might have been Turner. Anyway, when I rang the BSA offices (BSA stood for Birmingham Small Arms, but by now it was a general engineering company and manufacturer), I was told, 'Oh, Mr Turner has left us. He now works for a small Japanese company in Kingston upon Thames. You won't have heard of it. It is called Honda.'

It was true. I hadn't heard of Honda. But I *had* heard of Kingston upon Thames, where I was born. I duly rang Mr Turner and he invited me down to Kingston to lunch. 'The British motorcycle industry is finished,' he proclaimed. 'The future lies with the Japanese.' (It did indeed for a long time, but more recently there has been a recovery of the manufacturing of motorbikes in this country.)

I wrote feature articles on assorted subjects, including the motorcycle industry, for six months or so, and then received a telephone call from Patrick Sergeant, asking whether I should like to go back to the *Mail*. It was naked bribery. At the time, the *FT* was paying me £925 a year. Sergeant offered me £2,000.

Several colleagues said, 'You may never be offered such a huge salary again.'

I consulted someone for whom I had developed considerable respect: John Murray, the head of the three-man Lex team, who subsequently became finance director of the John Lewis Investment Trust. 'You've got to take it,' he said, 'you've just got to take it,' adding, 'Sergeant's lush pastures, eh?' (The Lex column specialised in financial comment and advice.)

I was enjoying the *FT* and getting on reasonably well as far as I could see. Newton said he could not possibly match that figure of £2,000, but he did offer to raise my salary from £925 to, I think, £1,125 or £1,225, the most he maintained that he could do without distorting 'differentials'.

I was in two minds. Always short of money, I found the £2,000 difficult to resist. I was twenty-five at the time, and colleagues maintained that Newton used to say, 'Anybody who is any good should be earning £3,000 a year by the time he is thirty.' There was also the consideration that the *Daily Mail*'s name was mud in our house when I was growing up – for good reasons. There had been the Zinoviev letter scandal of 1924. Allegedly written on behalf of the Comintern by Grigory Zinoviev, chairman of its executive committee, the letter urged the British Communist Party to sow subversion among the British armed forces. There is some controversy about what exactly happened, and it is now widely considered to have been a forgery. One story at the time, however, was that it was intercepted by the British secret service and deliberately leaked to the *Daily Mail*, which made a meal of it in an attempt to persuade voters to vote Conservative. It went into Labour folklore that this was a vital factor in Labour's loss of the 1924 general election. My father often talked about it.

However, it was not just the dubious role of the *Daily Mail* in that episode that prompted my parents' disapproval. It became notorious that in the 1930s, Lord Rothermere, proprietor of the *Mail*, developed fascist leanings. Quite apart from all this, my father was a strong Labour man. My acceptance of the *Daily Mail* job took some explaining!

There was one mitigating factor: the paper was now called the *Daily Mail and News Chronicle*, following what had been presented as a merger but was in effect a swallowing of the old liberal *Chronicle* – which *was* taken in our house – by the Conservative *Mail*. Patrick Sergeant himself had been a *Chronicle* man, and tried to be reassuring on this point.

I went back to the *Mail* in the spring of 1964 after six months with the *FT*. The Conservatives were still in office and the Governor of the Bank of England was Lord Cromer, who had family links with the Rothermeres, still owners of the *Daily Mail*.

Patrick Sergeant did things in style. He lived in Highgate, next door to Yehudi Menuhin. When I once said to his wife, Gillian, that it must be wonderful to live next door to the most famous violinist in the world, she said, 'Fortunately, the walls are soundproof.'

Sergeant had a chauffeur-driven car and dined at the best restaurants. His motto was 'An ounce of information is worth a ton of theory.' Thus, while he liked – indeed, boasted of – having graduates on his staff, he taught me a lot about the nitty-gritty business of acquiring and cultivating good contacts. Expenses on the *Mail* – for wining and dining contacts, and for taxis – were huge. Indeed, I don't think I have ever been quite so well off in my life as in that period from spring 1964 to spring 1967 when I worked for the *Mail*. He also taught me that one should not necessarily turn down an invitation to an event whose ostensible purpose was not of obvious or immediate interest. You often met interesting people at seemingly uninteresting events.

Sergeant had a staff of about ten journalists, who used to sit in an outside office. His own office had a red or green light showing, to let you know whether you could go in. Although the City office certainly produced news stories, the main thrust of his operation was the City page of comment. These comments would usually appear under his own name, whether written by him or not.

But most of the emphasis went on the lead comment. Sergeant would sit at his grand partner's desk and write the lead with one of an array of pencils, paragraph by paragraph, sheet of paper by sheet of paper, and hand the sheets one by one to his secretary, who would type out the lead as it came in. Often, dissatisfied with the first effort, he would crumple it up and hurl it into a waste-paper basket. If it was to be an economic lead, my job was to sit opposite him, contribute ideas and material, and offer an opinion on his judgements and phrases when asked. Or I might type an economic lead at my desk, and he would then go through it before it appeared under his own name. That was the deal, as they say these days.

Sergeant saw a lot of Maudling, who would often telephone him at his office. They frequently lunched together. The Chancellor would consult him on City matters and, because of their close relationship, Sergeant knew far more about what was going on in the Treasury than I – who was supposed to know. For this was a very early stage in my career, and Sergeant generously seemed to credit me with far more contacts than I actually possessed. Indeed, I would often meet John Palmer, a school friend who worked in the City office of *The Scotsman* and then *The Guardian*, for tea or a drink, and we would bemoan our lack of contacts as we exchanged theories and the minimum of what news we were supposed to have picked up. Later in his career, John became one of the best-connected Brussels correspondents of any newspaper, and in due course I built up my own network.

I have always been amused by the way once people get something into their heads they cannot be disabused of it, however often you try. An example was when the National Economic Development Office asked me to rewrite a jargon-filled pamphlet written for them by a well-known economist. They wanted it in plain English. I was too busy at the time and subcontracted it to a civil servant friend of mine. He produced a perfect piece of work, which went down well with the National Economic Development Office and the said economist. Often, when I met the economist in subsequent years, he congratulated me on my editing work. I tried at first to give credit where credit was due, but finally gave up. To his dying day he thought I had helped him with his pamphlets.

As Chancellor, Reggie Maudling had a government chauffeur. I heard enough stories from different Treasury officials to believe the following: Maudling had a tendency to err on the side of idleness, but he could read and grasp a brief at remarkable speed, often in the back of the car transporting him to a meeting or public event at which he was due to speak.

When I was working for Patrick, his chauffeur took me aside to complain that he had been asked to deliver a book to 11 Downing Street. I asked him, as a matter of interest, what it was. Back came the reply: *The Drinking Man's Diet*. Eric then produced the copy he was about to deliver. I opened the first page. The text began – I cannot recall the precise words, but they were something like this: 'Worried about your weight? Relax! We can help you. Pour yourself another drink...'

BACK TO THE *FT*, 1967–76

After my return to the *Mail*, Maudling's chancellorship was, though we didn't know it at the time, in its final months. Since one of the main focuses of attention was the poor state of the balance of payments (there was a huge and chronic deficit in the trade figures, with imports far exceeding exports), attention became heavily concentrated on the monthly trade figures. Sergeant wanted scoops about the figures, and I managed to establish a reputation in this field. I did not know it at the time, but many years later Sergeant told me he had been called in by a Board of Trade official, who told him the leaks were causing consternation but the enquiries into them had got nowhere.

Yet it became increasingly obvious that there was a limit to one's creative potential when writing mostly under the name of one's boss, generous though he always was to me, and from whom I learned many tricks of the trade.

I was not the only member of his staff to become restive. The space was very limited, and there were those at the *Mail*'s headquarters off Fleet Street who noticed that Patrick's City page empire was so large that we almost outnumbered the general reporters on the main news desk. But the suave Sergeant had a ready response to rumblings from above: expansion! He justified the large size of his staff by pioneering an expanded family finance section entitled Money Mail, in which there was far more use of staff bylines. Of course, this was not the only reason. In spite of the emphasis in economic news on trade figures and other difficulties, the fact of the matter was that the British economy was expanding, people were becoming more prosperous and there were opportunities to advise them on their investments.

But I was amused by the way Patrick introduced the idea to

his staff. He came into the office one day and proclaimed, 'I am sure people have lots of coins scattered around the house which they could put to better use.' From that tiny seed evolved the highly successful Money Mail with many imitations. In the very first issue I was required to write an article proclaiming, 'Now is the time to buy a house.'

My first wife and I were in fact negotiating to buy a house at the time. As part of my research for the article in Money Mail, I interviewed the chief executive of what was then the Alliance Building Society in Brighton. At the end, he said that any time I needed a mortgage I should get in touch – which I did. But the Alliance did not think a £10,500 loan for a Georgian house in Canonbury Square was worth the risk. These days they change hands for millions.

Working in the *Mail* offices in Angel Court and, later, Finsbury Circus, I was in the heart of the old, pre-Canary Wharf, City, and developed a feel for it, as well as, eventually, a growing contacts list. While my brief was to follow the economy, most of the coverage in the City page was of stocks and shares, takeovers and so on, with a heavy emphasis on share tipping. The quest for good information on the stock market involved my colleagues in a phenomenal amount of drinking in the local bars, and not just over lunch. This was two decades before Big Bang and the internationalisation of the City, which was still very parochial. The general atmosphere was still very Dickensian.

While being far from expert in stocks and shares, I was roped in by Sergeant to help predict a 'share of the year' at the beginning of one year. He went around his staff, asked for our views and then declared, 'Well, you are all wrong. I have just been playing squash with the chairman of [a well-known machine tool company] and they are my choice.'

When his chosen share duly appeared in the paper, one of

the City analysts specialising in the machine tool industry asked to meet me and said, 'Why on earth is your boss picking that company? They are in a terrible state. I was about to advise my clients to sell, but, given your newspaper's influence, I shall wait a bit until they go up.'

Labour won the general election of October 1964, and the new Chancellor was James Callaghan, whom Sergeant now began to cultivate. Sergeant would talk of the association as 'Stoker Jim' and 'Sailor Pat'. (Both had been in the navy.) However, with my own Labour leanings known to him, Sergeant now began to regard his relatively raw undergraduate recruit as his main conduit to Labour Party and government thinking. (At this stage I should like to emphasise that I have never been a member of a political party. Whatever people have been able to deduce about my views from what I write, I have always been anxious to maintain my independence. On the whole, this helped me to maintain reasonably good relations with all parties.)

But although it was useful experience, by spring 1967 I was ready to move on, or back, and could hardly believe my luck when I had a call from Bill Rodger, the deputy editor of the *Financial Times*, asking if I could go and see him. Rodger came straight to the point: *The Times* had started a separate Business section, with the intention, the *FT* feared, of doing nothing less than challenging the *FT*'s pole position as the leading daily paper on business and finance.

They need not have worried. *The Times*'s Business News became an established feature of Fleet Street, but the *FT* went from success to success. I did not know at the time, but *The Times* had actually approached Sergeant and offered him the Business editorship. He recalled years later, 'I told them nobody is going to dislodge the *FT*.'

Bill Rodger was a courteous man, immaculately dressed, with a pronounced tic – a repetitive jerk of the neck, as if his collar were too tight, but possibly related to the stream of alcohol that passed his lips. Yet he never appeared 'tight' in that sense. After his characteristically succinct explanation of the *FT*'s fears, he said they had decided to expand the staff, and were inviting certain people back.

Rodger's office was near Newton's, separated only by the shared office of their secretaries. Within a few minutes, Newton came in, affected to be surprised to see me, and invited me into his own office. 'Oh, it's you,' he said. 'I always liked you.'

The job I was offered was that of a City reporter, with an emphasis on getting scoops. Somehow or other, Patrick Sergeant's generous view of my work had got back to Newton. The last thing I wished to do was to focus exclusively on the City. But I had a colleague at the *Mail* who would be perfect for that role – a man called Christopher Gwinner. So it was arranged that we should both join the *FT*, with me returning to a general feature-writing role.

After the initial boost, my salary had stagnated at the *Mail*, so I was pleased when Newton offered Gwinner and me £2,750 a year. I was not so pleased later on hearing that Newton had told someone that our recruitment – in my case, re-recruitment – had been 'cheap'.

I had not yet embarked on a career as an economics correspondent or commentator. The world of Prime Ministers, Chancellors and Governors of the Bank of England was still at one remove. I was thrust back into the world of fast feature writing: I would go into the office mid-morning (10.30 or 11 a.m.) and be told, 'The National Provincial Bank and the Westminster Bank are merging. Can you write a feature on it by six o'clock?'

In those pre-internet days, physical files were very important. I would go to the *FT*'s library and ask for the relevant files, bury myself in them and then spend several hours on the phone. I would also compare notes with the chief leader writer, Robert ('Bob') Collin, who, to my mind, had one of the best brains among a galaxy of stars.

It was a very civilised, almost collegiate, atmosphere at the *FT* in those days. The older and more experienced members of the staff went out of their way to help the new recruits. Bob was especially kind, and would write his leaders (unsigned editorials) after attending conference, looking at the files and talking to whomsoever was writing the main story on which he was to comment. He did not cultivate contacts. At lunchtime he would usually repair by himself to the Skinners Arms by Mansion House Station, drink cider and read books on mathematics or how to learn Russian.

BANK OF ENGLAND, 1976–77

In 1976, I accepted what was meant to be a three-year contract with the Bank of England. This came after nine years of being the *FT*'s economics correspondent. Since then, I don't think anyone has done that reporting job for quite as long. The *FT* liked to move people around, and I was offered a post in the parliamentary lobby several times but did not relish the thought. In that role, one has to cover a multitude of political stories, many of which would not have interested me. If ever I had confirmation of this resolve, it was some years later, when I was on *The Observer*, and one Saturday evening my friend and colleague Adam Raphael, then *The Observer*'s political editor, was faced with covering an alleged scandal concerning the Conservative MP Jeffrey Archer and a prostitute. Lobby correspondents have to write about all manner of things, only some of which would interest me. I am a strong believer in the view that if what you're writing does not interest you, it is unlikely to fascinate the reader.

The *FT* also ventured the idea of a foreign posting. The paper's foreign coverage had been built up during the 1960s and early 1970s and was becoming a strength. However, my then wife did not relish such a move and it would have been complicated by the fact that we now had six children between us. At about this time, Christopher Dow, the economics director of the Bank of England, asked me to take a three-year contract with the Bank of England, to work for the Bank's quarterly bulletin and participate in the speech-writing process for the Governor, Gordon Richardson. 'Process' it certainly was, because I soon discovered that drafts of Governor Richardson's speeches mounted up well into double figures. Moreover, although Richardson had indicated to me that he liked the way I wrote in the *FT*, his speeches were essentially committee efforts. After a few contributions to speeches, my efforts were focused entirely on the economic commentary in the Bank of England bulletin. In those days there was plenty of inflation but no inflation report. These days there's little inflation but plenty of reports.

The process of being hired by the Bank involved so many lunches with Christopher Dow at the Reform Club that I lost count. Samuel Brittan, with whom I was still working at the *FT*, commented, 'If only the Bank spent as much time trying to sort out our economic problems as it is doing lunching with you…'

I have always, when asked, described my time at the Bank as a 'secondment', although the editor at the time made it clear that the three years involved would necessitate my formally leaving the *FT*. It was, in effect, a secondment from journalism rather than the *FT*, because, although I have always kept in touch with the paper, I did not return.

The Bank of England was a peculiar place in those days and there are those, including, as I write, in the Treasury, who think it still is, hence the determined pursuit in 2012 by the Chancellor George Osborne of the Canadian central bank governor Mark Carney to bring a new broom to Threadneedle Street. The Bank was and remains a very hierarchical place and it was thought that Carney might change all this. However, the fact of the matter is that the Bank of England, founded in 1694, did not get where it is today by being easily thwarted. Even as I write, one can detect tensions between the Treasury and the Bank. Governor Carney, despite being surrounded by various committees, remains at the apex of the Bank.

In fact, Gordon Richardson and Christopher Dow were trying to bring a new broom to the Bank back in the 1970s.

Policymakers are educated people, with their own view of the world. Some are self-confident, even arrogant; others are unsure of themselves. The old joke is that the views of some policymakers reflect the advice of the last person they talked to. There were even those officials in the Bank of England when I worked there who complained, only half-jokingly, that although the Governor had painstakingly built a formidable edifice of highly qualified advisers, what really mattered was the conversation he had had with the person he had sat next to at dinner the previous evening.

Richardson, Governor from 1973 to 1983, was an imposing figure, with, according to my female friends, the looks of a Roman emperor. He was a man of great presence, who looked taller than he really was. He lived to a ripe old age, but, sadly, lost his sight. When Eddie George, a later Governor, was given the Keynes Sraffa Award, he took me aside at the reception and asked me to look after Richardson. As various Bank and City names came up, Gordon would whisper in my ear, 'Is he still with us?' I seldom remember dreams or take notice of them. But I have a vivid memory of dreaming that night that I was wandering around a ghostly hall, with Gordon asking repeatedly, 'Is he still with us?'

My main job at the Bank was to assemble the constituents of the economic commentary from an array of talented economists who were working under the aegis of Dow and Leslie Dicks-Mireaux, who was in charge of the economics division. Some years earlier, while at the National Institute of Economic and Social Research, Dow and Dicks-Mireaux had written a celebrated (by fellow economists) article on wage inflation. This understandably misled some Bank economists, including Dicks-Mireaux, who had been recruited by the Bank well before Dow's arrival, into believing that when Dow got there the two would work together harmoniously. But this did not prove to be the case. In fact, they seemed to be on different wavelengths.

I soon realised that it had been a mistake for me in the past to use the phrase 'The Bank thinks...', as if there were a unified view. The Bank was full of good people and there were many differing views. Fantastic quantities of paper would cross one's desk, with Official A commenting on Official B's interpretation of Official C's draft of a gubernatorial speech.

There was an added complication. A delightful, old-style Bank official, Michael Thornton, who had been awarded a Military Cross in World War II, was in charge of the Economic Intelligence Unit. But he was certainly not an economist, and therefore not rated highly by Dow. Indeed, he once called me in with regard to a paper Dow was circulating and asked for advice, saying disarmingly, 'I am not sure what Dow is on about. I am not an economist.'

I had known Michael before my arrival there because he used to chair small press briefings on the eve of the publication of the quarterly bulletin, on which I was now working. When I arrived at the Bank and met him formally on a kind of courtesy call, he blithely said, 'Now, Keegan, I have to confess that although I have read you for years in the *FT*, the only article of yours I can remember was when you wrote about what it was like to own a Volkswagen Minibus.'

If the Bank was considered old-fashioned in 2012, it was even more old-fashioned and quaint in the mid-1970s. The Bank was generous in inviting a journalist in and trusting him, and I certainly do not wish to indulge in ungrateful criticism of my hosts. But there were certain amusing aspects of the daily routine that linger in my memory. For instance, whereas I think that these days the so-called work ethic has been stretched to its limits, the Bank, and City, that one experienced in those days was a fairly civilised and relaxed place. Until I got used to the hours, I would be baffled by the difficulty of making contact with people. There were no emails back then, but there was always someone at the other end of the internal telephone lines. Often, though, it was an assistant or somebody from Personnel – an outfit which was at the time known as Staff Posts.

'May I speak to X, please?'

'Oh, sorry, he's at coffee.'

'May I speak to Y, please?'

'Sorry, he's at tea.'

Usually this meant that the said person had crossed the road, Lothbury, to the Bank club, which, in addition to offering coffee breaks in the morning and tea breaks in the afternoon, boasted a rather good subsidised restaurant, with a flourishing bar. But my favourite memory of the Bank's paternalist way of looking after its staff was the discovery that if I worked after 5.30 p.m. I would be entitled to sandwiches and a bottle of Young's pale ale to keep me going.

Most of the junior staff seemed to live in the suburbs or beyond, and 5.30 p.m. was the time they headed for their commuter trains. By contrast, my *FT* routine had been to settle down to write my news stories between 5.30 p.m. and 7 p.m., and I took this routine with me to the Bank. This brought the advantage not only of good sandwiches and pale ale delivered by a courteous messenger, but also the freedom to work uninterrupted on the bulletin, or on the various internal papers that would eventually surface in the bulletin.

A notable difference was that, whereas for a journalist words flow fast and freely, every sentence in a Bank publication had to be drafted with the utmost care. My wife, a barrister and former Bank of England economist, says that she drafts and I write.

Given that the Bank was always playing cat-and-mouse with the Treasury, great efforts went into the drafting, once the tortuous process of arriving at a consensus had been brought to an end by deadlines. These days, hardly a week goes by without public comments from the Governor and members of the various monetary and regulatory committees, but there was a time under Richardson's governorship when his public statements were so rare that the City editor of the *Sunday Telegraph*, Patrick Hutber, christened the Bank 'The Tomb of the Unknown Governor'.

The general atmosphere is brilliantly described in the Dow diaries, a shortened version of which was published by the National Institute of Economic and Social Research. I recall Dow once observing in frustration, 'This place! Have you ever read

Stendhal?' There was an underlying conflict between Governor Richardson and Dow on the one hand, and the chief cashier of the Bank on the other, who really thought it was his right to run the place. There was an occasion when I was in the Governor's office, called a parlour, with Richardson and Dow. There were only three of us and we were discussing a forthcoming bulletin. Reflecting the underlying tensions, Gordon looked up and said, 'You know, we three are outsiders in this place.' Dow went to extraordinary lengths to get his essentially Keynesian views into gubernatorial speeches and in the bulletin's quarterly climax, 'The Assessment'. A few of us coined the term Dovian to describe his sometimes convoluted prose.

As a Keynesian, Dow was very suspicious of monetarism. Monetarism was a very old economic doctrine whose proponents held that the conquest of inflation was essentially a matter of controlling the money supply. In its modern version it was associated with the American economist Milton Friedman, of the Chicago School. We Keynesians always held the view that controlling inflation was much more complicated than Friedman and his disciples maintained. There was a great debate in the columns of *Newsweek* in the 1970s between Friedman and the eminent American Keynesian Paul Samuelson. Samuelson once said that Milton Friedman was 'the eighth or ninth wonder of the world depending on how you score the Grand Canyon'. But when the Keynesian approach ran into difficulty, and life became more difficult for policymakers, monetarism came into vogue. It is very much associated with Mrs Thatcher's government – quite rightly – but there are some who hold that it really began under the Labour government of James Callaghan, when he took over the reins from Harold Wilson and was faced with the 1976 IMF crisis.

The Bank had had its fingers burned earlier in the decade trying to apply a policy known as competition and credit control, and its economists knew that the job of controlling the money supply was rather more complicated than politicians realised. But there are always time-serving officials who will allow more leeway to misconceived ideas – and some who actually believe in them.

There is no getting away from the fact that the Keynesian economics that I had been taught at Cambridge, and still subscribe to, was in trouble during the 1970s, and exposed a flank to the rise of monetarism. The Keynesian approach was developed in reaction to the Great Depression which began in 1929, under which unemployment rose to 15 per cent in Britain. Essentially the Keynesian approach was, to quote a phrase much beloved of Denis Healey, 'When you are in a hole, stop digging.'

Originally the emphasis was on boosting public spending when the private sector was depressed and monetary policy was caught in what was known as a liquidity trap, so that lower interest rates were ineffectual in boosting demand. In the post-war years, rescue operations evolved into what became known as 'demand management', involving tax cuts as well as increases in public spending. During the relatively successful economic policies of the immediate post-war decades, Keynesian policymakers probably became overconfident. The idea was to apply policies of economic expansion where appropriate, but to rein back if there were problems with the balance of payments or inflation.

Controlling inflation became more difficult. In the US, the financing of the Vietnam War had aggravated inflationary tendencies, while in the UK it proved a problem to control inflation as the trade unions recognised their bargaining strength and flexed their muscles.

It was fashionable in the 1970s to conclude that Keynesians had lost the plot and that prices-and-incomes policies were ineffectual in curbing inflation. In came the monetarists, and Keynesian policies fell out of fashion during the period of Sir Geoffrey Howe's chancellorship in 1979–83.

A speech made by Prime Minister Callaghan to the Labour Party conference of October 1976 in which he said one could no longer spend one's way out of recession was seized upon by the monetarists as proof of the demise of Keynesianism. But his reference was entirely tactical, to appease a hostile US Treasury that was being difficult about the UK's negotiations with the International Monetary Fund (Crisis 3).

In his memoirs, published after eight years of Conservative rule, Callaghan made it quite clear that he was really a Keynesian and disagreed with the Thatcher/Howe/Lawson polices that were then contributing to a rapid rise in unemployment. As it happened, inflation and unemployment were both already falling by 1977–78, towards the end of Callaghan's premiership. It was only the Winter of Discontent in 1978–79 (see Crisis 3) that finally wrecked the Labour government's reputation for economic competence.

The fact of the matter, as became apparent all those years later in the wake of the 2007–08 financial crisis, is that Keynes was right all along: the only way to emerge from recession is to spend your way out.

As presented by the monetarist guru Professor Milton Friedman, it all sounded so easy. One of Dow's main tasks was to explain to Governor Richardson privately, and sometimes at great length, that the last City person who had bent his ear about the money supply at dinner the night before was not necessarily the perfect font of advice.

It did strike one sometimes that, for all the laborious recruitment that the Governor went in for, and for all the undoubted talent among his pool of advisers, he could be disproportionately influenced by the opinions and remarks of outsiders he met in the course of his very assiduous business and social rounds.

In addition to the frequent lunches I had enjoyed with Christopher Dow before I joined the Bank, I was subjected to the Bank's equivalent of the Foreign Office's traditional 'country house test', under which candidates were observed, at least in those days, for their general behaviour and standards of social decorum. In this case it was a townhouse test or, more accurately, a penthouse flat test: a dinner with Richardson and some of his colleagues at which he made a great show of his knowledge of proper, New York-style, martinis.

Several were served before a dinner at which there was no shortage of excellent white and red wines, with port or brandy to follow. The hospitality of the Bank was legendary then, and for decades after. But later, under the regime of Sir Mervyn King in 2003–13, wine was not spontaneously offered at lunchtime. The trick was to ensure that, when asked in advance for any dietary requirements, one made sure to say, 'Wine.' In Lord Lawson's case, I understand, the request was for 'fine claret'.

Before going to the Bank, I had been sounded out by *The Economist*. Andrew Knight, who was then in charge of their bureau in Brussels, offered me the post of jointly running the Brussels office. As a well-established *FT* correspondent, I would hardly have wanted to become his deputy, but the joint proposal seemed odd, and was subsequently explained when it turned out that all along he had been destined to return to London as editor of *The Economist* – something he did not tell me at the time. I was intrigued, but not particularly attracted, by the idea of the

Brussels job. In due course I was to make frequent trips to Brussels and other European capitals while covering our relations with Europe.

However, at Knight's suggestion, I went as far as agreeing to meet the editor, Alastair Burnet, at his London office. The 'interview' consisted of a most enjoyable conversation between 6 and 8 p.m. in Burnet's office. He sat behind his desk; I in front. In the course of the conversation, most of a bottle of malt whisky was consumed, mainly by him. When I voiced my concerns about the Brussels job, he explored at some length the possibility of my working in the London office, and left me to reflect.

The idea of my joining *The Economist* faded, but my association with *The Economist* did not. While I was at the Bank, I was telephoned one day by my friend Sarah Hogg, who was then the magazine's economics editor. She invited me to lunch at Manzi's, the fish restaurant just off Leicester Square. I accepted, but warned her that, as I was the most obvious suspect, I could not possibly give her any scoops.

This was agreed. Then, before the appointed day, I was approached by Rupert Pennant-Rea, Christopher Dow's personal assistant. He said he was looking for a job in journalism and asked if I could help him. I rang Sarah and mentioned this. She was looking for an assistant and asked me to bring Rupert along to lunch. I need not have feared being put in an awkward position between the Bank and Sarah over the kind of confidential information that, in Sarah's shoes, I would have been searching for. Most of the conversation consisted of an unofficial interview of Rupert by Sarah. At the end, she asked him for examples of his written work, and he was duly taken on by *The Economist*, where he rose to become editor.

The story did not end there. Many years later, when Sarah was head of Prime Minister John Major's Policy Unit at 10 Downing Street, in the closing months of 1992, the time had come for the government to decide on the successor to Robin Leigh-Pemberton as Governor of the Bank of England. Prime Ministers and Chancellors like to spring a surprise on these occasions, but there was little question that the next Governor had to be Eddie George, a career-long star of the Bank. Indeed, George had been marked out much earlier. When I arrived there for my stint in 1976, Christopher Dow told me that he would show me a paper he had commissioned from a bright young Bank man on the reorganisation of the Economics Intelligence Department. The bright young man turned out to be Eddie George, and the paper was the George Report.

Eddie rose and rose, via the economics division, the overseas division and, especially, the Bank's then-powerful markets division to become deputy governor. The question was: when Eddie was appointed to Governor, who was to be the deputy?

There were various internal candidates, but Prime Minister John Major and Chancellor Norman Lamont wanted that element of surprise. This was provided by Sarah Hogg, who suggested none other than her *Economist* recruit of all those years ago, Rupert Pennant-Rea, by now the magazine's editor. My impression was that this was not the choice Eddie George himself would have made, but he lived with it, and the two developed a working relationship until a certain event caused embarrassment all round.

The episode was epitomised by a memorable headline in *The Sun*: 'THE BONK OF ENGLAND'. Rupert Pennant-Rea was reported to have been discovered *in flagrante delicto*, making love to a girlfriend on the Governors' carpet. In those days there was one governor and one deputy, not two or, as later, three or four of the latter; internal communications were addressed to 'The Governors' (plural) and the said carpet on which the notorious 'bonk' was performed was accessible, as it were, to both Governors.

Kenneth Clarke, who was Chancellor at the time and a very broad-minded, relaxed man, could not quite see what the fuss was about. But to Eddie George, this was a disgrace; indeed, a sacrilege. Dishonour had been brought down upon the Bank. There was no question that Pennant-Rea would have to go.

Eddie was a happily married man and quite shocked by the whole episode. But as he had not been entirely enthusiastic about Rupert's appointment in the first place, I am not sure that he regarded it as a great tragedy, annoyed though he undoubtedly was.

Going back to 1976–77, however, I owe to Rupert the suggestion that, having published a couple of novels, I should join him in writing a book about economic policy. This work eventually appeared under the title *Who Runs the Economy? Control and Influence in Economic Policy*. The thesis we developed could be summarised as: 'It all depends.' Politicians come into office with ambitious plans, and sooner or later encounter Macmillan's Opposition of Events.

THE OBSERVER, 1977–

My three-year contract at the Bank did not last. Shortly after I had been there a year, I was approached by *The Observer* and offered what for me was an ideal job: to be economics editor of *The Observer*, the newspaper for which I had the most respect, and had done ever since discovering it on my newspaper round in the early 1950s. It was, among other things, the paper that had opposed the Suez venture of 1956, which brought down Eden and cleared the path for Macmillan to move from the Treasury to No. 10; it had also printed Khrushchev's denunciation of Stalin in full, taking up most of what was then a paper with few pages by modern standards.

In circulation and size, *The Observer* was then, as now, a poor relation to the massive *Sunday Times*. Although left of centre, it was much more 'liberal' than many on the left would have liked. David Astor, who had owned and edited the paper during its heyday, had stepped down by the time I was approached in 1977. Astor, although a millionaire, had never been particularly interested in business or finance. He was famous for once having asked, 'What is a mortgage?' and to have been horrified on being told, expressing concern that members of his staff were 'in debt'.

Under the new editor, Donald Trelford, *The Observer* was trying to build up the coverage of business and economics. There had been a long time when the main reference to business had been in a column called 'Mammon' – the very title of which always seemed to me to have a slightly contemptuous air to it. There had been a memorable example of *The Observer*'s attitude way back in the 1960s, when they had commissioned Roy Jenkins to write about the abortive bid by ICI to take over the rival textile company Courtaulds, and Jenkins had referred rather haughtily to the expensive property in the Bishops Avenue, Hampstead, where the chairman of ICI, Sir Paul Chambers, lived, as 'a businessman's mansion'.

My main interview with *The Observer* took place in the art deco pub called the Blackfriar, opposite Blackfriars station and round the corner from the *Observer* office, then in St Andrew's Hill. Over several pints, the deputy editor, John Cole, told me that the paper needed a full-time economics correspondent; at the time they were relying on a weekly article from Professor Alan Day of the London School of Economics, who was very distinguished but very definitely an academic, not a journalist who could do the rounds of press conferences and keep in touch with the Treasury, Bank of England and other contacts, let alone travel to, for example, economic summits such as the first one called by President Giscard at Rambouillet in 1975, which I covered for the *FT*.

It later turned out that the man who suggested *The Observer* approach me was the future political editor Adam Raphael. Our paths had crossed several times when Adam was covering parliamentary committees for *The Guardian* and I for the *FT*.

You can never be sure on these occasions, but my strong impression over drinks in the Blackfriar was that John Cole had already decided to hire me. There was, though, the little matter of meeting the editor, Donald Trelford. This meeting took place in Donald's office, some days later. He was relatively unknown at the time, and I was struck by his mop of black hair and very dark eyes. A most courteous man, he nevertheless had an impenetrable look about him. I got the impression he didn't know much about me, and was happy to accept the recommendation of John Cole and Adam Raphael. However, many people have underestimated Donald over the years, and I suspect that, being the very intuitive man that he is, he would have vetoed my appointment if he had any doubts. He also made a point of introducing me to Terence Kilmartin, the literary editor, who was a more influential figure than his title implied.

As it was, taking the job at *The Observer* was an important step in my career. First, however, there was the little matter of my three-year contract. The Bank were fine about this. Although my work editing the economic commentary in the bulletin had been going well, I think Christopher Dow had soon realised that I was not the kind of professional economist who wished to become part of the bureaucratic system. And when I saw Gordon Richardson to announce my departure, he immediately said, 'I have always thought of you as a newspaper man.' Any doubts I might have had were soon quashed by my friend John Bispham, who was in charge of economic forecasting at the Bank: 'You have got to take it.' Rupert Pennant-Rea, Dow's assistant, thought the same.

The *Observer* offer came in the spring of 1977, and it was agreed that I should see the next quarterly bulletin through, and leave the Bank in the summer. I had made good friends and contacts at the Bank, and was struck by the civilised way in which they trusted a 'journalist within the Bank'. I had had access to all sorts of confidential information, at a time when there was a serious economic crisis, and the financial markets and financial press were obsessed with the statistics for public sector borrowing and the official reserves of gold and foreign currency.

John Cole, when deputy editor of *The Observer*, once indicated that I might be relying too much on the words of officials and not paying enough respect to elected politicians. When I was putting a particular interpretation on some aspect of economic policy to him, John would say, 'But Roy Hattersley says...' as if Roy Hattersley were God. I got to know Hattersley well in due course, and was much impressed by his remarkable memory for events – always accurate, as far as I could tell. Hattersley told me that he had never kept a diary, and indeed was critical of those ministers who did – not least when they were writing them during Cabinet meetings. There was a hint here I think of a political version of Heisenberg's principle, whereby the observation might be affecting the quality of the proceedings.

The real problem for Labour in 1976 had been the way they had lost the confidence of the financial markets. Not only was

sterling under considerable pressure, the government was finding it impossible to sell government stock, or 'gilts', to finance
expenditure. It was what was known as a 'gilt strike'. The position
was reached where strikes by the trade unions had contributed to
the government's problems earlier in the decade and now there
was effectively a strike by the institutions needed to finance government expenditure.

Treasury officials with whom I was in contact, whether or not
they had faith in the financial markets, knew that the prevailing
views were inhibiting government policy. I was trying to reflect
this, but John Cole used to say, 'These officials of yours are not
elected politicians.'

John had firm advice on drink and broadcasting. On one occasion, I introduced my friend Richard Brown to him shortly
before Richard was due to appear on a BBC economic discussion with two MPs who were experienced broadcasters. 'Have
two gin and tonics before you go on,' John said. 'Not one and
not three.'

Through working as a financial journalist and having experience of being inside the Bank, I had got to know many officials
very well, at several levels. Nevertheless, their knowledge of me,
and mine of them, did not prevent the Bank from behaving in a
most extraordinary, indeed outrageous, way towards the woman
who was eventually to become my wife.

Hilary Stonefrost was a very bright graduate recruit who had
turned down offers from the Foreign Office and the Treasury
in favour of working as an economist at the Bank in 1979, after
graduating from the London School of Economics with a Master's degree.

Hilary and I were introduced in 1983 by our friend in common,
Richard Brown, a former IMF official, who was a colleague at the

Bank. At the time, Hilary was one of the Bank's experts on the US economy, which was much in the news, and one day when I was discussing the US scene with Richard, he said I ought to meet Hilary, who knew far more about the particular aspect of the US financial scene we had been discussing – her regular note on US matters was not only widely distributed within the Bank; it was also in great demand at the Treasury.

The three of us met upstairs at Le Poulbot in Cheapside for breakfast one day. Le Poulbot was a fashionable establishment run by the Roux brothers, with a good-value brasserie upstairs and a very expensive, Michelin-starred restaurant downstairs. The site is now occupied by a building society.

I can't recall much about the economic discussion, but certainly remember being impressed by Hilary. A few weeks later, a lunch was arranged at the Escargot in Greek Street, during which the attraction grew, and seemed to be mutual. We got on to port, and Richard made an excuse and left at about 4 p.m.

As we left the restaurant and walked up Greek Street, I noticed that Hilary was carrying a riding whip. I thought, 'This could be a bit embarrassing if someone I know sees me in Soho with a beautiful girl – sorry, my new feminist friend had instructed me always to refer to women, not girls – carrying a riding whip.'

It turned out that she had a horse stabled at Mill Hill and was on her way there.

Now, given that I had recently been separated and divorced from my first wife, I was concentrating on seeing as much as I could of my children, who lived with their mother during the week. I had read a frightening statistic that 50 per cent of divorced fathers lose contact with their children. I had occasional girlfriends, but was in no mood to try 'settling down' again. Anyway, for whatever reason, I did not follow up the successful lunch. Hilary took the initiative and dropped a letter through my door saying that as a feminist she believed in paying her way. As I had taken her out to lunch, she would invite me to dinner.

We have often joked about what would have happened if she had not written that letter. But the point is she did, and we started going out together.

Which brings me to the truly bizarre behaviour of the Bank in this matter. Some years later, Hilary told me that the Bank had offered her a promotion to work with the economist Charles Goodhart, who was heavily involved with monetary policy and monetary statistics. But this promotion would only take place if she stopped seeing William Keegan.

She dismissed this outrageous suggestion out of hand. The apparent justification for it was that monetary policy was central to the Thatcher government's strategy and the Bank was concerned that there would be breaches of confidence.

Their concern, like their behaviour, was absurd, a product of the mentality of a bureaucracy where at the time something like a quarter of the staff seemed to belong, one way or another, to the personnel category, overseeing the other three quarters. Frankly, I often wondered when I was at the Bank about the way the institution seemed to contain so many busybodies.

Monetarism, and the monetary statistics, were certainly central to the policy. When at *The Observer*, I myself was considered an outspoken critic of the policy, and regarded the precious money supply statistics as virtually meaningless. Moreover, I had such good professional relations with many of the Bank officials above Hilary in the hierarchy that I was more likely to be told indiscretions by them than by my new girlfriend. My good relations with these officials continued.

The episode was ridiculously insulting, especially to Hilary

– who, by the way, manifested immense discretion in not telling me about it until years later. She declined what was regarded as a good career move within the Bank – monetary policy being all the rage at the time – out of loyalty to someone who at the time was a mere boyfriend, in a situation where she could not be at all sure where our relationship would go.

Here we come to an interesting example of camaraderie among journalists, Chancellors and former journalists. Nigel Lawson, Chancellor from 1983 to 1989, had had a distinguished career in journalism, at the *FT*, the *Sunday Telegraph* and then as editor of *The Spectator*. When he became Chancellor, I was frequently critical of the policies he pursued and began, at first ironically, to refer to him from time to time as 'my old friend'. This seemed to go down well with readers, and also with Lawson, even though we were frequently at odds.

He would take delight, when meeting me, in saying, 'Still writing the same old rubbish,' to which I would reply, 'Still pursuing the same old policies.' On one occasion at one of the occasional drinks parties the Chancellor holds, a journalist from a right-wing paper tried to suck up to Lawson by saying, when I approached the circle around him, 'Why are you talking to *him*?' To which the Chancellor replied, putting his arm briefly over my shoulder, 'Because we *are* old friends.'

Lawson came to lunch at *The Observer* when, as happened from time to time, my job was under threat. Neither the bosses of Atlantic Richfield, who owned *The Observer* from 1976 to 1981, nor Lonrho, the owners from 1981 to 1993, were keen on my attacks on the Thatcher government. At one of these lunches, Kenneth Harris, one of the directors of *The Observer*, was present, and most certainly belonged to the camp who wanted to fire me. Towards the end of the lunch, he turned rather pompously to Lawson and said, 'Now, Chancellor, we are always criticising you; have you anything to say about us?'

At which stage Tony Howard, the deputy editor, nudged me and muttered, 'Wait for it.' But Lawson could not have been more helpful. He said, 'I know what you are referring to. I read William's column. I don't always agree with it. But I wouldn't be without it.'

Years later, Harris actually began to treat me like a long-lost friend. Ever since he had helped to save *The Observer* in 1976 by introducing David Astor, the owner, who had had enough of financing the losses, to Robert O. Anderson, the chairman of the American oil corporation Atlantic Richfield, Harris had organised an annual dinner in London so that Anderson and his colleagues could meet the great, the good and the not so good. Hundreds of guests turned up over the years to an assortment of smart London hotels, and various senior members of *The Observer* were invited, but not me.

There came a time, however, in 1993, when Lonrho sold *The Observer* to the Scott Trust, owners of *The Guardian*, and many of the senior members who used to be invited to the dinner had moved on, or, not to put too fine a point upon it, been fired. I myself was one of the few survivors of the old regime, and suddenly found myself in demand for the annual dinner, which had long since taken on a life of its own. Well, I have always taken the long view in these matters.

* * *

The Anderson regime was intent on cosying up to the Callaghan and Thatcher governments from 1976 onwards, not least with regard to concessions for the exploitation of North Sea oil. Atlantic Richfield were obviously in the North Sea for the money, but I myself, along with many other observers, was concerned that this great windfall was being wasted. It seemed to me that the North Sea money should have been used, as indeed it was by the Norwegian government, to plan investment for the future, when the revenues would inevitably diminish. Alas, the Treasury was against the idea of what they called 'hypothecation', devoting particular sources of revenue to a specific objective, rather than putting it into the general pot of tax revenue. And the Thatcher government ruthlessly used the revenue to help it with its problems with public sector borrowing. I was so concerned about this that I wrote a Penguin special called *Britain Without Oil* – essentially advocating an investment programme that was never implemented. The funny thing about the book was that Penguin illustrated it with a picture on the cover of an empty motorway with weeds growing on it – a slight contrast with the way our modern motorways are often chock-a-block.

I myself did not experience too much interference with my work at *The Observer*, and always thought that the editor Donald Trelford was skilful at fending off proprietorial criticisms of his staff. Indeed, I was invited as one of the *Observer* team to a lunch with some of the Atlantic Richfield people at Rules, a very traditional London restaurant, which it was assumed would impress the Americans.

It did so, but only up to a point – the point when our new owners, who were very much of the 'Perrier water only' brigade, noticed that the large fish course was a mere staging post, to be followed by a kind of Dickensian game dish.

When Tiny Rowland, head of Lonrho, took over the paper, in the face of hostility from most of the staff and readers, he was in the process of cultivating the Thatcher government in order to gain permission to buy Harrods. This was a long-running story, which captured the public imagination. Those of us on *The Ob-server* who were prominent opponents of the Thatcher regime were obviously in the firing line. Moreover, I led with my chin when Tiny addressed the journalists in *The Observer*'s gloomy basement canteen (we were still at 8 St Andrew's Hill) and I asked a question about his intentions, which was obviously not considered acceptable. 'Who is that man?' he apparently enquired of one of his lieutenants.

His takeover of *The Observer* was such a contentious issue that there were hearings before the Monopolies Commission. Despite what Tom Bower says in his book on Rowland, I was not one of those who gave evidence. John Cole, our deputy editor, was, and shortly after, he left for the job of political editor of the BBC. I was one of those who urged John to stay, blissfully unaware that by joining the BBC he would become one of the most famous and recognisable people in the land – for his Ulster accent as well as his appearance.

However, I stayed, and was a marked man. What followed was a marvellous example of Donald Trelford's skills as an editor. One Saturday morning, I arrived in the office to find a memorandum from the editor saying that I was being stripped of my duties as editor of the Business section, and my regular 'In My View' column was being removed from the front page of what was, in those more prosperous days for newspapers, a separate section for Business and Sport.

An exchange of letters went on all morning, but mine was a losing case. It could have been far worse. What Tiny really wanted, in common with the wish of certain *Observer* directors, was for me to be sacked. Donald had contrived a brilliant compromise. I was to be given the courtesy title of 'associate editor'.

Shortly afterwards, Donald's secretary came over to see me

and asked whether I was free for a game of snooker with the editor. Of course I was free! In those days there was a snooker club beneath the arches of the railway line that ran across the Thames to Blackfriars Station. It was called Duffers and was one of the editor's favourite haunts, where he could escape from the undoubted pressures of editing a paper owned by Tiny Rowland. (Incidentally, 'Tiny' Rowland was very tall, and Donald was small – although famously described by *Private Eye* as 'perfectly formed'. The two became known as 'The Two Tinies'.)

Donald was very keen on snooker: indeed, he wrote a book about it. I have always enjoyed the occasional game, but am not nearly as competitive as people like Donald. It was Alan Watkins, the great political columnist of *The Observer* at the time, who, in his book *A Short Walk Down Fleet Street*, observed that on every newspaper he had worked for there would be somebody known as 'the editor's friend' – someone who could be relied on to be available to accompany the editor to the pub at the boss's behest.

Curiously enough, although fired from my position as business editor, I now found myself in the position of the editor's friend – or at least one of them, because Donald was quite gregarious. It was, I think, during the first of our many games of snooker that I ventured to ask Donald what exactly was the job description of my new title of associate editor. Quick as a flash, he replied, 'People prepared to associate with the editor.'

PART II

THE NINE CRISES

ECONOMIC BACKGROUND TO THE CRISES

I should like briefly to sketch in the background to the British economy whose ups and downs I covered for half a century.

The first policymakers I met, whether Conservative or Labour, were of a generation that had experienced the Second World War – and, indeed, in many cases the interwar years. From an economic and social point of view, they wanted to avoid a repetition of the Great Depression of 1929–32 and the protectionism and competitive devaluation that accompanied or followed that period. The Second World War had brought all classes together, and the electorate's belief that Labour offered a fairer society proved a major factor in the Conservatives' defeat in the 1945 election, notwithstanding Churchill's magnificent war record and his contribution to the Allied victory. Among other things, the result of that election was also a convincing demonstration that we did not have a presidential system – if we had, it is difficult to believe that Churchill would not have been re-elected.

I refer to 'policymakers' but I should attempt to answer the question 'Who were and are these policymakers?' In Britain, when it comes to economic policy, we have to begin with the Prime Minister, our most senior elected representative, and the Chancellor of the Exchequer. The Prime Minister is also the First Lord of the Treasury, and the relationship between the PM and the Chancellor is vital. Nigel Lawson once said that this was the most important relationship in the government. He should know; he was Chancellor. For a time he had a good relationship with his Prime Minister, Margaret Thatcher, but when it broke down, it broke down with a vengeance – a breakdown that signalled the final stages of Mrs Thatcher's premiership, and the opening of a wound in the Conservative Party that festered for decades.

I was once taken to task by Alan Watkins, the political commentator, for using the word 'policymakers'. It is now widely used and I think Watkins thought I had coined the phrase, but I don't know. But an important point throughout the period of economic policy I have covered has been the relationship between the Prime Minister and the Chancellor. Most of the senior Treasury officials I have known have tended to say that things go wrong when the relationship between the Prime Minister and the Chancellor goes wrong. But the exception to this rule must surely be the relationship between Prime Minister Cameron and Chancellor Osborne in 2010–16. They thought they had learned the lesson of the problems that arose in the often fraught relationship between Tony Blair and Gordon Brown. But the 'good' relationship between Cameron and Osborne produced the appalling policy of austerity, whose consequences the country has finally woken up to, and the catastrophic decision to hold the EU referendum. Perhaps some creative tension between Prime Minister and Chancellor would have helped them – and the country.

The 1945–51 period – of the two Attlee governments – saw years of economic reconstruction and rationing, neatly epitomised in the title of the Philip French and Michael Sissons book *Age of Austerity*. The 1951–64 Conservative governments saw derationing, the end of many controls, and a general increase in the standard of living, which prompted Harold Macmillan to declare in 1957 that 'most of our people have never had it so good'.

This warning came from a Prime Minister who was, and still is, usually criticised for having been too keen on reflation and over-concerned about unemployment – the legacy from his horror at witnessing the social effects of unemployment on his Stockton constituency in the interwar years. The interesting thing is that the quotation for which Macmillan is most remembered was unscripted – and not sufficiently interesting to Macmillan for him to have recorded it in his diary.

Both in the international arrangements for economic policy coordination and rules, and in the domestic approach to policy, the emphasis was on economic growth, provided that this did not cause problems with inflation or the balance of payments – those trade figures – and, in popular parlance, Britain's ability to 'pay her way' in the world.

British economic policymakers had to come to terms with the huge cost of the war – we would be repaying American loans right into the twenty-first century – and the end of the empire, which had provided us with 'captive markets' and reliable sources of raw materials for centuries, and which had made a never-to-be-forgotten contribution to the war effort.

Notwithstanding Macmillan's spontaneous remark about never having had it so good, as the 1950s wore on, and the 1960s loomed, our policymakers looked across the Channel and became envious of the faster economic growth rates being achieved there, and the apparent success of French-style 'indicative planning' on the part of governments. This interested governments of both major parties.

Although now and again Prime Ministers and Chancellors present the rest of the Cabinet with a fait accompli, in theory, and on important occasions in practice too, policy must be approved by the Cabinet. (Thus, in the negotiations with the International Monetary Fund in 1976, the Prime Minister and Chancellor had to carry the rest of the Cabinet with them before formal agreement with the Fund could be reached.)

The decisions and policy advice of the Chancellor are dependent on the talent and accumulated wisdom of the Treasury, as well as other Whitehall departments with a direct interest in the economy, and the Bank of England.

Then there are the channels which flow into this sea of advice: the various pressure groups such as the Confederation of British Industry (CBI) and the Trades Union Congress (TUC); trade associations and chambers of commerce; major industrial corporations, whose bosses are seldom reticent in promulgating their views of what is good for the rest of the economy; and the City of London, with its view of what the financial markets want from economic policy – or what they are prepared to put up with. It is by now generally accepted that the financial sector – bankers! – exercised far too much sway over policy-making in the run-up to the 2007–08 financial crash.

In the background are the individual economic departments – the ultimate suppliers of formal and informal economic advisers

– and a proliferation of think tanks, not to say commentators and contributors to the media. Besides all this, one should never underestimate the importance of fashion, in general, and the prevailing economic orthodoxy – Galbraith's 'conventional wisdom'. Then, most important at crucial turning points, are the challenges to the conventional wisdom, such as the rise of monetarism and what the present author would regard as extreme free market doctrines in the late 1970s and 1980s. After monetarism came the fashion for the European exchange rate mechanism, and then inflation targets.

Recent history has been dominated by the banking crisis of 2007–09, with whose consequences we are still living – not least with the era of austerity that followed. The financial crisis took a complacent generation of economists and policymakers by surprise. Conquering inflation was supposed to be the ultimate achievement.

And then came the Brexit referendum...

1967: DEVALUATION: BEFORE AND AFTER

The devaluation of 1967 followed a sequence of events in which the Conservatives under Reginald Maudling began a 'dash for growth' which ended in what became known as the Maudling boom, whose consequences Labour had to deal with. The background to this was partly the general observation that the leading European economies were growing faster than ours, which was one of the factors behind the push to join the common market. The dash for growth was an attempt to raise the productivity of the economy permanently. This meant looser fiscal policy: higher public spending and lower taxes. It led to the most remarkable year, when the economy grew at the quite unsustainable rate of approaching 6 per cent in 1964.

The big issue when the Wilson government came in was whether to face the problem of the balance of payments by devaluing the pound immediately, as a number of the new Prime Minister's advisers urged. The main macroeconomic themes of the Wilson governments of 1964–66 and 1966–70 were the attempts first to stave off devaluation with a series of emergency alternatives, and then to 'make devaluation work'. The crunch came in November 1967, popularly remembered in the phrase 'the pound in your pocket has not been devalued'.

In Reginald Maudling, who laid the foundations of the boom, the Treasury had a Chancellor whom they liked and admired. Sir Douglas Allen, later Lord Croham, who worked with Maudling at the Treasury from 1962 to 1964, said, 'He was a gambler – a nice man to work for. He took risks and he was a bit unlucky. He expanded the economy at just the wrong time.'

Allen believed Maudling's Permanent Secretary, William Armstrong, should have persuaded him to be more cautious in spring and summer of 1964. And Sir Alec Cairncross, the chief economic adviser, observed that Maudling 'took risks with the balance of payments in the hope of a breakthrough in economic growth in which we had little faith'.

The irony about the Maudling boom was that until it became apparent, he had been criticised on all sides for being too cautious. Indeed, he was known as 'Dawdling Maudling'. Then came the boom. This led to a burgeoning balance of payments problem which Wilson and others played up in the run-up to the 1964 election. When Maudling handed the keys of No. 11 over to the new Chancellor, James Callaghan, he famously quipped, 'Sorry about the state of the books, old cock.' Maudling and Callaghan got on well and this remark did not get into the public realm until memoir time. This was quite a contrast to the handover many decades later between Labour's Chief Secretary to the Treasury Liam Byrne in 2010 to the incoming David Laws. It was Treasury tradition that outgoing ministers left friendly notes about the inheritance, but Laws shamefully chose to publicise Byrne's joke, 'I'm afraid there is no money', and this became cannon fodder for the coalition government. Treasury officials were not amused by Laws's abuse of a light-hearted tradition.

Maudling subsequently suggested that Wilson had created a rod for his own back by, in Maudling's view, exaggerating the scale of the balance of payments problem during the election campaign.

When Labour came into office in October 1964, the boom was nearing its end. Maudling was the last of a series of Chancellors whom Macmillan had appointed in his desire to stimulate economic growth and bring down unemployment. As noted, the high unemployment and social distress he had witnessed in his constituency of Stockton-on-Tees during the interwar years had depressed Macmillan and influenced him for life. Indeed, it became a joke among officials in Whitehall the number of times, both as Chancellor (December 1955 to January 1957) and as Prime Minister (1957 to 1963), Macmillan referred to Stockton.

Today, Macmillan is remembered as Chancellor for having introduced premium bonds and as Prime Minister for the statement that we'd 'never had it so good'. This was not an original line – the phrase had in fact been popularised by President Harry S. Truman – but at the time it was widely thought to be an invention of Macmillan's. Moreover, the phrase people remembered was a classic newspaper corruption of what Macmillan actually said. It was in a speech to a Conservative rally in Bedford in July 1957, and did not even appear in the original printed version of his speech.

How do I know this? I learned from a neighbour who recognised me in my local pub, and said he wanted to add to a reference I had made in my *Observer* column to Macmillan's quote. 'I was there in the hall,' he said, 'and Macmillan was in fact responding to a heckler.' Now, around that time, the character actor Peter Sellers had made some very funny records, including a brilliant take-off of a standard politician's speech. In one of these, someone interrupts and shouts, 'What about the workers?'

to which the Peter Sellers character replies, 'What about the workers indeed, sir?'

At all events, my informant told me that some wag in Macmillan's audience had shouted out, 'What about the workers?' prompting Macmillan to reply spontaneously, 'Go around the country, go to the industrial towns, go to the farms and you will see a state of prosperity such as we have never had in my lifetime – nor indeed in the history of this country. *Indeed, let us be frank about it – most of our people have never had it so good!*'

Ironically, given what was to come, one of Macmillan's themes was to warn about the dangers of inflation – then at what were subsequently remembered as very low levels. Nevertheless, the annual rate of increase in the index for retail prices had been creeping up that year, from 1.7 per cent in April to 2.1 per cent in May, 3.2 per cent in June and, indeed, reached 4.5 per cent in the month of that 1957 Bedford speech.

The British economy was in the process of entering a long period when, via 'pay pauses', 'pay norms' and other forms of incomes policy, governments of both major parties became preoccupied with trying to curb the wage demands of the trade unions. Indeed, work on incomes policy became a growth industry for the economics profession, including some of the economics professors and lecturers one encountered at Cambridge.

As Prime Minister, Macmillan would second-guess his Chancellors, occasionally firing them or provoking them into resignation – the classic instance being the resignation of Chancellor Thorneycroft and two junior Treasury ministers, Enoch Powell and Nigel Birch, in January 1958, when Macmillan overruled them over planned expenditure cuts – cuts they were advocating because of their concerns about inflation, the annual rate of which had reached 4.6 per cent in December 1956. Macmillan brushed this episode off as 'little local difficulties' and proceeded with a planned overseas tour. He had more style than his modern successors!

As we have seen, in Maudling, Macmillan found a Chancellor who was far less cautious than some of his predecessors; but not at first. However, by the time Maudling had really stoked up the economy, sparking the eponymous Maudling boom in 1963, Macmillan had retired on health grounds.

There is fashion in economics: during the more recent period of austerity under George Osborne (Chancellor 2010–16), the obsession of politicians, most economic analysts and the media was with 'the deficit'. By this was meant the budget deficit. The balance of payments deficit on physical and non-merchandise trade, which was the fashionable obsession of the 1960s and '70s, hardly got a mention – at least not until the threat of Brexit.

But in the 1960s it was the budget deficit that hardly got a mention in the public prints. The obsession was with that balance of payments deficit, which was expanding during what became known as Maudling's dash for growth.

Maudling's hope, along with that of many economists, was that the dash for growth would lead the British economy into a virtuous circle, in which higher demand would lead to more investment and a reduction in the balance of payments deficit. Unfortunately for the Conservatives, the reverse was true. The ballooning balance of payments deficit became a big story, and Wilson, as Leader of the Opposition, made a meal out of it.

Brian Reading, who was an economic adviser to opposition leader Edward Heath, maintained that Labour had only made an issue of the £800 million balance of payments deficit during the 1964 election campaign when they thought that they were going to lose the election. (A more recent example of promises politicians hope not to have to implement was Cameron's commitment to the EU referendum, which at least some of his advisers thought could be safely vetoed by the Liberal Democrats if there were to be another coalition in 2015.) Brian Reading maintained that it was this emphasis on the balance of payments that caused the collapse of confidence which came to dominate Wilson's government.

However, Maudling's quip to the incoming Chancellor may have taken years to emerge in public, but the state of the balance of payments was all too obvious. So there was Labour in October 1964, back in office after what Wilson had termed 'thirteen wasted years of Tory rule', with lots of plans – including the emergence of a 'National Plan' for industrial modernisation, not to mention the rallying cry to confront the 'white heat' of the scientific revolution – but immediately confronted with a balance of payments crisis.

There had been much preparation, and Labour had brought in their own chief economic adviser to the Treasury, in the shape of the Cambridge economist Robert Neild, who had come from the independent National Institute of Economic and Social Research. Neild was a firm believer in the need to address the balance of payments crisis by devaluing the pound, so that industry could regain price competitiveness in international markets.

Robert Neild's experience in 1964–67 was a classic example of an adviser finding their advice was not welcome, let alone followed. It has been well documented how Wilson was firmly against devaluation and ruled it out from the start, with Callaghan, the new Chancellor, agreeing with him. Neild finally lost patience with the ministerial veto on devaluation, and accepted an important job in Stockholm in the cause of nuclear disarmament – or at least the prevention of further proliferation.

Devaluation was eventually forced upon the government a few months after he had resigned.

You cannot keep a good man down. All these decades later, in his nineties, Robert Neild is still trying to give good advice to the body politic and wrote an interesting paper for the Royal Economic Society saying bluntly that in order to finance decent public services, the UK needs a significantly higher rate of taxation.

The previous decade had been a history of 'stop-go' and lurching from one balance of payments crisis to another. 'Stop-go' was a criticism levelled by the economic journalists of the time at what was seen as the jerky approach to the policy. Various metaphors were used: brakes off, brakes on, foot on the accelerator. The deficit Labour inherited was indeed huge by the standards of those days and, one way or another, the Wilson governments of 1964–70 spent most of the time coming to terms with the consequences of that deficit, and of their forlorn attempt to wish the obvious necessity of devaluation away. It is interesting that the balance of payments deficit in recent years, which receives far less attention than in the old days, has been significantly greater as a percentage of GDP than the notorious ones that led to the devaluation of 1967 and the IMF crisis of 1976.

The resistance to devaluation was powerful, but existed mainly at the ministerial level. Harold Wilson, who as a very young Cabinet minister had been at the Board of Trade in 1949, when the pound had been devalued from its pre-war level of $4.00 to $2.80, was scarred by that episode, and not at all receptive to the idea of another devaluation. His Chancellor, James Callaghan, was equally set against the idea. Callaghan was not an economist – Wilson was, but was also a proud statistician – and had been having private economic seminars at Nuffield College, Oxford, while in opposition. In government, he enjoyed the services of a formidable Whitehall advisory machine. But whereas one of the 'outsiders' he brought into the Treasury, Robert Neild, was a firm advocate of devaluation, Sir Alec Cairncross, the head of the Government Economic Service, was not – at least not at that stage.

However, the strains on the pound – which had been at a fixed rate of $2.80 since the previous devaluation fifteen years earlier – were such that the new government found itself introducing a surcharge on imports, and an export rebate scheme as a substitute. These were temporary measures and in effect an admission that the pound was indeed overvalued. There was constant pressure on the pound, sparking tension for a government with a very narrow majority. However, in the general election of March 1966, Labour gained a majority of nearly 100. This meant that it was in a happier parliamentary position, but the problem with the pound's overvaluation still remained. The next attempt to stabilise the position came with a deflationary package in July 1966, remembered ever after as 'the July measures' – very much a 'stop', not a 'go'. The seriousness of the position was such that they had also had to introduce a pay freeze.

Against the background of the balance of payments crisis, Wilson had fulminated against currency speculators, dubbing them 'the gnomes of Zurich'. But the speculation against the pound was as likely to be carried out by British businessmen, bankers and private individuals as by foreign bankers.

With regard to the issue of currency speculation, I had an interesting experience being interviewed on the *Today* programme by the well-known broadcaster Robert Robinson. On one occasion he took me for a coffee before the interview, said he knew absolutely nothing about the subject and asked if I could help him with some background, which I duly did. When we went on air, he began by saying, 'Now, everyone knows that...', drawing on what I had just told him, and proceeded to ask me a very difficult question which bore no resemblance to what he had said he would ask. I fumbled my way through my answer.

The next time I was interviewed by him, I was well prepared. 'Now, who *are* these speculators?' he asked on air.

'They are people like Robert Robinson,' I replied.

During the continual balance of payments crisis, the *FT* editor Gordon Newton saw quite a lot of Wilson. At a dinner held in his honour many years later, Newton recalled how he used occasionally to 'drop in at No. 10 on my way home'. There was an occasion when the FT index (the precursor to the FTSE 100) reached a new peak and the two celebrated the occasion with champagne. Wilson said to Newton, 'If anybody knew that a socialist Prime Minister was toasting the FT index, there'd be trouble with the party.'

Possibly because of the closeness of their relationship, and possibly out of a sense of national duty, Newton refused to advocate devaluation in the *FT*, even though Samuel Brittan and others thought it was both necessary and inevitable. I myself was a reporter at this stage, not an *FT* commentator. But I did advocate devaluation in *Socialist Commentary* – which was, by the way, on what was then the right wing of the Labour Party.

Earlier, when I was still on the *Mail*, I had attended a weekend *Socialist Commentary* talk by Tony Crosland, who was in the Cabinet, but not as Chancellor – a role he always wanted, thought himself eminently qualified for, but never achieved. I had been an admirer of his work for years – though not of his desire to abolish the grammar schools – and meeting him afterwards was a big moment. It also taught me the importance of discretion. I raised the subject of devaluation, having heard that he favoured it, and was hoping for an enlightening 'off the record' conversation – as, among other things, a fellow contributor to *Socialist Commentary*. Unfortunately, in my enthusiasm, I blurted out that I was working for the *Daily Mail*.

Crosland immediately clammed up. His face assumed a pained expression, and that was that. I had lost my moment. I had 'bogged' it. Years later, Conor Cruise O'Brien, who was then my editor-in-chief at *The Observer*, said to me over dinner about some regrettable moment, 'This, William, like everything else in my life, I have learned the hard way.'

Of course I didn't let Crosland down. I wouldn't have done. But I most certainly did not get the chance to. One of the oldest tricks of the reporting trade is to trap a public figure into an 'indiscretion' which becomes 'a story'. Sometimes the public figure walks blithely into the trap. Sometimes, more disturbingly, he or she is let down by a reporter who betrays a confidence given as 'background' or 'off the record' and not only quotes the source, but names him.

Shortly after I returned to the *FT*, I received an internal telephone call from Samuel Brittan asking whether I would accept if he suggested that I should become economics correspondent. Sam, as he is known to his oldest friends, had returned to the *FT* as economics editor, with the emphasis on writing a weekly column. This was after a year or so when he had been seconded to the newly created Department of Economic Affairs (DEA), which was intended to be a counterweight to the Treasury and a catalyst for faster economic growth. The Macmillan government had introduced the National Economic Development Office, overseen by the National Economic Development Council, in an effort to encourage improvements in the economy's productivity.

This brought members of the government, the employers' organisations and the unions together for monthly discussions, with papers prepared by the National Economic Development Office. But Wilson and his colleagues wanted a more formal body within government and set up the Department for Economic Affairs. It produced a national plan and in my opinion did better work than it has often been credited with. Nevertheless, it did not have much chance of counteracting the Treasury, and its efforts were frustrated by the impact of the 'no devaluation' decision on policy generally. The DEA was short-lived and was eventually wound up, being absorbed by other Whitehall departments at the end of the decade.

Although Sam has always had a good eye (and ear) for news, he wanted someone else to do the day-to-day coverage. But, oddly enough, I recall hesitating about accepting what became a dream job for me. Perhaps it was my suspicious attitude to economics, or sheer conservatism, or because I was really enjoying being a general feature writer and not knowing when I went into the office what subject I would be required to become an instant expert on that day.

My initial period as economics correspondent, in spring and summer of 1967, was relatively quiet. Indeed, in August, things were so quiet on the economic front that I was assigned to cover the threatened secession from the United Kingdom of the Isle of Man. Beneath the surface, difficulties were building up, however. The basic problem, as we have seen, was the overvaluation of sterling, which as noted was the major factor behind Britain's chronic balance of payments problem at the time. During this period when we were not allowed to advocate devaluation on the *FT*, a colleague of mine on the paper, Anthony Harris, kindly offered me some freelance work alternating with him to write an anonymous column for the *Oxford Mail* called 'Abacus'. So I was able to write about devaluation, under a pseudonym, though not for the *FT*. It was a particularly amusing exercise because I never saw what Anthony had written in the alternative weeks, but nobody appeared to complain about any inconsistency in the editorial line.

All hell broke loose in the autumn of 1967 with the devaluation of the pound. This had been a long time coming and constituted a belated acknowledgement of the inevitable consequences of the dash for growth under Maudling's chancellorship. This growth experiment had been the resultant of several contributory forces. There was general dissatisfaction with our economic performance vis-à-vis Continental Europe. There was also a new, strongly held feeling by Macmillan, when Prime Minister, that the Treasury was too powerful and exercised an unnecessarily deflationary and inhibiting influence on the economy. And there was a belief, encouraged by the influential economic commentators of the day, that policies of 'stop-go' played havoc with industry's investment plans. The 'stops' – tax increases; credit controls; emergency increases in Bank rate – were precipitated by balance of payments crises such as those under Peter Thorneycroft (Chancellor, January 1957 to January 1958) and Selwyn Lloyd (Chancellor, July 1960 to July 1962).

Wilson's statement that 'the pound in your pocket has not been devalued' is one of the abiding memories of the 1967 devaluation. It reminds me of a press conference Jim Callaghan gave as Chancellor when he announced that the government was in due course going to switch to decimalisation of the coinage – i.e. what we have been used to now for many years. Decimalisation was announced in the 1960s but introduced in the 1970s – it obviously took a lot of planning. (Brexit, meanwhile, was, according to the hard Brexiters, going to be introduced in a couple of years.) It may seem incredible to younger generations, but until decimalisation we lived in a world of 'pounds, shillings and pence' and there were 240 pennies to the pound. Moreover, the old penny was very bulky in one's pocket. At the press conference, I asked Callaghan whether they could do something about the extraordinary weight of the coins in one's pocket. He replied, 'If you feel so strongly about that, why don't you do what I do and get your tailor to give you reinforced pockets?'

In November 1967, Prime Minister Harold Wilson tried to soften the blow of the devaluation against which he had fought for so long. He resorted to a homely metaphor, which has gone down in history when many other statements have been forgotten. To this day, people refer to 'the pound in your pocket' when the name Harold Wilson comes up. It came in a broadcast announcement on the evening of the devaluation, and it was intended to be reassuring. But for the general public it had quite the reverse effect – and a consequent impact on Wilson's own and his government's reputations.

Devised by Treasury officials, the statement was meant to explain to the public that, while the currency had been devalued by 14.3 per cent against the US dollar – the currency against which most other countries valued their own – the impact on the general public would be much smaller than 14 per cent. The point being that imports were only a small proportion of most people's expenditure, and the effect would, on average, be more like 3 to 4 per cent on the cost of things people actually bought.

In his broadcast to the nation, Wilson said, 'Devaluation does *not* mean that the value of the pound in the hands of the British consumer, the British housewife at her shopping, is cut correspondingly. It does not mean that the pound in the pocket is worth 14 per cent less to us now than it was.' Wilson changed a phrase drafted by officials from 'money in our pocket' to 'pound in the pocket'.

The point may have been well intended, but it went down badly. I myself think Wilson was not only a consummate politician, but also something of a statesman. Among other things, despite huge American government pressure, he refused to send British troops to Vietnam, and did a great service to the nation in founding the Open University. But he had a slippery reputation – he was dubbed Harold 'Wislon' by *Private Eye*, and it stuck. There had been an earlier example when the cartoonist Vicky (Victor Weisz) referred to Harold Macmillan as Supermac. This was meant to be ironical but actually proved to work to Macmillan's advantage. By contrast, the dubbing of Harold Wilson as 'Wislon' was never seen in the same light.

The problem with the use of the notorious pound or money in your pocket concept – of which the officials who devised it were quite proud at the time – was that it was too clever by half, and, in any case, not strictly true because it *had* been devalued, albeit not to anything like the extent of 14 per cent. But it was not entirely their fault. One of those closely involved told me years later that Wilson had put such emphasis on the first half of the phrase that the second half, the rider, was not remembered.

It was natural for Wilson to grasp an opportunity to try to soften the blow. Apart from anything else, when the devaluation finally came, it was a blow to him personally. For years, Labour had been terrified of being considered 'the party of devaluation' – just as, after the onset of the financial crisis of 2007, Gordon Brown, haunted by accusations that Labour was the party of nationalisation, was slow to accept the advice of his officials that he would have to nationalise Northern Rock.

As president of the Board of Trade, Wilson had presided over what he referred to as 'a bonfire of controls', left over from the recent war. Unlike most economists, he was more tuned intellectually to physical, supply-side measures such as import controls to cure a trade deficit rather than to use of the price mechanism for a currency adjustment. Moreover, the devaluation of August 1931, when Britain came off the gold standard, may have taken place under the National Government, but the Prime Minister and Chancellor in that government were the Labour politicians Ramsay MacDonald and Philip Snowden. The memory contributed to the criticism that Labour was the party of devaluation.

In addition to Wilson's personal distaste for devaluation, he was able to cite powerful international considerations at the time. Early on, he insisted in a speech at the Guildhall that resistance to devaluation demonstrated loyalty to the Commonwealth, many of whose members held sterling balances in London.

While most of the economists in the Treasury and 10 Downing Street in 1964 favoured devaluation, Thomas Balogh, from Balliol College, Oxford, preferred import controls, and Sir Alec Cairncross, head of the Government Economic Service from 1964, opposed devaluation when it was first mooted immediately after Labour came to power. Wilson's opposition to devaluation was so vehement, however, that all talk of the subject was banned, and relevant papers were supposed to be destroyed.

But the price of Wilson's stand was, as his biographer Ben Pimlott pointed out, giving moral support for American foreign policy, not least in Vietnam, because propping up the pound required US intervention in the foreign exchange markets. Moreover, US officials were concerned that a devaluation of the pound could have repercussions elsewhere – which did eventually happen later, at the turn of the decade, when the cost of the

Vietnam War put strains on the dollar, opening the floodgates, and ending with the break-up of the Bretton Woods fixed exchange rate system (see Crisis 6).

However, despite the fact that UK support for American foreign policy was deeply unpopular at home, instigating many an anti-war demonstration on the streets of London, Wilson does go down in history with credit for resisting American demands for him to send British troops to Vietnam. Denis Healey, Defence Secretary at the time, claimed to me years later that he had stiffened Wilson's arm in this matter, insisting that Britain's support should be purely vocal.

In November 1964, shortly after the election, there was one of many panics over the pound, and a brief hiatus to the 'no devaluation' policy, when economic advisers Robert Neild and Sir Donald MacDougall were asked to consider the relative merits of devaluation or floating the pound. MacDougall, who strongly favoured devaluation, recalled sarcastically in his memoirs that the pound had just been 'saved' (temporarily) by means of a huge $3 billion loan raised by the Bank of England Governor Lord ('Rowley') Cromer, working the telephone, from central bank colleagues around the world. Robert Neild regarded this episode as a 'financial Munich'. From then on, as MacDougall observed, until the fatal day in November 1967, the subject of devaluation was taboo.

But a 'devaluation war book', advising on the appropriate currency adjustments and handling of announcements, was wisely kept by civil servants, and locked away in a safe for the day when they were almost certain it would have to be used. By November 1967, Britain's 'Rolls-Royce' civil service machine had unwisely managed to lose the code for the combination lock on the safe that contained the war book. The Treasury frantically telephoned

Peter Jay, who had been private secretary to its top official at the time, and was now economics editor of *The Times*. Luckily for them, Jay remembered the code, which was the date of the 1949 devaluation, with the digits reversed.

Jay did the honourable thing: he told the Treasury the code, but did not embarrass the government and his former colleagues by revealing what had happened, or taking journalistic advantage of it. I myself first heard about the episode decades later, when Jay told the story at an academic seminar on the 1967 devaluation. He did not embarrass his father-in-law either; he had been married to Callaghan's daughter Margaret since 1961 – when Labour were, of course, still in opposition.

As for Callaghan himself, as Chancellor he had many times been forced to indulge in what one can reasonably describe as a finance minister's 'forgivable lie'. Having felt it necessary to issue repeated denials of any intention to devalue, Callaghan found he had little option but to resign when the intervention was finally forced upon him – indeed, he had promised his Cabinet colleagues some months earlier that he would resign if his sterling defences were seen to be finally down.

Callaghan revealed in his memoirs that one of the big influences on his acceptance that the game was up was a private memorandum from Sir Alec Cairncross on 2 November in which the latter confessed that even he had become a 'convert to devaluation'. In Callaghan's words, 'He continued by saying that world opinion would have condemned devaluation at an earlier date but would now be understanding because it was known how hard the government had fought to avoid it.'

The November 1967 devaluation of the pound was preceded by many scare stories and nervous moments. At the *FT*, we had to be absolutely sure about our information. The editor had taken the decision not to rock the boat by calling for devaluation. But there was also a danger of causing trouble and being accused through sensationalism of precipitating a crisis. Indeed, Gordon Newton was so cautious that he seemed to adopt a policy of 'when in doubt, let the main feature article be about the aircraft industry'. In which context, my father-in-law at the time rang me one day and asked irately, 'Has the *Financial Times* turned into the *Aeroplane Gazette*?' Newton's approach was a variation on the traditional Fleet Street advice: 'If in doubt, leave it out.'

Financial crises can be a big test of relations between reporters and their contacts. In the period before the 1967 crisis, there were reports from the news agencies of a large loan being arranged for the UK through the central banking network based at the Bank for International Settlements in Basle. They were rumours, not hard reports. But the news desk rang me at home at around ten o'clock one evening to ask me to write the story. I certainly did not want to take any chances. Early on in my feature-writing spell at the *FT*, the editor, Gordon Newton, had charged into our office and barked, 'Keegan, you made a mistake!' Before I had got very far with my shamefaced apologies, he interrupted me: 'All right, that's enough. I don't like mistakes. Just don't do it again.'

On the evening of those rumours from Basle I telephoned an important source at the Bank of England, and at first received a very guarded response to my questions. After a few minutes of oral shadow boxing on the telephone, I found myself asking, 'Will I lose my reputation if I write this story?' The answer, to my relief, was no. This meant that I was happy, the paper was happy, and my interlocutor could not be found guilty of a direct 'leak'. This was an approach I confess I had to resort to from time to time in years to come.

The devaluation on Saturday 18 November, from $2.80 to $2.40, came at the height of Harold Wilson's intensive efforts to achieve what Macmillan had failed to do in 1963: to overcome President de Gaulle's resistance to our application to join the European Economic Community. In a note to George Brown, who had moved from being head of the Department of Economic Affairs to the Foreign Office, Wilson wrote that the devaluation 'ought to help' in regard to the application to join the EEC.

The point was that, in the closing weeks of the Bank of England's battle to fend off the speculative forces against the pound, the government was also frantically trying to break down French resistance, and one of the French objections had been the vulnerability of the pound. Indeed, there was a sense in which the French were doing their best to aggravate the pound's vulnerability. I recall that we at the *FT* were not alone in avidly awaiting every report and comment in *Le Monde* by their correspondent Paul Fabra. The Treasury and the Bank were also hanging on Fabra's every word. For some reason, we imagined that Fabra was a commentator of mature years and judgement. When I eventually met him at some European conference we were covering, it became obvious that he must have been very youthful at the time. He was very charming and I often compared notes with him at subsequent international conferences. It was not so much that he had had his ear to the ground as that the French government seemed to have chosen him as the unofficial mouthpiece of their every thought on the pound.

But with regard to any improvement in Britain's bargaining position resulting from the devaluation, and thus the collapse of one French objection, Wilson was realistic enough to say, 'I doubt whether it will in any way affect the General's long-term strategy' – which was, bluntly, to keep Britain out. De Gaulle always harboured suspicions of Britain's trustworthiness because of its links with America and concerns that it would fundamentally alter the nature of an EEC which was very much a French creation.

And so it proved. In the words of Sir Stephen Wall, the historian of our various efforts to join the EEC, nine days after the devaluation, 'on 27 November, categorically and contemptuously, de Gaulle dismissed Britain's application'.

For Callaghan, the failure of policy – which was as much Wilson's as his; indeed, more so – there was no question of resigning from the Cabinet altogether. He merely swapped jobs with Roy Jenkins, who went from what history has regarded as a most successful Home Secretaryship to his more controversial time as Chancellor of the Exchequer. At the Treasury, Jenkins's job was, to use the catchphrase of the time, 'to make devaluation work'.

At the *FT*, from November 1967 until the 1970 general election Samuel Brittan and I were almost as obsessed as the new Chancellor by the objective of 'making devaluation work'. I recall Sam, who had made the need for devaluation almost a personal crusade, declaring immediately after the event that, now that it had been achieved, he could turn his attention to other, more interesting issues than macroeconomic policy. On one occasion, he came into the office excitedly and announced, 'I have suddenly discovered the beauty of trees.' Yet, as it turned out, the aftermath of devaluation was to preoccupy us, and macroeconomic policy continued to be an obsession of British policymakers, and those of us covering it, for decades.

I realise nowadays that most people seem to think that everything is available on the internet. People such as myself, who like hard copy and press cuttings, are considered Neanderthals. But when embarking on a look back at the 1960s, I was eternally grateful to the way that at the *FT* at the time it was our practice to keep massive scrapbooks of our day-to-day coverage. Being something of a hoarder, I had kept my cuttings of the 1967–70 period in the study at my Snowdonia retreat. Going through the day-to-day coverage of those times was quite a revelation. One's broad memory was of Roy Jenkins's cautious policies finally paying off by the early 1970s, but all the efforts being ruined, from Labour's point of view, by a freakish set of trade figures just before the election. This gave rise to headlines such as 'Britain Back in the Red'. Certainly, it turned out that I had written seemingly endless reports about continual problems with the trade figures, more often than not as the main story on the front page – the 'splash'. It seemed to be a case of one embarrassing set of trade figures after another, with measures designed to squeeze consumer spending not working as well as expected, and Chancellor and Bank of England Governor Sir Leslie O'Brien frequently having to lecture the high street bankers – nearly all British in those days – to rein in their lending to private individuals – usually referred to by economists as 'consumers'.

However, there was some truth in the 'back in the red' story. The improvement in Britain's trade performance was not sustained and led up to the 1976 crisis.

The poor trend of the balance of payments figures in 1964–67, and the dire pre-devaluation forecasts of what lay in store for 1968 onwards, were the final nail in the coffin of the arguments of those politicians, not least Prime Minister Harold Wilson, who were still trying to resist devaluation. Eventually the pressures on the pound in the foreign exchange markets became overwhelming, and no amount of borrowing from other central banks could stave off the inevitable.

In his book *The Politics of Harold Wilson*, Paul Foot emphasised that the poor state of the balance of payments and the obvious vulnerability of sterling were perfect pretexts for the French to veto Britain's second application to join the European Economic Community. The French, driven by their obsessive quest to damage the dollar through the pound, insisted that entry to the common market would not be possible without a savage sterling devaluation followed by drastic deflationary measures.

The strategy was to restore industry's price competitiveness by making exports cheaper and imports more expensive. The 14.3 per cent devaluation meant that pounds were 14.3 per cent cheaper to those buying them. But, arithmetically, this also meant that foreign currency would cost British buyers almost 17 per cent more than before.

Moreover, it would take time for the hoped-for beneficent effects of devaluation to work through the system. The higher price of imports and cheaper exports would inevitably make the trade and balance of payments deficits worse before they got better, when, it was hoped, via the workings of the price mechanism and the impact on profitability, the volume of exports would rise and the import bill would be lower than it might otherwise be.

There were many nervous moments. The essence of the policy was to move resources into exports (or 'import saving'). In an economy close to full employment, this required restraint on domestic spending – both public and private. The sense of urgency was communicated to the public by restrictive budgets and tight controls on hire purchase (HP) agreements; arrangements which may seem bizarre to a modern age. The phrase 'hire purchase' meant what it said: instead of waiting until they had saved enough money to buy a car or what became known as 'consumer durables' (refrigerators, washing machines etc.), people could enjoy their use from the start, hiring them until they had paid off the price and were able to own them outright. There is nothing new under the sun: in recent years, the concept seems to have been revived in all sorts of complicated car lease deals.

As part of the July measures of 1966, aimed at staving off devaluation, people had initially been required to put down a deposit of 40 per cent on HP deals, reduced not long after to 33.3 per cent. But the Treasury noted that between the second halves of 1967 and 1968 the volume of consumer spending had not fallen, a development, or lack of development, which was not quite in keeping with the greater emphasis on exports and investment for future export capacity. I see from the archive that by early November 1968 I was reporting in the *FT* that the required down payment for HP deals was being raised from 33.3 per cent back up to 40 per cent – an episode I had long since forgotten.

Later that month I was reporting on a freeze on bank lending to individuals, so that banks should lend more to exporters – something that did not go down well with the banks, not least because it soured relations with their customers.

Most people of a certain age, and students of the period, are aware of the embarrassment of Labour's resort to the IMF almost a decade later, in 1976. But another largely forgotten feature of the 1967–70 years was the extent to which we were in the hands of the IMF even then. On 2 April 1969, I was apparently reporting in the *FT* that the British government still owed \$1 billion to the IMF on a loan taken out in 1965. Meanwhile, new 'standby arrangements' for loans were being negotiated with the IMF, which was insisting on a limit to what it called domestic credit expansion (DCE).

In 1976, the IMF was to become obsessed with the public sector borrowing requirement. But in 1967, and for the rest of the decade, its lodestar was this measure called DCE, which was a broader concept, covering the change in the stock of money *and* the balance of payments deficit. As British policymakers struggled to 'make devaluation work', they had to show interest in the IMF's targets for DCE – a concept that the predominantly Keynesian economic service had hardly paid attention to.

In the end, Chancellor Roy Jenkins's cautious Budgets led to a rare Budget surplus in 1969/70. In January 1970 (an election year), Jenkins declared that it was 'not a year for dissipating the achievements' – the balance of payments was improving and the Budget surplus was in sight – and that people must not pitch their Budget hopes too high.

True to his word, in his April Budget he introduced a 'moderate stimulus' of minor tax cuts, too moderate for his colleagues, who tended for a long time to blame him for Labour's election defeat in June.

It has gone into folklore that a fundamentally improving overseas trading balance was, unfortunately for the government, distorted by the importation of two jumbo jets in May, leading to a deficit and tabloid headlines proclaiming 'Britain Back in the Red'. Jenkins admits in his memoirs that, when consulted by Wilson about the timing of the election, he (Jenkins) ignored the advice of his own right-hand man, John Harris, that there could, indeed, be a freak set of figures.

But the unfortunate truth is that the beneficial effects of a devaluation that was a necessary condition for improving the UK's international competitiveness were gradually being eroded. Militant trade unions were putting in large wage demands in response to the squeeze on incomes that had made devaluation seemingly successful. This led to an inflationary trend which would have bedevilled a re-elected Labour government, and which ultimately floored the new Conservative government of Edward Heath.

One has to conclude that although the 'Britain back in the red' headlines were an exaggeration, and undoubtedly affected the result of the election that Wilson had expected to win, the improvement in the balance of payments after the 1967 devaluation was not sustained. The consequences can be seen in the events that led to the three-day week of 1973–74 and the IMF crisis of 1976.

1973: THE OIL CRISIS AND THE THREE-DAY WEEK

It is a cliché these days that journalists tend to be chained to their desks, slumped over their computers and trawling the internet. In the 1970s, we were encouraged to get out and about, and lunches with the great and the good were considered an essential part of the work.

However, I began to feel I needed a contrast to the daily round of economic statistics, and developed the habit of disappearing from the *FT* at lunchtime, driving home for a quick lunch to nearby Islington, and spending half an hour or so in my study writing what I hoped would be a bestselling comic novel. In those days there was no congestion charge and parking near the office was cheap and easy. At lunchtime there was very little traffic, and I could be home within ten minutes, and back at the office by 3 p.m. What a leisurely existence it now sounds! At the *FT* in those days one did not have to show one's face until 11 a.m., and could disappear after the editor's morning conference. I seldom worked later than 7 p.m.

Under Gordon Newton, my editor for the earlier period, accuracy was prized above scoops. When *The Times*'s Business News appeared on the scene in 1967, it rather overdid the search for scoops, and developed a reputation for unreliability. When Hugh Stephenson was made editor some time later, his brief was to 'cool it' and rebuild the section's reputation – once newspapers get a bad name for mistakes, it lingers. Indeed, in *The Guardian*'s case, memories of misprints in the early 1960s linger on, and people still refer wickedly to *Private Eye*'s great invention *The Grauniad*.

Alas, my part-time novel-writing absences were spotted, and I was taken aside by the editor and one of the assistant editors, Joe Rogaly, and told that the economics correspondent needed to get out and about a little more, and come up with some scoops. This was under the new editor, Fredy Fisher, who happened to have a strong interest in the economic news and was quite well connected himself.

Rogaly was deputed to take me in hand and show me how to do it. A lunch was arranged with the Chief Secretary to the Treasury, Patrick Jenkin, at a discreet hotel off Sloane Square. It was early summer and we were at the high point of what became known as the 'Barber boom', after Anthony Barber, the Chancellor, although it was really the Heath boom, because Barber, a nice man, was a relatively weak Chancellor in the face of the brusque, no-nonsense Heath. A strong Prime Minister, Heath had for a time the added advantage vis-à-vis the Treasury of the presence of Sir William Armstrong, who had been the Treasury's top civil servant and was by now the head of the civil service. But in the end, as we shall see, this close relationship ended in tears for Heath, Armstrong and the government. However, that was eight months later – during the three-day week. The episode I refer to here was at the peak of the boom, with Heath's dream of a sustained improvement in UK economic performance not yet shattered by the government's mishandling of the miners' dispute.

It was a Friday in May 1973. In the course of the lunch, Jenkin told us that, despite worries about the sustainability of the boom – the aim for some time had been 5 per cent real growth, well above the economy's long-term potential – the growth policy was to remain unchanged.

On our way back to the office, Rogaly, my senior, and appointed my mentor by Fredy Fisher, became excited and declared, 'This can be Monday's splash.' At this stage I should emphasise that half the Monday paper would be prepared on the Friday and they were always searching for news to fill the paper.

I protested, saying that I did not think 'no change' in policy was exactly a story, whereas he thought that given speculation about the unsustainability of the policy, 'no change' *was* a story. My doubts also extended to the fact that I hardly knew Jenkin, and had no idea how reliable he was. Alas, I was browbeaten into writing the story as a front-page splash and – surprise, surprise – the Treasury announced a package of public expenditure cuts on the Monday. Much as I liked Rogaly as a person, and admired his own journalism, that was an important moment in learning things the hard way, and marked the end of his role as my mentor. When the Chief Secretary rang me personally to apologise for having misled me, I managed to restrain myself – just.

In the story of relationships between Prime Ministers and Chancellors, and the balance of power, the chancellorship of Tony Barber stands out. Barber became Chancellor only by accident, after the sudden and unexpected death of Iain Macleod.

Macleod was an impressive man, both intellectually and in presence, though slightly below medium height. He suffered from a spinal complaint which caused him considerable pain, yet he gave the impression of physical strength. On one occasion when he came to lunch at the *FT* he dominated the conversation without monopolising it and deeply impressed the lot of us.

We all thought he would be an outstanding Chancellor, who would stand up to his Prime Minister. He had, after all, taken a brave stand some years earlier in resigning over the traditional way in which the Conservatives chose their leader – 'the customary processes of consultation', which led to the elevation of Alec Douglas-Home – and calling for a more democratic process of selection. The subsequent reforms had led to the election to the Conservative leadership of Edward Heath, a grammar school boy. Heath had been Chief Whip, and heavily involved in the abolition of retail price maintenance (RPM) as well as the ultimately unsuccessful trade negotiations during earlier efforts under Macmillan to join the EEC. His involvement with abolishing retail price controls had led *Private Eye* to christen him 'Grocer Heath'. Younger readers may be surprised by the phrase 'retail price maintenance', but for many years prices were strictly controlled in many areas and shops, and there was little competition. With the Conservatives gaining more confidence in the years after the war to indulge their free market principles, the abolition of RPM became quite a cause; indeed, it was a subject for most economics courses at the time.

Heath made Macleod his Chancellor. Alas, his chancellorship lasted a mere four weeks, part of which was spent in hospital. In his outstanding biography of Macleod, Robert Shepherd points out that after a routine operation for appendicitis, Macleod suffered a heart attack when he returned to No. 11. His death came as a shock and was quite unexpected.

Tony Barber was Chancellor for the remainder of Heath's premiership, which was to see the worst period for industrial relations since the war, the worst economic crisis – precipitated by the quadrupling of the price of oil in autumn 1973 – and one of the most ill-timed policy decisions in living memory, namely the indexation of wage increases to the retail prices index, on the eve of the oil crisis.

In fact, there was subsequently another increase in the oil price, so that over a short period it quintupled, having been so low ever since the Second World War that, although oil companies were often in the news, the price of oil was not, except when the duty on petrol would go up in annual Budgets. I recall John Llewellyn, then one of the economists at the Organisation for Economic Co-operation and Development (OECD), who was involved in the preparation of the OECD's influential Economic Outlook, remarking, 'For decades we just took cheap oil for granted.' It was hardly a factor in macroeconomic policy.

It had been because oil was so cheap that successive Chancellors saw the price of petrol at the pumps as a ready milch cow for extra duty. But the quintupling of what was known as 'the posted price' was, as they say, 'something else'.

There were two factors behind this quite dramatic increase in the price of oil. The first was that, after the devaluation of the US dollar associated with the break-up of the Bretton Woods fixed exchange rate system in 1971–73, the oil producers were noticing the impact on their revenue – the price being quoted then, as now, in dollars. But the real force was imparted by the outbreak of the Yom Kippur War between Arab states and Israel between 6 and 25 October 1973.

Israel was invaded by Egyptian and Syrian forces. With the West, led by the US, supporting Israel, the Saudi king called for Arab solidarity, and the Arab states imposed an embargo on shipments of oil to the oil importers. What made it so serious was that Saudi Arabia was the world's biggest exporter of oil. This precipitated the use of 'the oil weapon' by the Arab oil producers generally, and spread to the other oil-exporting countries and the rise of OPEC (the Organization of the Petroleum Exporting Countries) as a serious economic and political force.

Then Iran got in on the act, seizing on the growing shortages. The market for current, real-time prices was known as the 'spot' market, but in technical terms the relevant price was known as the 'posted price', on which all oil company prices were based. This sounds crazy, but because of the arcane way in which posted prices were calculated, the actual spot price doubled when the Iranians increased their rates, although the official posted price went up by only 20 per cent.

Adrian Hamilton, our energy correspondent, was an expert on the oil business and he knew both the oil companies and the Middle East well. He seemed to be the only British journalist to appreciate that because of the abstruse price calculations, a 20 per cent rise did indeed signify a doubling in the actual price. He wrote this up, but the BBC and other newspapers reported that there had only been a rise of 20 per cent. This was the version also being put out by 10 Downing Street. The unfortunate fact of the matter was that this doubling in the price of oil was obviously going to drive a coach and horses through the government's economic strategy, even before the next batch of price increases. This exercise in procrastination did the government no good. It might have been wise to get their excuses in early about the way the oil shock was going to damage their economic strategy, but they chose not to own up immediately to the full impact.

There can be something funny about even the most authoritative of newspapers – a curious lack of confidence and a temptation to believe that the truth lies elsewhere. When the *FT*'s editor, Fredy Fisher, noticed the difference between his own correspondent's version and that of the others, he summoned Adrian and told him to print an apology the following day. But

Adrian held his ground and at a later editorial conference Fisher said that Adrian had told him – and 'he'd better be right' – that this was indeed a doubling of the price, in which case the story required Budget Day treatment.

I highlight this reminiscence not just because Adrian was a close colleague and friend of mine. I believe the episode showed the value of specialist correspondents on newspapers, who cultivate the important contacts in whatever line of reporting they specialise, but are not 'run' by them. Adrian had wonderful contacts in the oil business and was respected by them. Anyone who was not a specialist, such as members of the parliamentary lobby at the time, could be forgiven for missing the true significance. They have to rely too much on official 'briefings' – which was one reason I myself always turned down suggestions that I should move on to become a parliamentary lobby correspondent.

Of course, the policymakers who had come up with the idea of calming the trade unions by linking wage awards to prices had no idea that they were on the verge of a price-wage-price upward spiral caused by the drawn-out process by which, month by month, higher energy prices seeped through the economic system, causing increases in the prices of many goods and services dependent, one way or another, on the price of fuel. The policy was well-intentioned.

This inflationary process was not good news for Edward Heath's plans to revive the British economy and permanently raise its rate of growth. The increase in the price of oil imposed by the OPEC group had the effect of increasing the bargaining power of all the energy producers, not least the miners. This was a classic case of Macmillan's 'events, dear boy, events'.

As noted, the seemingly clever device by which the unions were to be tamed was known as 'the threshold agreement'. Once prices as measured by the cost of living index, known then as the retail prices index (but also covering many services not purchased in retail shops), reached a certain 'threshold', a rise in wage rates would be triggered. I vividly recall being approached, after the press conference explaining the policy – late in 1973 but crucially before the oil crisis – by Sir William Armstrong, for a brief private word. The great man seemed remarkably pleased with the policy and took some delight in pointing out to me that the threshold – 7 per cent – was quite high and might never be reached. Of course, the bombshell from OPEC would soon destroy the policy – and, eventually, the Heath government. Inflation went on up and up, peaking at 26.9 per cent in August 1975, by which time Wilson had been Prime Minister for eighteen months and was trying to cope with the dreadful inheritance from Heath.

Ask people who lived through the 1970s what they remember most about the economy, and nine times out of ten they will include 'the three-day week'.

The three-day week was called by Prime Minister Edward Heath on 13 December 1973, to come into operation at the beginning of January 1974. It was in response to serious concerns about energy shortages – concerns that were so serious that, shortly before it was announced, the Conservative government had alerted 'the alternative government machine', whose brief is to assume responsibility for running the country in an extreme national emergency, such as a nuclear attack. The revelation about the government's emergency fall-back preparations came in a series of *Sunday Times* articles some two years after the dramatic events of winter 1973–74, later reprinted in a pamphlet entitled *The Fall of Heath*. Written by the journalists Stephen Fay and Hugo Young, the articles revealed that nobody outside the inner circles of government knew of the plans at the time.

With oil shortages precipitated by a crisis in the Middle East, and the powerful mining union operating an overtime ban in protest against the government's incomes policy, it was undoubtedly a national emergency. There was not the proliferation of television channels we have these days, so that, in the interests of energy conservation, the government felt able to order the main channels to limit their hours of broadcasting, and switch off at 10.30 p.m. Without exactly imposing a wartime blackout, ministers told the public to economise on use of electricity. One minister (our old friend Patrick Jenkin again) even urged people when going to bed to brush their teeth in the dark. This advice, pretty ludicrous anyway, prompted a popular newspaper to send a reporter and photographer up to London's Highgate, where Jenkin lived. The following day, they printed a picture of the house with all lights blazing. January and February 1974 were a boom time for candle makers, and prices rose accordingly.

The three-day week and the failure of Heath to resolve a dispute with the powerful National Union of Mineworkers marked the nadir of his government. The essence of the problem was that the Conservatives, believers as they were in 'market forces', were the victims of the impact of the energy market on the miners' bargaining position. Heath was reduced to calling an election he did not wish to hold, which was effectively conducted on an issue he never wanted to arise. That issue was, in popular parlance: Who governs? Heath or the miners?

Unfortunately for Heath, it was the miners. No, not really: the chaos created by the impasse between the government and the miners most certainly brought down the Heath government, and the inheritance for Labour – from an election its leader Harold Wilson did not expect to win – was a poisoned chalice. But the worst fears of those in high places were not confirmed.

A minority of communist leaders intent on wrecking the normal processes of democracy did not conduct a coup. It sounds crazy even to say this, but at times during the economic troubles of the 1960s and 1970s there were fears of such coups – usually nurtured by extreme right-wing millionaires discussing plotting their own coups!

* * *

It was a long fuse that led to the three-day week and the collapse of the Heath government. The fashionable Keynesian weapon for fighting inflation in the 1960s had been incomes policies – that is, government attempts to control wage inflation either by appealing to the trade unions for 'voluntary restraint' in wage bargaining or, from time to time, by statutory controls.

This must seem odd to a younger readership, in an age of the gig economy, where so many people feel lucky to have a job at all, and the thought of an annual round of wage bargaining sounds quaint, but in those days most employees belonged to trade unions, who bargained regularly – usually annually – on their behalf. The unions were a power in the land and gradually sowed the seeds for a reaction, as they overplayed their hand, becoming too powerful.

It was the failure of the British governments of the 1960s and 1970s to cope with the problem of excessive union wage demands that led to the election of Mrs Thatcher in 1979. Most observers felt that the rot set in when the Wilson government drew back from implementing the legislation to control the unions advocated in a White Paper, 'In Place of Strife', in 1969. This paper was overseen by Barbara Castle, Employment Secretary, whose left-wing credentials could hardly be faulted. If she thought the unions needed to be restrained, then it was well worth considering. However, the proposal was considered, and then rejected. One of the key Cabinet figures against legislating to rein in the unions was James Callaghan, who had a strong union background. This left the field open for the more hostile approach to the unions by Mrs Thatcher in later days.

One will never know what would have happened if the Wilson government had gone ahead with legislating to bring the unions within the law. Most commentators and 'middle-of-the-road' people at the time seemed to think that, by drawing back after all the work that had gone into the White Paper, Labour missed a golden opportunity. My late colleague the political commentator Alan Watkins used frequently in subsequent years to blame James Callaghan, then Home Secretary, for his crucial intervention. Labour's links with the unions were powerful, and Callaghan was a union man.

Be that as it may, the Conservatives under Heath were determined to rein the trade unions in, and to weaken their power via a mixture of legislation – the Industrial Relations Act of 1971 – and exhortation, as well as moving towards a macroeconomic policy that at first tolerated an anti-inflationary policy of allowing unemployment to rise. This was accompanied by early declarations that, unlike Labour, they would not be 'interventionist' – epitomised in the frequently cited quote from Trade and Industry Secretary John Davies that the government would no longer prop up 'lame ducks'.

But the efforts of the Heath government Mark I soon came to grief, and the experience suggested that any attempts to implement 'In Place of Strife' might have met the same fate. As Edmund Dell wrote in *The Chancellors: A History of the Chancellors of the Exchequer*: 'The [Conservative] Industrial Relations

Act was found to create more problems than it solved. Bitterly resisted by the trade unions, it was in the end also condemned by the employers.' Dell added: 'Barbara Castle's legislation might well have proved equally unworkable.' I wonder.

Indeed, the background to the onset of the three-day week and the fall of the Heath government can be pinned down to three factors: first, the succession of events that led to the collapse of what was known as the Selsdon Man approach; secondly, the way in which the oil crisis – or 'oil shock', as the Japanese christened it – compounded the government's economic problems; and thirdly (in my opinion), a missed opportunity during crucial talks at a meeting of ministers, employers and unions under the auspices of the National Economic Development Council on 9 January 1974.

Selsdon Man was the phrase with which Harold Wilson had derided the policies that lay behind the Conservative manifesto in the 1970 general election – supposedly hammered out at a weekend meeting at the Selsdon Park Hotel, Croydon, Surrey. There is some controversy as to just how important that particular meeting was, but the label, used to describe the Heath government's early free market agenda, stuck.

It was a dramatic succession of events that undermined the Heath Mark I approach. Less than a year on from the June 1970 election, the most famous symbol worldwide of British industrial success, Rolls-Royce, was on the verge of collapse: on 4 February 1971, the government announced that, to save the aero-engine and luxury car giant from bankruptcy, it would be nationalised.

Then came a six-week miners' strike in January and February 1972, 'resolved' with a highly inflationary wage settlement. On top of this, the Chief Constable of Glasgow telephoned No. 10 to inform the Prime Minister that he could no longer be certain of maintaining public order while Upper Clyde Shipbuilders was threatened with closure. National unemployment had reached the hitherto unheard-of level of one million in December, and unemployment was an especially serious issue in Glasgow. This precipitated the rescue of Upper Clyde Shipbuilders – again, as in the case of Rolls-Royce, with public funds. Ironically, the rescue was announced by the minister who had not wanted to prop up 'lame ducks', Trade and Industry Secretary John Davies, on 28 February 1972. Davies was a decent man, but one of a number who have not found the transition from industry to politics that easy.

Not to put too fine a point on it, there was now, in the winter of 1971–72, panic in the ranks of the Heath government. The phrase 'U-turn' came into popular parlance. It was applicable not only to the reversal of the previous attitude towards intervention in industry and in wage bargaining – Heath and Barber had disavowed incomes policies as failed policies of the Labour government – but also to macroeconomic policy. The emphasis was once again on 'growth', with targets of 5 per cent over the next two years, and much of the economic reporting focused on whether the government was achieving this goal. The brakes were off, with regard to both tax and public spending.

'U-turn' was a phrase that went down in history, and was subsequently employed by successive oppositions to describe many a change of policy. Harold Wilson, as Leader of the Opposition, said about a particular Heathian policy that the Prime Minister had 'nailed his trousers to the mast'. In those days I was often invited to the (Communist) Chinese embassy in London and quizzed about the economy and government policy generally. But there came a moment when the suspicion dawned on me that they were less interested in my economic views than in my explanation of various pieces of jargon that cropped up in the newspapers. Certainly I recall being asked about the meaning of 'U-turn', and one question parked itself vividly in my mind: 'Mr Keegan: Mr Wilson – what does he mean when he says Mr Heath has nailed his trousers to the mast?' On one occasion my first wife was also present at a small dinner in the embassy, when a (female) Chinese diplomat gave her a stern and extraordinarily rude lecture on the supposed irresponsibility of having more than one child. I think that incident brought my relationship with the embassy to an end.

There followed another 'dash for growth' reminiscent of the Maudling boom in 1963–64, this time called the Barber boom, even though, as noted, the real drive for another 'growth experiment' came from the Prime Minister himself. There was yet another macroeconomic factor: the Bank of England had been working on a new policy based on a research document called 'Competition and Credit Control'. Its basic message could be summarised as 'lots more competition and a lot less credit control'. Quantitative controls on bank lending were abolished, and in theory credit growth would be controlled by increases in interest rates. But those were the days when the government, not the Bank of England, made decisions on interest rates. In keeping with the policy U-turn, interest rates were kept low for too long, and monetary policy for a time became grist to the mill of the dash for growth. The chief economic adviser to the Treasury then was Sir Donald MacDougall, who, although no monetarist, later described the policy as 'inherently inflationary'.

Thus most of the brakes were off economic policy in the run-up to the oil crisis and the three-day week; indeed, in a sense, when Patrick Jenkin misled Joe Rogaly and me at that lunch in May 1973 about 'no change in policy', he proved to be partly right. Because although Tony Barber announced public spending cuts the following Monday, these were aimed at reducing total output in 1974 by a mere 0.5–0.7 per cent of gross domestic product, at a time when the economy was booming away and inflationary pressures intensifying. Indeed, in the month of January 1974, when the three-day week began, the retail prices index was running at 12 per cent above the rate of a year earlier and there was a huge balance of payments deficit even before the impact of the oil crisis. Minor reductions in public spending plans were calculated to make little difference.

The three-day week had been in operation for, well, just a week when the government, in the shape of Chancellor Barber, rejected an olive branch offered by the TUC which might just have settled the miners' dispute and saved Heath's government. Because of the impact of the oil price on the price of energy generally, the miners were in a strong bargaining position. In the words of Sir Donald MacDougall, who had moved on from being chief economic adviser to the Treasury to become chief economic adviser to the CBI, and who attended the fateful meeting, 'It is just possible that a chance was missed of changing the course of history.' MacDougall doubted it, but Sir Douglas Allen, who was also there as Permanent Secretary to the Treasury, told the historian Peter Hennessy and me many years later that he thought a chance was genuinely missed.

The fatal day was Wednesday 9 January 1974, and the occasion was a meeting of the National Economic Development Council, popularly known as Neddy. I referred earlier to the way Neddy had been set up way back in 1962 by Prime Minister Harold Macmillan and one of his many Chancellors, Selwyn Lloyd. Worried about wage inflation and low productivity in the British economy, they hoped that by bringing government, employers and unions together they could improve our industrial performance.

Macmillan's (failed) application for us to join the EEC was born of the same analysis and desire.

Now here was another Conservative government, twelve years later, in the course of losing its grip over an industrial dispute, in an atmosphere where inflation was a lot worse than when Neddy was set up. The crisis provoked by the miners' overtime ban and three-day week was the obvious topic for discussion.

There was much to-ing and fro-ing between ministers, union leaders, government officials and the director-general of Neddy's permanent staff in the run-up to this crucial meeting and after. The key issue was whether other unions would try to cash in on any exception the government might grant to the miners, whose bargaining power had been strengthened enormously by the quadrupling of the oil price. Younger people these days might find this hard to believe, but after their six-week strike in 1972 the miners had secured a 27 per cent wage rise, and now they were asking for no less than a 35 per cent increase.

There were several phases to the requirements on employers and unions imposed by the incomes policy. Industry was in what was known as 'Phase 3' of the latest incomes policy. I used to report on the Neddy meetings for the *FT*. At the time, the director-general of Neddy was the respected former senior civil servant Sir Ronald McIntosh. We are indebted to him for the fact that, for what he said was the 'one and only' time in his life, he had decided to keep a daily diary of events from November 1973 as 'the sense of impending crisis in the economy was almost tangible'.

At a Neddy meeting on Wednesday 5 December 1973, one Cabinet minister, Dick Marsh, said the nation was faced with the most dangerous situation since the 1930s and that it was no time to dismantle the prices and incomes policy. I asked at the subsequent press conference whether the government's ambitious growth target was now unrealistic, to which McIntosh replied that he thought it was. This answer was reported in some papers as being the stated view of Chancellor Barber. The Prime Minister and Chancellor were furious, but when Barber accepted McIntosh's explanation that he had not attributed that view to the government, Barber then criticised him for having said anything at all on the subject. Those were sensitive times, and Barber himself was particularly sensitive.

McIntosh recorded in his diary that in an analysis presented at the 9 January Neddy meeting, it was concluded that if the three-day week lasted only until the end of the month, 'the consequences would be manageable and recovery reasonably quick'. But beyond that, 'the effects on output, exports and eventual recovery would get quickly and cumulatively worse'.

It was then that one of the leading trade union leaders, Sidney Greene of the National Union of Railwaymen, came out with a serious offer from the TUC. According to McIntosh, he said 'that if the government made a settlement with the miners possible (i.e. outside Phase 3), the TUC and the trade union movement would not use this in other negotiations or quote it as an excuse for other exceptional settlements'.

McIntosh had remarkably close access to all the key union leaders. Although Fay and Young in their brilliant account of *The Fall of Heath* emphasise the ill intentions of certain union leaders, not least the communist firebrand Mick McGahey, vice-president of the National Union of Mineworkers, the most senior union leaders, including the TUC's secretary general Len Murray, were anxious about the potential damage of the three-day week and taking a statesmanlike view of the need to calm things down.

Greene, speaking for the TUC, added to his presentation of

the offer by insisting that it was intended, in McIntosh's words, 'to get the miners' dispute out of the way and so bring three-day working to an end'.

There had been so much bad blood between the Heath government and the unions in the early stages that an atmosphere of suspicion was inevitable. Nevertheless, in my view this offer was a golden opportunity to get the government off the hook and bring the three-day week to a swift conclusion – and even to ward off that fatal subsequent election on 'who governs'.

This is not just my view. It was also the view of Sir Douglas Allen, a tough man and nobody's fool. Allen could be relied upon to be as sceptical, indeed cynical, as any heir to the Doubting Thomas of the Gospels. He was sitting two rows behind his Chancellor, and tried to pass him a note. Allen had quickly come to the conclusion that the TUC's offer was worth considering. Alas, his note was not passed to the Chancellor in time, and Barber emphatically dismissed the offer. From that moment on, it was, as they say, all downhill.

There is little doubt that the three-day week had an enormous impact on the public's perception of the competence of the Heath government. Ironically, there were suggestions that productivity went up during the period, and that in some cases industries were producing in three days what had previously taken five.

It was also downhill for Sir William Armstrong, head of the civil service, who was working so closely with Edward Heath that he became known as the Deputy Prime Minister. Armstrong was very hawkish with regard to the miners' claim: on one occasion that January, while giving ministers dire warnings about the consequences of 'giving in to the miners', he apparently more or less prevented the others from speaking. On another occasion, he locked the doors behind a meeting of permanent secretaries and, according to the then Cabinet Secretary John Hunt, it became obvious that the strain was too much for him. He had a nervous breakdown and was sent off to the West Indies to recuperate.

Mercifully, he duly recovered and returned to became chairman of the Midland Bank. I remember that he was present at a dinner of the independent Institute for Fiscal Studies in the City in the late 1970s. He and I ended up at the bar, and when we left he said we must have lunch before long and he would tell me the whole story. Sadly, he died before either of us got around to arranging that lunch.

The other Treasury Armstrong – no relation – was Robert Armstrong, later Lord Armstrong of Ilminster. Having moved from the Treasury – where he was involved in the post-1967 devaluation policy – to 10 Downing Street, where he was Ted Heath's Principal Private Secretary, he was generally considered to have done sterling work in very difficult times. As the former civil servant Alun Evans discovered when interviewing Armstrong, the latter was amused to hear that, when the Treasury wanted him back, the Prime Minister refused to let him go, on the grounds that he was invaluable. This was a judgement that the gruff and taciturn Heath had not previously got around to sharing with his treasured private secretary.

Heath's government ended in tears in the 'Who Governs?' general election of February 1974. There was a strong view that, if he had called the election earlier, he might have won. Ironically, Wilson, who had expected to win the 1970 election and lost, was surprised to win this one. Unfortunately for him and Labour, the economic inheritance was to prove horrendous and led inexorably to the next crisis.

1976: THE IMF CRISIS

J. K. Galbraith's book *The Great Crash 1929* is usually considered the classic account of that crisis, yet it was published a quarter of a century later.

The British IMF crisis of 1976 has spawned library shelves of books and academic papers, and I have lost count of the number of relevant seminars I have attended on the subject. But Sir Douglas Wass, Permanent Secretary to the Treasury at the time, was sufficiently dissatisfied with what he had read on the crisis that he felt it necessary to publish his own version over thirty years later, in 2008.

Sir Douglas was a kind and courteous man, and a friend of mine. But there was undoubtedly a hint of Treasury arrogance in the way that, in his preface, he dismissed previous efforts, which were damned with faint praise. As far as he was concerned, memoirs and diaries 'contribute to an understanding of the economic problems faced by the government in 1976 – and what is more to the dilemmas it had to resolve. They also provide a valuable perspective on the purely political aspects of the crisis.' But 'they fall well short of an objective account of what happened and indeed many of them contain notable errors of fact'.

Since this is a personal memoir, I do not intend to go into the many accounts of 1976 available, but note with some amusement that Sir Douglas does not list the contribution that my fellow author Rupert Pennant-Rea and I made to discussion of the crisis.

It happened like this. While I was at the Bank, Rupert, who was then Christopher Dow's personal assistant, before leaving to join *The Economist*, suggested that we should combine our resources to write a book on British economic policy. In the course of the project, I wrote a chapter entitled 'Sterling and the Balance of Payments: 1976 and all that...' I had the good fortune to be able to interview many of the key participants in the events of 1976 and, on re-reading all these years later, I like to think that those interviews threw at least some light on what happened at some of the key moments.

The concerns about public spending and inflation of the early 1970s led to an obsession with the behaviour of what became known as 'the monetary aggregates' – various measurements of the money supply. Notes and coins in circulation were known as M1; wider measures were known as M2 and M3, giving rise to lots of jokes about motorways. The other obsession was with the size of the budget deficit and the public sector borrowing requirement (PSBR). The PSBR financed that part of the public spending which could not be covered by receipts from taxation and other duties. There was endless discussion and analysis in the Bank of England while I was there, but it was the government, led by Prime Minister James Callaghan and Chancellor Denis Healey, who were in the firing line. And the general loss of trust in a Labour government – always suspect in the eyes of the financial markets at the best of times – was not helped by the conspiracy theories that surrounded the surprise resignation of Harold Wilson in April 1976, which propelled Callaghan to No. 10. Some observers connected the resignation with these conspiracy theories. There were rogue elements in the security services who had deluded themselves into thinking that Harold Wilson was a communist agent. It was all nonsense, but Wilson himself seems to have become quite paranoid about it. The truth was that his resignation was not a surprise to his closest confidants. His solicitor, Lord Goodman, was told very early on after Wilson was re-elected in February 1974, and Callaghan certainly knew too.

The strategy adopted by the economic policy machine was to borrow its way through the perfect storm of serious inflation and mounting concern about public spending. On the horizon was oil wealth for the UK from the fruits of oil exploration in the North Sea.

Public sector entities, such as the nationalised industries and local authorities, were encouraged to borrow in foreign currency, to boost the foreign exchange reserves. But, in the end, the Achilles' heel of the country's financial position was the sterling balance problem.

This reflected the historical fact that Britain had depended on vast funds of Empire and Commonwealth countries' reserves during and after the Second World War. Callaghan had not wanted to let such depositors down. This preyed on his mind both in the initial decision not to devalue in 1964 and when he was forced to devalue in 1967. Indeed, the guilty feeling that he had let these countries down with his broken promises was one of the reasons Callaghan gave for his resignation in November 1967.

The eventual 1976 sterling crisis was postponed as domestic problems mounted in 1974–75 by the accrual of extra deposits from the newly rich Middle Eastern and African oil producers after the quintupling of the price of oil at the end of 1973 and beginning of 1974. And, once I moved from the *FT* in April 1976 to the Bank, I had access to just how serious was the drain on these deposits as the oil producers diversified their investments to New York, Zurich and other safer havens.

I also had access in advance to the figures for the PSBR. This produced an awkward moment for me when lunching with one of my old *FT* colleagues who was searching for a scoop and was trying out various guesses on me. But as poacher turned game-keeper I had to be holier than thou.

The 1976 IMF crisis is well remembered. It is far less well known in folklore that Britain had already had to borrow shortly before Christmas 1975, from what was known as the IMF oil facility, which was designed to help importing countries like the UK who were suddenly hit by the higher oil prices. But this did not involve the strict conditions that would be imposed later. Having sounded out the IMF about another 'tranche' – in IMF jargon – of borrowing, the government was hoping to get through 1976 with credits from the central banking network based in Basle.

They fell into a trap of agreeing to apply for further IMF loans if they had problems repaying the central bank credits. Alas, it became apparent that this would be the case – not only were oil producers diversifying, but other sterling balances were being withdrawn from London. Indeed, some two thirds of the out-flow in 1976 was due to withdrawal of sterling balances.

A major problem was that, given the impact on competitive-ness of soaring wage inflation – as we have seen in Crisis 2, the year-on-year inflation rate had peaked at 26.9 per cent in August 1975 – the Treasury was considering the need for a minor depre-ciation of sterling early in 1976.

Unfortunately, while this tactic was still under discussion, the withdrawal of some sterling balances by Nigeria early in March

1976 gave the markets the impression that the Bank was deliberately trying to edge the pound down. The cat was thrown among the pigeons the day after, when a pre-arranged cut in bank rate – then known as minimum lending rate – was announced. From then until the IMF loan towards the end of the year, confidence and trust in the British economy on the part of investors in sterling evaporated.

It had been quite an experience going from covering the burgeoning economic crisis in 1975–76 for the *FT* to a central bank where the reserves and sterling balances were under siege. This was a delayed reaction to the way the countries for whom the quintupling of the oil price was not a crisis but a bonanza had been raking in the money and depositing it, in 1973–75, in the traditional home for their reserves, namely London. These were principally the oil-exporting countries in the Middle East and Nigeria.

But, as we have seen, there came a point when they began to diversify their holdings, redepositing in New York and Zurich, for instance. All that was required was for an inevitable need to diversify to coincide with much-publicised economic problems, and the seeds were sown for what was then the biggest British economic crisis since the Second World War.

The storm was brewing before I arrived at the Bank in April 1976. Although we all thought at the *FT* that the official reserve figures on which I had to report every month were heavily massaged, or 'figments of the official imagination', I had no idea just how serious were the drain on the sterling balances and the true downward pressure on the pound until I started working at the Bank.

A senior Treasury official who was considered mischievous by some had encouraged me to write a front-page story in the autumn of 1975 that the UK might eventually have to apply for help from the IMF. But the cat did not really get out of the bag until those two days in March 1976, when, after much private dithering and discussion about whether the Treasury and Bank should initiate a devaluation of the pound, the financial markets did it for them. The virtual concurrence of a reduction in interest rates and some prominent selling of the pound caused the markets to speculate that the monetary 'authorities', as the Treasury and Bank were known, had deliberately embarked on a policy to force the pound down.

I don't think they had. I think they were still dithering. But the timing of a sale of sterling on Thursday 4 March 1976 by the Bank, on behalf of the government of Nigeria, and the cut in the official interest rates on Friday 5 March, gave the market the impression that they certainly had. (Oddly enough, this was only bringing the bank rate, then known as minimum lending rate, into line with market rates!) When I arrived at the Bank, almost everyone involved wanted to give me his or her version of events, often at great length. Sir Douglas Wass even wrote an exhaustive account of the events of 1976 (referred to above) with the clever title *Decline to Fall*. This title managed to epitomise the way that the pound had at first declined to fall when some officials, including Wass, had wanted it to, and then really did fall, out of control, taking the reputation of the Labour government with it. Indeed, the Conservatives were able to taunt Labour with the charge that it had had to go 'cap in hand' to the IMF for many years after.

In his book, Wass went to great lengths to challenge Healey's repeated assertion that if only the Treasury had got its forecasts right, he would not have had to apply to the IMF. Indeed, Wass once told me that the application to the IMF was made *before* those forecasts. Nevertheless, Healey made a great hit for years afterwards with his joke that he would like to do to economic forecasters what the Boston Strangler had done for the reputation of door-to-door salesmen.

Before the decision to apply to the IMF, Callaghan tried various devices – including approaches to his friend Chancellor Helmut Schmidt and the redoubtable Henry Kissinger – in the hope of warding off the next approach for a loan, which would involve 'conditionality' – i.e. strict and humiliating terms.

It was to no avail. Britain was going to be taught a lesson. It mattered not that the government had been taking various restraining measures, such as planned cuts in public spending, before it finally applied for the loan that would have strings attached. It was the Treasury official closest to the Americans, Sir Derek Mitchell, who warned that what Labour regarded as savage spending cuts would be needed. Mitchell was close to Ed Yeo, the hard-line US Treasury official who was urging penal cuts in public spending. In a negotiation with the Fund, it was not good enough to say, 'Look what we have already done.' The other side always wants more. The problem in such situations is that whatever measures a government takes, unless these impress the financial markets, they will not be enough and the IMF will demand more.

It was by any standards a dramatic summer and autumn. The pressure on the pound and the drain on the reserves were such that Denis Healey and Governor Richardson famously had to turn back at the airport and cancel a flight from Heathrow to Manila, where the annual meetings of the World Bank and IMF were taking place. This turnaround was on Tuesday 28 September 1976. Given the speed at which the pound was collapsing, one American observer said to me, 'The interesting question is not why they turned back from the airport, but why they went there in the first place.'

Treasury officials had decided early in September that there was no way that confidence could be restored in the British economy without an application to the IMF, although the politicians were naturally resistant. But with the pound under such pressure, and confidence so low that it was difficult to sell government bonds – a situation known as a gilt strike – the government decided that the game was up and they had to apply to the IMF immediately. The announcement was made on Wednesday 29 September 1976 and the following day Healey had to face the Labour Party conference, where he got a rough reception from the troops. Such was the state of the Labour Party at the time that Denis Healey, the Chancellor of the Exchequer, was not even on its national executive committee and had to address the conference from the floor. He was allocated a mere five minutes, but made a powerful speech, amid some booing but many a cheer.

Ed Yeo had chosen to fly to Manila via London to see Healey, and he was the hard man. But if he and his boss, US Treasury Secretary William Simon, had had their way with really savage cuts, the suspicion in the White House was that the outcome would have been so disruptive politically that the Callaghan government might well have fallen.

The point was that the US administration had a lot of influence with the IMF, of which it was by far the largest shareholder. However, Simon and Yeo had to answer to the President, and, at a summit in Puerto Rico in June 1976, Callaghan had a sympathetic hearing from Ford about his political problems and what he was attempting to achieve in Britain.

The head of the National Security Council was Brent Scowcroft, and Robert Hormats was the economist. As I wrote in *Who*

Runs the Economy, 'Ford's closest advisers in the White House were not unaware of the memories of the fall of the Labour administration in 1931. They had the impression that Simon and Yeo would not greatly worry if the Labour government fell as a result of excessively tough terms from the IMF.' But they also argued that there was no guarantee that, if the terms were excessive, a left-wing government even less to Simon and Yeo's liking would not emerge.

Which brings us back to the speech Callaghan gave to the Labour conference on Wednesday 29 September justifying the application to the IMF, something deeply offensive to large sections of the party, with the memory of the 1967 crisis still very much in people's minds. In a seminal passage, he asserted that the days of Britain's reflating to ever higher levels of inflation were gone, and that such policies no longer worked, if indeed they ever had. His actual words were:

> We used to think that you could spend your way out of a recession and increase employment by cutting taxes and boosting government spending. I tell you in all candour that that option no longer exists, and that insofar as it ever did exist, it only worked on each occasion since the war by injecting a bigger dose of inflation into the economy, followed by a higher level of unemployment as the next step.

This passage was drafted for Callaghan by his son-in-law Peter Jay, who at that time had lost confidence in the Keynesian tradition and was a leading advocate of the monetarism that we shall discuss in the next chapter. Peter Jay once told a seminar that he had offered his father-in-law quite a long speech, but that was the only passage Callaghan used. It was tactical and, as we have noted, very successful in regard to the US administration's eventual support for the IMF loan.

In his memoirs, Callaghan noted, 'My speech was quoted extensively and approvingly throughout Europe and America and more recently has been misused by Conservative spokesmen to justify their malefactions in refusing to increase public expenditure at a time of recession, of low investment and low inflation, and of record levels of jobless.' He wrote this in 1987 and added, 'I see no reason to retract a single word of what I then said.' But you do not have to be a linguistic philosopher to detect that there is a certain inconsistency between the two passages. Callaghan was very upset by the Thatcher government's cavalier approach to unemployment – epitomised some years later in Norman Lamont's phrase when Chancellor that unemployment was 'a price well worth paying'. The point is that, as the Western world found during the financial crisis of 2007–09, the only way to get out of a recession is by spending. Keynes was rediscovered!

The tactical usefulness of Callaghan's speech soon became apparent. The White House strategy was to back Callaghan and Healey against the hardline US Treasury, who were afraid of a more extreme left-wing British government under Tony Benn. For Scowcroft and Hormats, and hence for President Ford, Callaghan's speech was crucial. As Hormats said, 'That speech, which was echoed by Healey subsequently, demonstrated to us that the UK had changed course. Without that speech it would have been difficult to obtain support [for the IMF loan] in the US. With it, we could point to a genuine turnaround in thinking in Whitehall which merited our support.' US President Gerald Ford and West German Chancellor Helmut Schmidt telephoned Callaghan the following day to congratulate him on the speech.

There followed a gruesome couple of months for the Callaghan government, which have been well documented elsewhere. Since I was then at the Bank of England, I was obviously not covering the story as a journalist. But the economics editor of the *Sunday Times*, Malcolm Crawford, suffered a blow to his fine reputation when a front-page report of an IMF recommendation of $1.50 as the appropriate exchange rate for the pound was resoundingly denied by the Treasury. This became something of a *cause célèbre* in Fleet Street at the time. But many years later a former senior official at the Treasury admitted to me that Crawford had been 'broadly right'.

What apparently happened was that Crawford's editors had seen his regular column in proof and urged that his delicately phrased information be 'hardened' into a sensational front-page story. This was a classic example of the difficulties financial journalists, especially columnists, can encounter. An item which is not too embarrassing to the Treasury or Bank of England if it is used discreetly in a column can cause trouble if it is blown up. In this instance, the former Treasury official confessed to me that the delicacy of the negotiation with the IMF was such that they felt compelled to dismiss a report that was fundamentally accurate. 'I have always felt sorry for Malcolm Crawford over that episode,' he said.

Although the Labour Party's reputation suffered from the humiliation of the 1976 episode, it was a huge achievement on James Callaghan's part to hold the Cabinet together, helped not least by private meetings Callaghan and Healey had at weekends, which, Healey told me years later, officials back in Whitehall knew nothing about. They lived not far apart from each other in Sussex.

Part of the rescue operation for the pound involved, in addition to the IMF loan, loans from a group of leading US banks.

The *FT* got hold of the story before the official announcement and ceremony, and I was called down, in my capacity as a journalist on secondment to the Bank, by a Bank of England director who was livid that the *FT* had stolen the Bank's thunder. What did I think? Should he send a letter to the editor expressing his outrage? I am delighted to say that I managed to calm him down by saying that, in my opinion, the *FT* had missed the real story. 'How do you mean?' he asked. Well, I said, if I had still been at the *FT*, I should have focused on the fact that one leading New York bank had declined to participate in the operation, apparently because it believed that the British government was still not credit-worthy. He took the point.

One seemingly tiny, and very anecdotal, episode in 1976 during the negotiations took place when the IMF team visiting London to look at the books went out of their comfortable West End hotel – Brown's – to find somewhere else for dinner. They had spent all day being told by Callaghan's team how difficult things were, and what a bad idea it would be to impose IMF-style hardship on a nation that was already suffering so much.

The IMF team of three or four, led by Englishman and former Bank of England official Alan Whittome, strolled over to Wheeler's, off Jermyn Street – a famous fish restaurant at the time – only to find the place was chock-a-block and there was no chance of a booking. The same happened at several other restaurants before they could find a spare table. They concluded that they were being spun a line by the Labour Cabinet and things were not all that bad.

Such anecdotal experiences tend in my experience to have quite an impact on officials who in theory are meant to be swayed in their judgement only by hard data. There was the famous occasion at the *FT* when Sir Douglas Allen, Permanent

Secretary to the Treasury, came to lunch during the 'squeeze' that was supposed to be part of the policy to 'make devaluation work' in 1968–69, when another Labour government was in the hands of the IMF.

'I don't know that it is that severe,' he told us. 'I was in a show-room in Croydon on Saturday and there seemed to be a lot of people out there buying.' At seminars in recent years I have come across revisionist theories that the Callaghan government did not really need to resort to the IMF at all in 1976. One will never know, but frankly I do not believe them. Confidence in the government had completely collapsed; there was what was known as a 'gilt strike' in the market for government debt – i.e. investors at home and abroad were getting out of the pound and not buying government stock. To coin a phrase, 'Something had to be done.'

After that, there was a huge turnaround in the markets and the problem became the strength of the pound as opposed to the weakness.

Shortly after I joined *The Observer* in July 1977, the atmosphere surrounding sterling switched from a very negative one to great enthusiasm for the currency. We had got through the 1976 crisis and it was as if the financial markets suddenly discovered that Britain was in possession of North Sea oil – although the oil and gas had been in their sights earlier. In contrast to the position in 1976, the agreed official policy now was to hold the pound down by intervening in the foreign exchange market to take dollars and other currencies into the reserves, rather than to let the pound rise too high for the competitiveness of British industry, which was the point on the IMF's mind during the Malcolm Crawford incident about the appropriate exchange rate.

But the pressure was such that the more monetarist-minded Bank of England and Treasury officials were worried about the effects on monetary expansion and hence, according to their way of thinking, inflation.

One week, my *Observer* colleagues Adrian Hamilton and Adam Raphael and I came to the conclusion that the government was going to 'uncap' the pound. We duly wrote the story and, sure enough, the deed took place the following Monday. Our scoop led to an official leak inquiry, and one official who shall remain nameless telephoned my home and told my wife that, no matter how late I returned, he wanted me to phone back that night. I duly did – after midnight – when he implored me to write a letter in which I should make it clear that he was not the source of the leak.

I tried to dissuade him, on the obvious grounds that by doing this he would be drawing attention to himself. However, he insisted, and I duly wrote the letter. On going through my archives recently, I discovered a nice note he wrote to me afterwards, expressing deep appreciation. At all events his career did not suffer from that episode.

Basically, Adam, Adrian and I had put two and two together from the situation of sterling and various hints and comments we had received. There was an added source of concern for some officials, because I had attended a party at the Bank of England on the Friday evening at which the key officials involved in an earlier Whitehall meeting concerning the pound were present, and I spoke to several of them.

Months later, I was thanked for the story about the plan to lift the cap by an old *FT* colleague who was now working in the City. He had placed his faith in our contacts and made a lot of money over the weekend dealing in sterling in Hong Kong. There was a plot there for a financial thriller.

Another happy memory of the unwelcome strength of the

pound in 1977 is the way that a Treasury friend, Mike Mercer, and I managed over lunch one day to coin a new word – 'euphobia' or 'fear of good news'. Many years later I picked up a copy of Chambers Dictionary to discover that euphobia had made it into the lexicon.

'Euphobia' may have been the mood of the moment, but the Callaghan government of 1976–79 never recovered from the episode that preceded the euphobia, namely the collapse of sterling in 1976 and the humiliating episode with the IMF.

Denis Healey was Chancellor from 1974 to 1979. That is to say, he was one of the few ministers who were not shuffled by his Prime Ministers – first Harold Wilson and later James Callaghan. This remarkable record echoed the 1964–70 experience, when Healey remained Secretary for Defence throughout.

It was no secret that Healey was very knowledgeable about foreign affairs, and always wanted to be Foreign Secretary, just as Foreign Secretary Tony Crosland was much more au fait with economics and always wanted to be Chancellor. These formidable politicians certainly made their mark; neither achieved his particular ambition, yet both were rounded characters, with what Healey famously described – perhaps a little too often, some felt – as a 'hinterland'.

It was fashionable in what are now known as neoliberal circles to laugh in the mid-1970s at Healey's obsession with a 'social contract' with the trade unions over economic policy – which basically amounted to an attempt to stave off the pressures of wage inflation by offering union leaders a share in the formation of economic strategy.

As noted previously, wage increases had been linked to changes in the cost of living at the worst moment possible, when oil prices were shooting up. Also the Labour government's public spending plans were far too ambitious, although the government's relationship with the financial markets was not helped by some disastrous double counting, which made the situation look far worse than it was. Some Treasury officials were cynical about the influence of the unions – 'We are off to see the Politburo again,' one only half joked – while others, including Sir Douglas Wass, as Permanent Secretary, were more sympathetic to the Chancellor's dilemma, and supported an 'industrial strategy', which did not get very far.

An important part of my job as economics correspondent at *The Observer* was to attend the annual meeting of the World Bank and IMF. In 1977, it took place in Washington via the Commonwealth Finance Ministers meeting in Barbados. It was in Barbados that Denis Healey gave a formal press conference on the state of play, after which one of my colleagues asked me to see whether the Chancellor would give a separate briefing to the British press.

I duly approached Denis, who, with his characteristic air of bonhomie, said he would be glad to, provided we bought him a drink. So we repaired to a bar on the beach, where the Chancellor happily gave us quite a story – in effect leaking plans of one of the many 'mini' Budgets that were all the vogue in those days. Unfortunately for *The Observer*, it was mid-week, so there was nothing for me to report immediately.

Or, rather, there was: my former colleague Jurek Martin was there to cover the conference for the *FT*, but had other things on his mind. He approached me and said, 'Bert Lance has resigned.' The name Bert Lance will mean nothing to modern British readers, but he was a member of the US administration and his resignation was big news at the time. Jurek said, 'London have asked me to write a 2,000-word feature about this for tomorrow.

Do you mind if I subcontract the Healey story to you? It will obviously have to appear under my name, but frankly you know more about the UK domestic scene at the moment than I do. [Pause] I'll give you seventy dollars.'

It was a deal, and although I had left the *FT* in 1976 to go to the Bank, after writing hundreds of front-page stories, I wrote one more, under the byline Jurek Martin.

I got on well with Healey and kept in touch with him until his death at the age of ninety-eight. As time has gone on, I think more historians have realised what a formidable job Healey made of the chancellorship in appallingly difficult circumstances. This is not a universal view, but I am inclined to agree with them.

A government and its Prime Minister can be in office for many years, achieve or fail to achieve many ambitions, yet be remembered for a few chance phrases.

Such was the fate in folk memory of the Wilson governments of 1964–70. The phrase 'the pound in your pocket has not been devalued' is one of the abiding memories of the 1967 devaluation. As often happens, the original words were somewhat different, but the way of the world, encouraged by the desire of the media for snappy headlines, is to elide and sometimes distort the original, while nevertheless bestowing on posterity the essence of the truth. Thus in January 1979 James Callaghan returned from a heads of government summit in Guadeloupe during what became known as the Winter of Discontent and was ambushed by reporters at the airport, and before he knew where he was the headlines screamed 'Callaghan – "Crisis? What Crisis?"'

Younger readers must picture the circumstances. The Prime Minister had just returned from the sunny West Indies, where, as far as the general public was concerned, he had been hobnobbing with the other leaders of the G7 in some comfort – not to say Caribbean luxury – although in fact he had been involved in serious talks on Western nuclear strategy and other matters of international concern with President Ford of the US; Giscard d'Estaing, President of France; and Helmut Schmidt, Chancellor of West Germany. Callaghan considered this meeting so important that he devoted a good dozen pages of his memoirs to the subject. But all that most people remember is the invented 'Crisis, what crisis?' This is the kind of experience that goes with the job! He arrived back to a British winter, where the news was all about strikes and the breakdown of the government's pay policy, and there would even be reports in days to come that in Liverpool and elsewhere strikers were refusing to bury the dead.

Crisis, what crisis? It was a gift to satirists and a largely hostile press. But what Callaghan actually said was, 'I don't think other people in the world would share the view there is mounting chaos.' The problem was, as had happened with Edward Heath's government in the winter of 1973–74, that yet another government's pay policy had broken down.

Referring to this in his memoirs, Healey acknowledges that the government was probably overambitious in setting the targets for pay policy which fomented union demands and led to the Winter of Discontent. There can be little doubt that having to go 'cap in hand' to the IMF in 1976 and mishandling pay policy in 1978–79 – with the unfortunate episode of the Winter of Discontent – were big factors in Labour's loss of the 1979 election and the rise of Thatcherism.

CRISIS 4

1979–82: SADOMONETARISM AND THATCHER RECESSION

When the Thatcher government came into office in 1979, they were deeply suspicious of the Whitehall machine that was associated with the perceived failures of the 1970s, and not least with 'Keynesian' economic advisers. Much influenced by Nigel Lawson, the new Financial Secretary, and his long-time friend Sir Samuel Brittan, they opted for a monetarist from the London Business School, a young man called Terry Burns, to be the Treasury's chief economic adviser.

When Sir Geoffrey Howe, the new Chancellor, arrived at No. 11 and the Treasury, he and Mrs Thatcher were determined to make a big thing of reducing the top rate of income tax, which was then at the absurd level, even for lefties such as myself, of 83 per cent, or 98 per cent on investment income. The latter rate was, I suspect, one of the few cases where the notorious Laffer Curve really applies. Arthur Laffer, the American extreme right-wing economist, once drew on a Washington restaurant napkin a curve purporting to demonstrate that lower taxes would rake in more revenue for the Reagan administration. What they actually did was contribute to the vast increase in defence spending that swelled the budget deficit, but Ronald Reagan had a Teflon quality and a broad smile, and he got away with things a Democrat would have found difficult. As Reagan once quipped, 'The deficit is big enough to look after itself.' It certainly looked after the Cold War. The increase in defence spending under Reagan was enough to convince the Soviets that they could no longer compete – a development I referred to in my book *The Spectre of Capitalism* (1992), which covered the reasons for the collapse of Soviet and Eastern European communism. I tried to warn in the book that after Reagan and Thatcher we might be in the era of capitalism unchained, and to some extent the subsequent financial crisis made the point. Strangely enough, I had hoped that the very title, a play on Marx's famous remark that the spectre of communism is haunting Europe, would make my book a worldwide bestseller. I fear it did nothing of the sort, but it did manage to attract the attention of the Chinese communists, who produced an edition for which I was not paid a penny, and, at the other end of the political spectrum, it was apparently being read by the Chilean dictator Augusto Pinochet when he was held in captivity in London.

It was soon decided that if the new Thatcher government was going to reduce the top rate of income tax, it had better accompany this with a gesture to all those Middle Englanders who had voted them in, namely by reducing the basic rate as well. In order to finance this, they would have to counterbalance the cost with a rise in indirect taxation, i.e. in VAT. During the election campaign, Labour had accused the Tories of planning to double VAT, a prophecy the Cabinet wished to falsify. So the Jesuitical compromise was that VAT would be raised from 8 per cent to 15 per cent.

Treasury officials warned proselytising tax cutters that this would have a dramatic impact on inflation, going, as it undoubtedly would, directly onto the index of retail prices. But Mrs Thatcher, Chancellor Howe and the very influential junior minister at the time, one Nigel Lawson, had become evangelical about monetarism, and were under the influence of monetarist economists who maintained that all one had to do to control inflation was control the money supply, and that the Treasury was stuffed full of 'Keynesian nonsense'.

Thus it came about that a new government that had been elected on a platform of bringing inflation under control presided over a year when the RPI rose from an inherited 10 per cent or so to over 20 per cent. Another important factor was a promise made by Mrs Thatcher in the heat of the campaign to implement the recommendation of an independent commission which had advocated a very costly pay award for public sector workers – the so-called Clegg Awards.

An advance report of the key Budget measure with regard to VAT turned out to be a great scoop for us at *The Observer*. I was working closely on news stories at the time with Adam Raphael and Adrian Hamilton, and, prompted by them, telephoned a Treasury official at home on the Saturday before the Budget, and said, 'We hear that VAT may go up to 12 per cent.' To which my mandarin friend responded, 'Why stop there?'

This was just the hint we needed to produce quite a good scoop. It was also a classic example, as far as we were concerned, of the civil service at its best. My interlocutor could subsequently claim, should there be a leak inquiry, that he had not leaked anything. This was unattributable 'guidance' at its best, from a trusted source who knew that we should never land him in the soup.

The 10 per cent inflation rate inherited by a newly arrived Thatcher government that had vowed to be firm on inflation was soon followed by a spiral of price increases that were directly attributable to the mistakes made in Sir Geoffrey Howe's first Budget of June 1979. By November, the retail prices index was well on the way to its peak of 21.9 per cent, which it hit in May 1980.

The position in November 1979 was so serious that the Treasury and Bank felt they had little option but to raise the bank rate, or minimum lending rate, as it was then called, from the already high rate of 15 per cent to 17 per cent.

Now, this was around the time that it became known that Sir Anthony Blunt, the Surveyor of the Queen's Pictures, had been a Soviet spy and recruiting agent. The news was half broken in a book by the BBC interviewer Andrew Boyle – I say 'half' because Boyle referred to the existence of this spy in high places, but for legal reasons – or at least for a particular interpretation of Britain's strict libel laws – Boyle's book did not actually name Blunt.

The Times had a go, but managed to get the story hopelessly and hilariously wrong. They had a tip-off that the name of the Cambridge don who was about to be unmasked contained five letters, beginning with the letter B. They ran a prominent story about the completely innocent King's College don Donald Bevis. It was *Private Eye*, under Richard Ingrams, who got the story: it was not Bevis, but Blunt.

Journalists are always looking for new angles. The 'shock' rise in interest rates had been covered during the week, but attention had been somewhat diverted by the unmasking of Blunt, which, thanks to *Private Eye*, had become a huge story. I suddenly had the idea of writing a column in a parody of John Le Carré's style, the message being that the powers that be had deliberately kept the unmasking of Blunt back for the final part of a deal they had done with him, and that the revelation was timed to divert attention from the hugely embarrassing increase in interest rates. Incidentally, I never met Blunt, but knew people who thought they knew him well. They were absolutely amazed to discover that he had been a spy – 'Such a shy, diffident man.'

As we have seen, the Conservatives came into office in 1979 in the wake of Labour's 1976 IMF crisis and the 1978–79 Winter of Discontent. But they proceeded to cause another crisis of their own. That June 1979 Budget and associated measures severely aggravated the inflationary tendency of the British economy that they had made such a song and dance about when in opposition.

The logical arguments made by Treasury officials cut no ice with the new administration. Howe and his confident colleague, Financial Secretary Lawson, had come under the influence of the monetarists. They had indeed managed to convince themselves that all they needed to control inflation was to control the money supply – or, more strictly, the stock of money. Their ultimately abortive efforts to control various measures of the money supply led them to raise interest rates higher and higher. This made London a very lucrative financial centre in which to deposit money, with the result that the pound rose, and rose, and rose, making it very difficult for British manufacturers to compete. The result was ever higher unemployment, and the biggest recession since the Second World War.

As a traditional Keynesian, I was deeply suspicious of the doctrine on which the policy was based, and especially critical of the zealous tone of what became known as Thatcherism. The public and media reaction to the perceived failures of the Labour governments was such that at times one felt quite isolated in opposing what I eventually dubbed sadomonetarism. Denis Healey – by then back in opposition, of course – coined the term 'punk-monetarism', but 'sadomonetarism' first appeared under my name in *The Observer*, and it struck a chord with some of my contacts in the Treasury and Bank of England, who were charged with conducting policies they did not really believe in.

Certain enlightened officials at the Bank conducted covert operations to help otherwise sound companies whose very existence was threatened by the combination of high interest rates and a seriously overvalued pound. Much of British industry, however, went under. Mrs Thatcher and her band were like evangelicals.

*   *   *

One of the great moments of my journalistic career was meeting J. K. Galbraith, the man whose book *The Affluent Society* I had read all those years ago before going up to Cambridge, and which had influenced me from then on. One should always be wary of what he called 'the conventional wisdom'!

In 1979, during that first monetarist phase of the Thatcher government, my editor Donald Trelford had suggested to me that it would be a good idea to commission a written debate between Galbraith and the most vociferous propagator of monetarism, namely Milton Friedman. When I wrote to Galbraith – no emails in those days – I received a reply to the effect that Friedman would probably not agree to this. His message was: Milton and I recognise that he is better on his feet than I am, but I am better in print. He won't agree to a debate. But if you were to commission an article from me and send him a copy, you could offer him the right of reply.

Galbraith's article duly appeared in August 1980 and was syndicated around the world. It was the occasion on which he wrote:

Britain has, in effect, volunteered to be the Friedmanite guinea pig. There could be no better choice. Britain's political and social institutions are solid, and neither Englishmen, Scots nor even the Welsh take readily to the streets ... There are other advantages in a British experiment. British social services and social insurance soften what elsewhere might be intolerable hardship. British phlegm is a good antidote for anger; but so is an adequate system of unemployment insurance.

I wrote to Professor Friedman and received a reply, dictated by him and signed in his absence by an assistant. For us at *The Observer*, it was what one of my colleagues used to describe as 'pure gold'.

He declined the offer of writing for us, but said that, if it was any help, he was enclosing a copy of some written evidence he had been asked to submit to a parliamentary committee. In fact, he landed a major scoop on our desks. The evidence had not yet been published, but it contained a remarkable message: Milton Friedman, the high priest of monetarism, and one of Mrs Thatcher's heroes, dissociated himself from the government's policy of reducing the budget deficit at a time of recession.

For the result of this exercise in sadomonetarism, set off by Geoffrey Howe's 1979 Budget, was to be the biggest recession since the war, with unemployment rising and rising to over three million by 1986. For the wartime and post-war generation, this was a big shock – something that was never meant to happen again after the horrors of the 1920s and 1930s. Manufacturing industry was particularly affected, with the Midlands and the north especially badly hit. This was in contrast to the subsequent recession of 1991–92, when the south of England bore more of the brunt.

At one stage, things got so bad that the chairman of ICI went to Downing Street to ask Mrs Thatcher whether she wanted ICI to remain in Britain. During that time, I got to know Sir John Harvey-Jones, who later became chairman of ICI. Sir John subsequently became a television star with a programme that involved visiting British companies and telling them in no uncertain terms what they were doing wrong. He never went to university himself but relished becoming Chancellor of Bradford University. He once told me that the greatest influence on his career had been 'Professor Parkinson'. It was Professor C. Northcote Parkinson – an eminently memorable name – who went down in history with Parkinson's Law: 'Work expands so as to fill the time available for its completion.'

Unfortunately, the Thatcher government, while ostensibly obsessed with the work ethic, became past masters in pursuing economic policies that put millions of people out of work. In its early days I was invited to meet the Secretary of State for Employment, Jim Prior, in his office opposite St James's Park Station. Over a gin and tonic, Jim, a prominent member of the Cabinet, asked me, 'What on earth is this government up to?' Jim was one of the – in my opinion, honourable – group of ministers in Mrs Thatcher's first government whom she dubbed the 'Wets'. He would have liked a gentler approach towards the unions and had been more sympathetic towards Edward Heath than Thatcher.

There was a lack of balance and perspective about the Thatcherites and the sadomonetarists. They went on about the putative past failures of Labour governments, and indeed the Heath government, in their attempts 'to back winners'. They seemed blithely ignorant of the way that other countries' governments enjoyed successful relationships with industry, and that intervention need not be all bad.

As if the 1973–74 oil crisis were not enough, another one came along in 1979–80. The rise in prices contributed to a slowdown and indeed recessions in most oil-importing countries, but the damage was nothing like as severe as in the UK, where the economic crisis was largely self-inflicted. In his memoirs, Jim Prior relates a damning observation:

> All through the early period of Margaret's government I felt the Treasury team were out of their depth. They were all theorists – either barristers or, in the case of Nigel Lawson, a journalist. None of them had any experience of running a whelk stall, let alone a decent-sized company. Their attitude to manufacturing industry bordered on the contemptuous. They shared the view of the other monetarists in the Cabinet that we were better suited as a nation to being a service economy and should no longer worry about production.

As Prior added with feeling and what proved to be justified foreboding, 'I could not see how this could be reconciled with the employment of a potential workforce of around 23 million people on a small island.'

It was this extraordinary approach that lay behind the biggest UK recession since the war, and untold misery for hundreds of thousands of people who became unemployed. My criticisms of the government, however, were not going down well with either Atlantic Richfield, who owned *The Observer* from 1976 to 1981, or their successors, Lonrho. When he heard that my job was threatened, John Harvey-Jones invited *The Observer*'s editor, Donald Trelford, and some colleagues, including me, to lunch. Trelford was always protective of my role, but after that lunch I learned on the grapevine that Harvey-Jones, pretty well our leading industrialist at the time, had deliberately supported me in front of the editor just in case rumours of my professional demise were true.

A European development which was going to have a big influence on relations between Mrs Thatcher and her Chancellor Nigel Lawson began in the late 1970s. After the collapse of the Bretton Woods system, the French and the Germans decided to introduce a European exchange rate system. There was a false start earlier in the decade, but the European Monetary System (EMS) was set up in 1978–79, the key champions being Chancellor Helmut Schmidt of West Germany, President Giscard of France and Roy Jenkins, who had left British politics temporarily to become President of the European Commission. The principal public manifestation of the EMS was the exchange rate mechanism (ERM), which Labour refused to join and Lawson became obsessed by in the course of his chancellorship.

One of the ironies of the overvaluation of the pound associated with sadomonetarism was that a principal factor contributing to Denis Healey's veto on sterling's entry to the ERM in 1978–79 was the view that the UK needed from time to time to devalue the pound – as we have seen in the chapters on the 1967 devaluation and the 1976 IMF crisis.

True, the ERM was supposed to be a 'fixed but adjustable' exchange rate system, but Healey was impressed by the way the senior West German politician Manfred Lahnstein had confessed that he regarded the ERM as a way of preventing other European currencies from devaluing against the D-Mark.

By not joining the ERM, British economic policymakers retained the freedom to allow the currency to depreciate when UK inflation got out of line with the inflation rates, and therefore the price competitiveness, of other countries. What they had not bargained for was a dramatic rise in the exchange rate despite the fact that our inflation rate was running well ahead of our competitors.

In which context one must not overlook what Sir Geoffrey Howe regarded as one of his greatest achievements, namely the abolition of exchange controls in 1979. These exchange controls had lasted since the Second World War, and had been reinforced temporarily at the time of the 1966 July measures by an (understandably!) unpopular limit on the amount of foreign currency British holidaymakers were allowed to take abroad – rather sarcastically named officially as the £50 travel allowance.

The abolition of exchange controls had been urged for some time by certain high-ranking Bank of England officials. Of course, it was not quite so welcome to the lower-ranking officials whose function it was to administer the nitty-gritty of the controls. The latter group, not surprisingly, were worried about their jobs.

Abolition of controls fitted perfectly with the free market beliefs of Mrs Thatcher, her Chancellor Geoffrey Howe and the Financial Secretary Nigel Lawson. Somewhat ironically, it was supported by Treasury officials who thought it would help to counteract the upward thrust of the pound associated with high interest rates.

I confess that I myself thought the abolition of controls was a rash move, which would inevitably have to be reversed, and I made the mistake of saying so rather forcibly in one of my columns. As it turned out, the controls remained in abeyance, and Sir Geoffrey never tired of reminding me, in public and in private, that I had been wrong. Indeed, there were certain anniversary meetings of the free market think tank the Institute of Economic Affairs when Sir Geoffrey did me the dubious honour of giving me a public name check on how wrong I had been.

*　　*　　*

Early under the new regime, a colleague at *The Observer*, Lajos Lederer, became anxious that one of my targets was Sir Keith Joseph, then Secretary for Industry, who was a friend of his. One evening, Lajos invited me to dine with Sir Keith and him at the Connaught. While your correspondent tucked into several courses, Sir Keith confined himself to a plate of oysters for the entire meal.

The object of the exercise seemed to be to bring Sir Keith and me closer together. He kept going on about 'common ground'. However, since he was a right-wing monetarist and I was not, we did not make much progress, although it was a perfectly civilised evening and Sir Keith was courtesy itself. At the end, Lajos claimed that we had somehow made progress, and it would be a help if the Secretary of State could give me his direct line, so that the dialogue could continue. At which point Sir Keith scrawled something on the back of an envelope and gave it to me. The following morning I looked at the number he had given me and realised that he had written down the number of the DTI switchboard.

Sir Keith was so eccentric that he believed his own department of state should be abolished. He seemed not to realise that most other governments, including the 'free market' United States, had close relations with industry, not least via what President Eisenhower had christened the military–industrial complex. It is noteworthy that the internet, which has transformed life as we know it, was not the result of the kind of market force Sir Keith believed in, but of US government expenditure on the military.

In the end, this non-interventionist minister moved on. His department was not abolished, but he became Secretary for

Education. When, a few years later, I was working on my book *Mrs Thatcher's Economic Experiment*, I went to him in his office and he was very generous with his time as I enquired into his version of the origins of what became known as Thatcherism. The idea for the book had come from both Ian Gilmour and Peter Walker, who, as members of her Cabinet, could not publish such a work themselves, although they gave me plenty of help. As Walker said over lunch one day, 'You have got to write that book.' 'What book?' 'The one I can't write.'

In the book, I described Sir Keith as John the Baptist to Mrs Thatcher's Messiah. What happened was that at one stage Joseph saw himself as a potential leader of the Conservative Party; his campaign was dubbed the counter-revolution to what he described as the 'corporate' orthodoxy of the early and mid-1970s, under both Harold Wilson and Ted Heath. However, Sir Keith made some ill-advised speeches in which he advocated higher unemployment to deal with the problems of inflation, and came dangerously close to advocating eugenics to break 'the cycle of deprivation' among working-class families. One Tory MP commented unkindly, 'First he wants to make them unemployed, then he wants to castrate them.'

Funnily enough, some of the officials who were having to carry out policies they did not believe in were happy to meet me, but only in secret. It was more than their professional lives were worth to be seen with 'the enemy' in public. There was one very important source for me who insisted on meeting in a curry house near Leicester Square where we were both quite certain that we would meet no one we knew.

Unemployment went on rising throughout 1980 and into 1981, reaching 10 per cent, but this did not stop Sir Geoffrey Howe from introducing an apparently deflationary Budget in March

1981 which has been the source of controversy in many a book and seminar ever since, and was most certainly hugely controversial at the time.

The focus of policymakers at the time was not the need to do something about unemployment, but to reduce a public sector borrowing requirement which was high precisely because of the depth of the recession. The recession inevitably affected tax receipts, rendering them lower than they would have been in more normal times; it also meant that unemployment and social security disbursements were bound to swell the deficit.

The 1981 Budget gave rise many years later to a collection of reflections on it, rather sarcastically entitled 'Expansionary Fiscal Contraction'. That phrase was coined by one of the people – among whom I counted myself then and indefinitely – who argued that cutting the public sector borrowing requirement at a time of recession was the reverse of what was required. Fiscal contraction? Expansionary? You see the point...

The view that this was all wrong was famously aired in a letter to *The Times* from 364 economists in March 1981. Ever since then, the supporters of the 1981 Budget have lost few opportunities to deride those economists, arguing that they could not have been more wrong, and adding that that Budget marked the beginning of the subsequent recovery.

Well, up to a point: the fact of the matter was that unemployment carried on rising until 1986. The Thatcher government's re-election in 1983 had more to do with the weak state of the opposition and the revival of Mrs Thatcher's fortunes after the Falklands War in 1982 than any miraculous economic recovery.

The Labour Party had moved too far to the left for the bulk of the electorate – and also for some of Labour's centrists, who broke off under the leadership of Roy Jenkins to form the

Social Democratic Party (SDP). Then there was the thorny issue of Labour's 1983 election manifesto, described by the prominent Labour MP Gerald Kaufman as 'the longest suicide note in history'. Among other things, under the leadership of Michael Foot, the manifesto called for withdrawal from the European Economic Community – as it then was – along with import controls and unilateral nuclear disarmament by the UK.

Given the domestic economic crisis, and her apparently uncaring approach, Mrs Thatcher had been the most unpopular Prime Minister since records began. She had enjoyed, if that is the word, an early burst of unpopularity under the Heath government when she was known as Margaret Thatcher the milk snatcher for removing free milk from schools. But her hardline adoption of monetarism and seeming disregard for the social problems caused by unemployment and public expenditure cuts made her something of a pariah. It was the Falklands War that marked the turning point in her political fortunes and, ironically, Michael Foot had strongly supported her in this venture.

The person who first pointed out to me that she possessed that dubious record of prime ministerial unpopularity was Sir Ian, later Lord Gilmour. Gilmour, a prominent member of the 'Wets' – the label she applied to dissident members of the Cabinet who questioned her approach – was sacked in September 1981 for expressing his discontent, not least towards those 1979 and 1981 Budgets. Early on in the Thatcher government, Gilmour and I met for lunch at the RAC Club, through the good offices of my colleague Adam Raphael, *The Observer's* political editor.

We warmed to each other immediately and became firm friends. I shall never forget that first meeting, when I arrived, was introduced and was offered an aperitif. I declined at first, pleading a hangover. 'Don't be ridiculous,' said Ian. 'What you need is a hair of the dog!' Gilmour was a friend of the Cambridge economist Professor Wynne Godley, also a friend of mine. We were all critics of the government, and there were frequent lunches and supportive phone calls.

Which brings us back to the 1981 Budget. Godley was one of the 364 economists who wrote to *The Times* condemning the deflationary appearance of the Budget. This is where the plot thickens. What the 364 did not know was that, in the background, there was an undeclared plan to bring the exchange rate down from its dizzy heights. Along with the associated cuts in interest rates, this was definitely an expansionary move, which the 364 knew nothing about. One suspects that if they had known this, the letter would not have appeared.

Essentially, there was a change in economic policy. The strict monetarist approach began to be relaxed, although so much political prestige had been invested in it that the change of strategy was never admitted. A key figure in this relaxation was Sir Alan Walters, who combined his role as Mrs Thatcher's personal economic adviser with a job with the World Bank in Washington. This meant that he was a frequent flier across the Atlantic and a close student of the overvaluation of the pound against the dollar.

To cut a long story short, Walters did not accept the conventional rationalisation of the strength of the pound – that it was due to Britain's relatively new-found status as an oil producer. A study, he suggested, had come to the conclusion that our status as a 'petro currency' could at most account for 15 to 20 per cent of its strength.

The depreciation of the pound over the next few years, together with the interest rate cuts, counteracted the deflationary influence of the 1981 Budget, as did the abolition of hire purchase and credit controls. None of this information was available to the 364 economists when they put their names to the famous letter. Moreover, although many supporters of the 1981 Budget maintain that it marked the beginning of the recovery, that recovery was hardly sensational, as demonstrated by the way unemployment continued to rise until 1986.

The 1981 Budget was controversial at the time and has somehow continued to remain so in academic circles. It was delivered by Sir Geoffrey Howe in the face of criticism not only from Keynesians but also from the arch-monetarist Milton Friedman that it was wrong to cut public sector borrowing at a time of recession. A similar issue arose during the Osborne chancellorship of 2010–16, when the phrase 'expansionary fiscal contraction' came into vogue. But the expansion can only really come from a counteracting relaxation of monetary policy. The dispute continues to this day. For instance, supporters of Osborne tried to justify his fiscal contraction in the early years by pointing to monetary expansion. But not much of the money seemed to get through to industry, and the recovery was painfully slow.

It was not to be long before what had become the biggest recession since the war, in 1979–82, was followed by what became known as the Lawson boom. But it was over a decade before Milton Friedman, the high priest of monetarism, finally repudiated the economic doctrine on which Thatcher and Howe had based their early economic policies. In 'Lunch with the *FT*' in June 2003, Friedman confessed, 'The use of quantity of money as a target has not been a success. I'm not sure I would as of today push it as hard as I once did.'

1983–89: LAWSON BOOM AND BUST, AND FALLOUT WITH THATCHER

When it comes to anything European in British economic policy, there are always several dimensions to the politics. Also, there are usually divisions between parties and within parties, with strong emotions seldom far beneath the surface, as the chaos since the 23 June 2016 referendum has demonstrated with a vengeance.

Moreover, whichever major party was in power during postwar decades, policymakers had to work through departments of state that were often at odds. For example, with respect to decisions and negotiations over the exchange rate mechanism, the Foreign Office was always far more pro-European than the Treasury. This to some extent reflected another division, namely that between economists and non-economists.

But economists too were divided over the euro. I think the majority of those I encountered were unhappy with the structure of the Eurozone, believing that politics had indeed triumphed over economics. There were some notable exceptions. Willem Buiter, a brilliant economist, who was a founder member of the Bank of England's monetary policy, was passionately in favour of our joining. He even gave me a present of a tie decorated with euros to try to win me round.

I had first met Buiter through my wife Hilary, when he taught at the London School of Economics. He produced the tie when we were having dinner with him and his wife at Granita, the Islington restaurant where Tony Blair and Gordon Brown met to seal arrangements for government. The acoustics in Granita were not ideal – which is, I fear, not unusual in modern London restaurants – and given the mistrust and feuding that developed between the two, Buiter remarked, as we struggled to hear one another, 'Do you think the acoustics here were the origin of the misunderstanding between Blair and Brown over the succession?'

Although at the time there were many references to the Granita Agreement – or lack of it – both parties subsequently said that the die had already been cast by the time they had dinner together in Islington. Gordon Brown makes this clear in his memoirs, and, in accordance with my reporting duties, I did once ask the owner of Granita whether she could add anything. She replied that it looked like a very boring occasion and 'they spent most of their time poring over spreadsheets'.

Buiter is Dutch, and like so many Continental Europeans he felt very emotional about uniting Europe by economic means – which had, after all, been the object of such founding fathers as the French bureaucrat Jean Monnet.

I met Monnet once, when he was guest of honour at a *Financial Times* anniversary celebration at a Park Lane hotel. When my turn came to meet him briefly in the receiving line, he asked me whether Britain was serious about Europe. I found myself saying, 'I am not sure.'

The pound had an ill-fated, and very brief, adventure in spring 1972 with the prototype European fixed exchange rate mechanism – known at the time as the currency 'snake'. That effort fell apart. The question of combining with other currencies did not come up again until 1978, during the preparations for setting up the exchange rate mechanism. It was the usual suspect, speculative pressures in the exchange markets, that forced the pound's escape from the 'snake'. After that, economists such as Nicholas Kaldor celebrated sterling's prospective freedom from balance of payments constraints. But as we have seen in an earlier chapter, things did not turn out too well.

As noted, the next episode was when, led by Chancellor Schmidt of West Germany and President Giscard of France, preparations were being made for the construction of the European Monetary System and the exchange rate mechanism. They were encouraged by former British Chancellor Roy Jenkins, who was by now President of the European Commission.

The question was: would Britain join?

In this instance it turned out that both the politics and the economics were at one. The build-up in the press was huge: it was known that Britain's Prime Minister James Callaghan and West Germany's Chancellor Helmut Schmidt got on extremely well. After seemingly endless European summits and bilateral meetings, the climax was expected to be a bilateral in Bonn where the two would announce that the pound was going to join the proposed European Monetary System.

There was a press conference at the Chancellery in October 1978, which I attended for *The Observer*. The two leaders entered the hall. We waited for the announcement amid a hushed atmosphere. Then came the anti-climax: 'We have been discussing the situation in Namibia...'

Despite all the frenzied speculation, one minister in Callaghan's government expressed the essence of the problem for the British fairly bluntly. Writing sometime after the event, or non-event, Edmund Dell, who had been a junior Treasury minister and then Trade Secretary, concluded, 'The politics of the question were clear enough. Joining the ERM would divide the party and the government. It could not afford to be divided once again on a European issue at such a time.' The Labour Party had been divided over entry to what was then the European Economic Community in 1973 – when the decision had in any case been in the hands of Edward Heath's Conservative government – and again in 1975, when the Labour Prime Minister Harold Wilson had skilfully handled the referendum which endorsed our entry. Although that hurdle was successfully crossed, doubts about European adventures resurfaced when the subject of the new European monetary system came up.

The institutional background also weighed against joining. The powerful Treasury was traditionally suspicious of most things European – although, when it came to the Brexit crisis all these years later, the Treasury, in my opinion rightly, was strongly opposed to sacrificing our membership of the institution we had spent decades trying to join, for all the concerns about the way Brussels operated. But in 1978–79, the Treasury, despite the horrors of the 1976 sterling crisis, was – again rightly in my opinion – principally concerned that, by putting the pound in the exchange rate system, the British government would lose the flexibility to devalue the currency from time to time.

There were at least two ironies here: first, the ERM, while intended to provide a 'zone of monetary stability' in Europe, was designed as a 'fixed but adjustable' system, rather like its more ambitious ancestor, the Bretton Woods system. So in theory the option of a devaluation would always have been there – and it was certainly used by the French.

PART II: THE NINE CRISES

Secondly, as it turned out, the main problem facing British economic policy in the next few years was the rise and rise of the pound, which would undoubtedly have been restrained if we had joined the ERM. The then president of the Bundesbank, Otmar Emminger, described what happened to the pound in those few years as 'by far the most excessive overvaluation which any currency has experienced in recent monetary history'.

There is a deep-rooted myth that the dramatic rise in the pound in 1979–81 was due to the arrival of North Sea oil and sterling's role as a 'petro currency'. But, as we saw in the previous chapter, other countries in the possession of oil did not experience similar episodes. A subsequent study established that possession of oil accounted for less than a fifth of the rise in the pound, which was largely caused by the enormous increases in interest rates required by adherence to the then fashionable doctrine of monetarism.

Now, often in economic policy, a few private conversations can exert an influence on ministers that no amount of official documents and drawn-out meetings can match. As referred to in the previous chapter, there was a classic example of this in Denis Healey's judgement about the ERM. Healey, a strong Chancellor, revealed in his memoirs that for him the decisive discussions were when the German State Secretary Manfred Lahnstein made a frank admission to him about his real motives for setting up the exchange rate mechanism. His own enthusiasm for the ERM was that it would put a lid on any market tendency to raise the value of the Deutschmark (DM), 'thus', as Healey says in his memoirs, 'keeping Germany more competitive, and other countries less so'.

With the Foreign Office strongly in favour of our joining the ERM, and the Bank of England, in Healey's words, 'mildly in favour, since they thought it would exert a useful discipline on

British governments', Healey, whose opinion was the crucial factor, said, 'I was fairly agnostic until I realised, from long discussions with Lahnstein and others, how it was likely to work in practice; then I turned against it.'

Eventually, in a classic diplomatic compromise, the British government agreed to join the European Monetary System, or EMS, but not its principal component, namely the European exchange rate system, or ERM.

So when things blew up all those years later on Black Wednesday, 16 September 1992, Labour, although by that time very pro-European, was not to blame – as we shall see in the following chapter. The ignominy of joining the ERM and mishandling it fell to the Tories, as a result of the abject failure of the Thatcher government's flagship counter-inflation policy – namely monetarism. This led to a classic example of the fusion of the search for panaceas in British economic policy and the influence of fashion. The ERM became the latest fashionable panacea. For, as Sir John Major ruefully reflected in his memoirs, in 1990 it was difficult to find anyone in the British political, financial and industrial establishment who was not in favour of entry to the ERM – in sharp contrast to the comments so many of these people made after the event.

The build-up to ERM membership provided a wonderful illustration of the historical practice of the Conservative Party of shamelessly shifting its ground when newly adopted doctrines prove wanting in practice. It was not just that, in the 1979–81 phase, inflation, instead of being brought under control by attempts to reduce the growth of the money supply, actually doubled: it was also that the faith of Mrs Thatcher and her powerful new Chancellor Nigel Lawson in the wonders of market forces was severely tested by events in the foreign exchange market.

There were two seminal episodes during the 1980s that prompted Mrs Thatcher and Chancellor Lawson to adjust their views about the wisdom of the financial markets. The first was in January 1985 when the value of the pound threatened to sink below the 'virility symbol' level of £1 to the US dollar. It must be emphasised that this was less to do with lack of confidence in sterling than with overconfidence in the dollar. That overconfidence led later that year to the Plaza Agreement, when the G7 leading finance ministers (not forgetting their central bankers) embarked on a collective policy to halt the rise in the dollar, and indeed to lower it to a level that was not threatening to cripple US exports and cause deindustrialisation.

The dive in the pound led to an hilarious episode featuring Bernard Ingham, the hard-nosed and bluff Yorkshireman who was Mrs Thatcher's chief press officer, and a Friday briefing of the weekend press. *The Observer*'s political editor was my friend and colleague Adam Raphael. He returned to our offices, then opposite Battersea Park, with the news that, as far as the loyal Ingham was concerned, his political mistress believed in market forces, and if the pound fell to $1 or below, so be it.

Adam was rightly suspicious of this line and sought my view. I agreed with him, and a few private phone calls persuaded us that we could write a story on the Sunday saying that the Treasury, via its agent the Bank of England, would intervene in the markets to ward off the humiliation of a $1 pound. Mrs Thatcher even sought the help of her friend President Reagan that month to support sterling.

There were farcical aspects to that weekend. Most of the other papers ran with the Ingham version of the policy and were not helped by the fact that at the time the Treasury had a brilliant but laid-back press secretary. So far from being proactive that weekend, the press officer was rumoured to be unavailable on his allotment.

The pound did not sink to $1, and eventually recovered. I subsequently met a banking friend who expressed more confidence in our report than those of the rest of the media and said he had made a lot of money in the foreign exchange markets that weekend.

It was during 1985 that, having accepted that his attempts to control the money supply had been an erratic and unreliable navigational guide, Chancellor Lawson became obsessed with the idea of putting the pound into the ERM as the next panacea for controlling inflation.

He tried privately with Mrs Thatcher, and in meetings with other ministers and officials, to persuade her, including in a meeting in autumn 1985 when most of his colleagues were won over. At the end, Mrs Thatcher summarised: 'Ayes seven, Noes one – the Noes have it.' She was in a kind of continual battle with most things European and always enjoyed the fight, but with regard to the ERM, she was heavily influenced by Professor Walters, who dismissed the ERM contemptuously as 'half-baked'.

The early months of 1986 saw a sharp fall in the price of oil. Lawson and the Treasury used the opportunity to embark on a tacit policy of allowing a gentle devaluation of the pound to boost the competitiveness of exports, on the assumption that the fall in oil prices would counteract any impact on prices of a lower pound.

However, not for the first time in post-war British economic policy, a Chancellor found himself in the classic position of someone who should have been, in that familiar phrase, 'careful what he wished for'. The same financial markets that had produced, in the early 1980s, 'the most excessive overvaluation … in recent history' now lost confidence in the pound once again.

During the course of the annual meetings of the World Bank and International Monetary Fund in Washington in September 1986, Lawson approached Emminger's successor at the Bundesbank, Karl Otto Pöhl, for assistance.

The British Chancellor suffered the embarrassment of being told that it was not Bundesbank policy to hold sterling in its reserves, but, to support the rate, the German central bank would happily buy pounds as agents for the Bank of England.

At a second meeting, Pöhl offered the UK a D-Mark loan. Although I was in Washington myself covering the annual meetings, my memory is that these private meetings – one of which, I think, took place in the Bundesbank's plush suite in the Four Seasons Hotel – did not reach the public gaze until a lot later. Lawson, a proud man, felt humiliated by this episode, and became all the more conscious of the disadvantages, as he had begun to see them, of not having the currency within the ERM – the point being that with monetarism having proved a failure in regard to control of inflation, the attractions of the stability afforded by the ERM began to appeal to him. To add insult to injury, he was only too well aware that earlier that year Pöhl had made a speech urging the UK to join the ERM!

Lawson subsequently admitted that 1986 had been 'a terrible year for the pound'.

The next stage in his attempts to win over a reluctant Prime Minister came in February 1987. This was the month when the G7 decided that enough was enough in the exchange markets. The Plaza Agreement of September 1985 had achieved its purpose: the dollar had fallen to a more sensible level, and concerns that an overvalued US currency would cause massive deindustrialisation in the US economy had dissipated. There had been enough adjustment. What was now needed in the currency markets was a period of stability.

The meeting at which G7 finance ministers and central bank governors agreed on a policy of concerted intervention to steady the markets took place at the Louvre in Paris, and the resulting agreement became known as the Louvre Accord.

Lawson enjoyed the international financial stage, and got on particularly well with James Baker, the US Treasury Secretary. The G7 discussions and agreements led him to embark, when he returned to London, on a policy that became known, much later, as 'shadowing the D-Mark'.

The remarkable thing is that the shadowing experiment went on as long as it did before being rumbled. Lawson had been hoping to demonstrate the virtues of future ERM membership by showing that the pound could live happily in a close arrangement with the German currency. It was, in a sense, from his point of view, a trial run. But when Mrs Thatcher finally woke up to what he and the Treasury's agent, the Bank of England, had been up to, all hell broke loose.

This was in spring 1988. I had broken the story in *The Observer* in March 1987, the month after the Louvre Accord. The headline was 'Secret Sterling Deal Ahead of Budget', and the piece featured the following passage:

> It is understood that a secret target zone for the movement of the pound against the D-Mark was agreed between the UK and West Germany around the time of the Group of Five meeting in Paris last month ... It is thought that the Bank of England and the Bundesbank have an agreement to intervene to keep the pound broadly within a range of DM 2.75 to DM 3.05.

A fortnight later this was augmented by the revelation that 'the government is now operating economic policy as if the pound were already in the exchange rate mechanism of the European Monetary System. Nigel Lawson would like to put sterling formally into the ERM shortly after a June election...'

I quote this at length because on going back in my files I made an amazing discovery. The above appeared a year before Mrs Thatcher discovered what was going on, and all hell broke loose. But evidently Mrs Thatcher did not read the *Observer* Business section, and her press secretary did not draw it to her attention. Now, they say memory plays tricks, but I like to think that I have a reasonably good memory. However, my report in March 1987 made so little impact that even I forgot it. Thus when, a year later, a senior official asked me over coffee after lunch whether I had noticed that we were shadowing the D-Mark, my reaction was as follows:

'Wow! No, I certainly hadn't. What a story!'

Both Mrs Thatcher and her economic adviser Sir Alan Walters realised now what the Chancellor was really up to, and were hopping mad. The Prime Minister did not like the European exchange rate mechanism partly because it was European and partly because it was an exchange rate mechanism. This was the time when she came out with the much-quoted phrase 'You can't buck the market' – notwithstanding that earlier episode in January 1985 when she had successfully ordered intervention to prevent the pound from falling to $1.

As a consequence of the worst British recession since the Second World War, inflation had come down from a peak of 21 per cent in 1980 under the first Thatcher government to around 3.5 per cent by the time of the 1983 election. After that, it had begun to rise again. It was given added impetus by Nigel Lawson's tax-cutting budget of 1988. Notwithstanding his damaging flirtation with monetarism, Lawson was at heart an expansionist.

By 1988 he was extremely popular, and he will go down in history as the Chancellor who lowered the bar for rates of taxation to a level that even Gordon Brown, years later, was nervous about raising. As we saw in Crisis 4, the top rate had been absurdly high until 1979, when Geoffrey Howe had brought it down to 60 per cent. Lawson's 1988 Budget reduced it further, to 40 per cent, where it remained for most of New Labour's stewardship, until the financial crisis. This had an amazing impact on the general attitude towards taxation levels and rather stymied the efforts of those of us who argued that UK tax rates ought to be far closer to Continental levels in order to improve our public services.

Unfortunately for Lawson, however, he has already gone down in history as yet another Chancellor, like Maudling before him, who let a boom get out of control. But his dramatic resignation in autumn 1989 had less to do with the boom than with his differences with Mrs Thatcher and her adviser Alan Walters over the ERM question.

1992: BLACK WEDNESDAY

Both the Treasury and the Bank of England had a habit of referring to people on paper by their initials. Gordon Richardson could never get Christopher Dow's initials right and used to write to him as C. J. R. when the correct order was J. C. R. D. Initial confusion reigned briefly in Whitehall when it was learned that, after Lawson's resignation, his successor was to be J. M. Those initials surely stood for John MacGregor, a prominent Conservative MP who had always shown a close interest in economic affairs, and who had indeed previously served in the Treasury as Chief Secretary, with responsibility for control of public spending. But it turned out that Mrs Thatcher had chosen John Major to be Chancellor. The Prime Minister seemed to have mistaken John Major's natural politeness for agreement with everything she stood for, and chose him believing, in one of her favourite phrases, that he was 'one of us'.

When Mrs Thatcher was ousted in 1990, she let it be known that she favoured Major as her successor. But she and her acolytes spent the greater part of his premiership undermining his authority, believing him to be far too 'European', despite the way Major successfully negotiated Britain's opt-out from the single currency at Maastricht in December 1991.

Major was Chancellor for a mere year before, to many people's surprise, becoming Prime Minister. I used to joke that Major did only three things as Chancellor: he presented one Budget; he kept interest rates at the same level for eleven months; and he took the pound into the European exchange rate mechanism – that is to say, he achieved what Nigel Lawson could not, in wearing Mrs Thatcher down, and finally persuading her to drop her resistance to ERM entry.

It was not, of course, just Major. He was at the head of what by then had become an establishment consensus that we should join. Motives were mixed. Lawson and others saw the ERM as the 'lodestar' the British economy required in order to control inflation, monetarism having proved an abject failure. Others, not least the Foreign Office, were moved primarily by pro-European motives.

The Treasury, the Bank of England, the Confederation of British Industry and much of the serious press were in favour of ERM entry. I heard some interesting and not entirely irreconcilable accounts of the immediate background. One version was that Mrs Thatcher was finally worn down. Another was that, contrary to the general impression, she was, in the end, almost enthusiastic about ERM entry, asking officials excitedly, 'When are we going to do it? When are we going to do it?' The Thatcherite version was that ERM entry was forced upon her, and the subsequent debacle on Black Wednesday, 16 September 1992, proved she had been right all along to oppose it when Chancellor Lawson was advocating it. The version to emerge from the Bank of England was that at the time, autumn 1990, she was desperate to cut interest rates and repeatedly asked the Bank to do so. But, after the general loss of credibility in the government's monetary policy, the Bank maintained that a cut in short-term rates would provoke an increase in long-term rates, because the markets would believe the Treasury and Bank had 'gone soft' on inflation. By contrast, it was argued, entry to the ERM would lead to lower, German-style levels of inflation. Unfortunately, the inflationary consequences of the contemporaneous unification of Germany were not taken into account.

In the preparation for the fatal day, Mrs Thatcher and her adviser Sir Alan Walters had made it a condition of the ERM decision that, among other things, inflation should be coming down when Britain joined – 'the Madrid terms', taking their name from the location of an EU summit. But inflation was not falling in the early autumn of 1990 – indeed, the annual rate rose from 10.6 per cent in August to 10.9 per cent in September.

At the annual meeting of the World Bank and IMF in Washington that October, Major, in the British delegation's offices, gave the Chancellor's customary press conference. On such occasions the agenda is supposed to concentrate primarily on what has been going on at the international meetings, but there is nearly always an intense focus on what is going on back home. Sensing that the approach to the ERM was almost upon us, I asked Major whether the Madrid terms had been 'seasonally adjusted'. He laughed, and I deduced that they had – i.e. that the government had decided to apply to put the pound into the ERM. I was tempted to write a predictive news story about this, but a fellow financial journalist urged caution, and I refrained. I am sure his advice was well meant, but I should have had more confidence in my own judgement.

The decision was announced shortly afterwards and I felt rather isolated when attacking it in my column, arguing that we were going in at the wrong exchange rate, for the wrong reasons and at the wrong time.

Sometime earlier, the Bundesbank president Karl Otto Pöhl told me, only half-jokingly, that the only way for the UK to get control of inflation was to join the ERM, and that waiting until inflation fell before doing the deed could take a long time.

Mrs Thatcher was known to listen to Pöhl, although her admiration for him diminished somewhat after she told Bank Governor Robin Leigh-Pemberton to follow Pöhl during the Delors Committee discussions that preceded the formation of the European single currency. While harbouring doubts about the whole thing, Pöhl in the end went along with it, to Thatcher's surprise, and, in obeying instructions and following him, Leigh-Pemberton, in the words of one official, 'went native'.

But Pöhl got his own back by insisting that the planned European Central Bank should be founded on statutes that made it at least as rigorous as the Bundesbank. This meant that, taken with the European stability and growth pact, the single currency had a deflationary bias from the start. It was not for nothing that the word 'stability' assumed precedence over the word 'growth'. The object of the pact was to encourage 'sound' non-inflationary economic policies. A favourite word in many a European communiqué was 'sustainable'.

Pöhl was a gift to British journalists because he was open, frank and engaging. On one occasion in mid-week he told me that the Bundesbank was going to change interest rates the following day – hot stuff for the financial markets – but as I was writing for Sunday he knew he could trust me not to tell anybody. I also got to know one of his predecessors, Otmar Emminger, who was so keen to disabuse me of what he thought of as my rampant Keynesianism – vainly as it turned out – that he went on for hours and I missed my plane. However, I found a press office at Frankfurt Airport which made me at home during the long wait for the next flight.

One of the themes of these reminiscences about British economic policy is that, at the macro level, British policymakers had continual concerns about the economy's proneness towards inflation. For a long time this was connected with attempts to control what were regarded as the excessive wage demands of trade unions. The crises associated with the three-day week, the Winter of Discontent and the miners' strike all reflected failures of one sort or another of counter-inflation policy – which took various forms, often in desperation.

A related theme was provided by sporadic attempts to improve productivity. The idea was that if productivity could be raised, then not only would general living standards improve but inflationary pressures would be less. Unfortunately, such attempts – the National Plan of the 1960s; the dash for growth under what became known as the Barber boom in the early 1970s – did not eliminate the inflation problem, which would show up in the impact of cost inflation on the international competitiveness of our exports, and hence balance of payments problems.

It is, incidentally, one of the great ironies of our economic performance that there was a breed of economist, principally monetarists, who argued that once inflation was under control everything would be fine. Now, as I write in 2018, inflation is not an obvious problem, but many other aspects of the economy certainly are.

The Black Wednesday fiasco was of especial interest to me because throughout my career covering the economy – usually the British, with obvious interest in Europe and the world economy – I have always been fascinated by exchange rates.

My interest arose from small beginnings. When at the age of eleven I won an essay prize from the *Cork Weekly Examiner*, my prize constituted a half-crown – two shillings and sixpence

– Irish postal order. I was shocked, indeed horrified, when, on presenting this to the Raynes Park, London SW20, post office, I was given in return the princely sum of two shillings and three halfpence (we are talking here of 'old money', and not the 'old money' associated with the aristocracy).

The cost of foreign exchange transactions, and the ever-present danger of being ripped off, has interested me ever since. So have movements in exchange rates. Indeed, one of my regular daily tasks as economics correspondent of the *FT* in 1967–76 was to report on exchange rate movements during the more exciting bouts of speculation in the markets. And what one discovered early on, in a variation of Scott Fitzgerald's famous quip that 'the rich are different from you and me', was that the big handlers of investment and speculative funds in the markets operated on much finer commission or transaction charges than members of the general public.

These days people think nothing of movements in one day of several per cent in, say, the sterling/dollar or sterling/euro rate. But in the late 1960s and early '70s, under the Bretton Woods system of 'fixed but adjustable exchange rates', I would find myself writing front-page stories about changes of a fraction of 1 per cent between, say, the pound and the dollar or D-Mark or French franc.

In a sense, I was brought up as an economic journalist on the Bretton Woods system, which had been set up under the influence of Keynes in reaction to the economic horrors of the interwar years. To work properly, it required controls on movements of capital: such movements can far outweigh the impact of currency flows precipitated by ordinary trade. We have seen the lengths to which the Wilson government went to try to avoid changes, such as the devaluation of the pound in 1967, which were in fact necessary. But when the Bretton Woods system broke down in 1971–73 – with the Nixon administration no longer being prepared to support the rates of other currencies against the US dollar, which was itself devalued – the world embarked on not so much a system as a non-system of 'floating rates'.

Once the major nations embarked on a world of floating exchange rates, there could be wild gyrations in those rates. It was concern about these in the course of the 1970s that contributed to the decision on the part of Chancellor Schmidt, President Giscard and Roy Jenkins to press for 'a zone of monetary stability' in Europe, which led to the setting up of the European Monetary System.

When Chancellor Lawson was conducting his campaign for the UK to join the ERM, one of the principal objections put forward by his *bête noire* Sir Alan Walters – Mrs Thatcher's political adviser – was that the ERM was 'half-baked': the abolition of capital controls meant that the ERM was inevitably subject to what could become intolerable speculative pressures; by contrast, the proposed single currency, the euro, would not – at least for those within the system. (Though obviously there could still be large movements of the euro against the US dollar and other currencies.)

I myself had some sympathy with the school that wanted reasonably steady exchange rates, agreeing with some of the captains of industry I knew that wild fluctuations could be bad for business, just as could rigid adherence to a fixed rate that had become uncompetitive.

I became interested in the idea that, although the Bretton Woods system had long since been abandoned, there might be a case for the Group of Seven leading industrial nations adopting a system of 'target zones' for exchange rates. They would attempt to intervene to restore order and keep exchange rates between the dollar, the Japanese yen and the ERM currencies within certain defined limits (the Chinese currency had not at this stage become such a major force in the markets) but not such narrow bands as operated within the ERM.

At one of the international seminars I used to attend in Washington, I had heard the eminent American economist and policymaker Paul Volcker express similar views, so on one occasion I sent him a copy of one of my columns advocating target zones. I received a warm reply, one sentence of which was to the effect that he and I appeared to be the only people in the financial world we frequented who believed in target zones.

At the time of the intense discussions that took place after our adventures with the ERM, when the pioneers were preparing to embark on the single currency – which began for the banking system in 1999 but for the European public, with notes and coins, in 2002 – much was made of the convenience the Eurozone would provide for both business and the public: no need to change into another currency within the euro area, and no transaction costs!

This was of obvious appeal to the general public, not least for making holiday travel easier. The same issue arose when the Blair–Brown government went through the laborious process of weighing up the pros and cons of joining the single currency. But there were many other considerations than the convenience of travel, not least the sacrifice of sovereignty over monetary policy, and the freedom to devalue the currency against others – the loss of which the Italian economy has suffered from vis-à-vis competition from the much less inflation-prone German economy. These and other considerations came up in Gordon Brown and Ed Balls's famous 'five tests' exercise, which ended in a decision not to join the euro and involved no fewer than twenty-three exhaustive studies.

For the key mainland European economies of Germany, France, Italy and the Benelux countries, the EMS and ERM were staging posts on the way to the single currency. For the British governments of Mrs Thatcher and Chancellors Lawson and Major, joining the ERM was the last resort after all their other attempts at controlling inflation had failed. Labour under the leadership of John Smith had flirted with the idea of ultimately joining the single currency. Smith, when shadow Chancellor, once told me that, while he was certainly pro-European, one of his reasons for toying with the idea of ultimately joining the single currency was simply to embarrass the Major government, which was having such problems with its Eurosceptics.

As it happened, when in opposition Labour was decidedly pro-ERM, but, not being responsible for the actual decision to join, they escaped all the obloquy that descended on the Major government on and after Black Wednesday. Similarly, during Gordon Brown's chancellorship and premiership, the Tories under David Cameron and George Osborne went out on a limb to support the public spending levels of the time, but managed to forget this commitment when the financial crisis occurred. Indeed, disgracefully and absurdly, they blamed the global financial crisis on the same Labour plans that they themselves had supported.

The crucial influence on Labour's approach to the single currency was provided by the young Ed Balls, recruited as an economic adviser from the *Financial Times* by Gordon Brown, shadow Chancellor, in 1994. When interviewed by Gordon, he pointed out that he had a very different view from the Labour leadership about the ERM and the idea of putting the pound into the single currency. Indeed, he had written a Fabian pamphlet two months after Black Wednesday outlining his analysis, in which he also advocated giving the Bank of England independence over monetary policy. This, in due course, turned out to be the precursor to the eventual New Labour government's approach to the single currency and to the establishment of Bank independence.

It was at about this time that I first met Ed Balls. He rang me out of the blue and we met for lunch at the El Vino branch in New Bridge Street, Blackfriars. (This was an offshoot of the famous El Vino in Fleet Street. It had opened in 1982, around the corner from St Andrew's Hill, where *The Observer* was then housed. It has been known ever since as 'the New El Vino's'.)

Ed explained that he was a leader writer on the *FT*, but had been offered a job by Gordon Brown. He asked my advice as to whether he should take it. I already knew Gordon well. My advice was 'yes'. Labour were almost certainly going to win the next election, and he was in any case – in his mid-twenties – young enough to return to journalism if things did not work out. Years later, I asked him if he had consulted any other journalists. He named two. I asked what their advice had been. 'One said "don't" and the other could not make up his mind.'

His interview with Gordon Brown had taken place after Black Wednesday, when the Labour Party was rethinking its position on something that Brown had advocated so strongly.

Black Wednesday, 16 September 1992, assumes enormous significance in these reminiscences of covering the British economy. By a devious route, it was by far the most dramatic consequence of the failure of the Thatcher/Lawson government to control the British economy's inflationary tendencies. And, ironically, it was Mrs Thatcher and her colleagues who had successfully castigated the Labour governments of 1974–79 for the failure of their counter-inflationary policies.

The humiliation of the forcible ejection of the pound from the European exchange rate mechanism on Black Wednesday played a key role in the events leading up to the biggest economic crisis I have covered in these past fifty years. For it was Black Wednesday which galvanised the Eurosceptic wing of the Conservative Party into forming the movement which finally led to the referendum of 23 June 2016 and the threat of Brexit.

John Major was never forgiven by the Eurosceptic wing for championing the ERM and for proclaiming that he wished to put Britain 'at the very heart of Europe'. This reinforced the opposition of the Eurosceptics to most things European, and was a crucial link in the chain that led to the EU referendum. Major had done brilliantly in negotiating the UK's famous opt-outs from the Eurozone and the Social Chapter. Exemption from membership of the Eurozone pleased many observers and commentators such as myself, because, however pro-European we were, many of us were concerned about the economic policy restrictions imposed by Eurozone membership.

On the other hand, in common with the Labour Party and the TUC, I myself regarded the opt-out from the Social Chapter as a retrograde step, and, of course, when Labour was returned to power in 1997, Tony Blair was quick to opt back into the Chapter, which was essentially concerned with protecting the rights of workers.

But, from the point of view of the Eurosceptic group in the Cabinet – whom Major, in an unguarded moment, described with feeling as 'the bastards' – the opt-out from the Social Chapter marked progress in their right-wing agenda, and something of a minor triumph. Their ultimate triumph – the 2016 referendum – was over two decades away.

The Maastricht Treaty was signed in March 1992, but the meeting where everything was negotiated was in December 1991. I covered it with my colleagues Alan Watkins, *The Observer*'s great political commentator, and Nicholas Wapshott, the political editor. The meeting was early in the week for a Sunday paper. Watkins had the bright idea that the three of us should lunch the following day in the hotel restaurant where the EU leaders had lunched the day before – 'Let's absorb the atmosphere, chaps,' he said.

On the way to the conference hall, we were introduced to the Dutch concept of 'the green wave' – a remarkable sequence of green traffic lights. A more pertinent memory of that conference is Major's claim that the result was 'game, set and match' for the UK – a remark fed to him, rumour had it, by Gus (now Lord) O'Donnell, who was then his press secretary.

This claim was much repeated in Parliament and the British media. For a time, Major looked as though he might triumph over the Eurosceptic 'enemy within'. Moreover, against the odds, he won the election of April 1992. I say 'against the odds' advisedly. I am a racing man – horse racing, that is, not jogging; I retired from cross-country running many moons ago, when I discovered the joys of walking. It so happened that I was at Ascot the day before the general election with the economist Roger Bootle, and we were so sure that Labour would win that we did not take up the bookmakers' offer of 6 to 1 against the Conservatives – that is, six pounds for every one pound staked! We have been kicking ourselves ever since.

David McKie, then at *The Guardian*, was on night editorial duty that week and maintained that it was clear that things were going against Labour even before the Sheffield rally, at which Labour leader Neil Kinnock was considered to have been fatally triumphalist.

It was an amazing feat for Major to win a general election

while the economy was still bogged down in the second biggest recession since the 1939–45 war. The Tories seemed to be good at this. Had they not won the 1983 election after the biggest recession since the war, with unemployment high and still rising? Of course, then the opposition had been divided between Labour and the SDP, and Labour itself had campaigned on a wildly unpopular manifesto.

Major was helped in 1992 by the dubious but effective campaign run by the Conservative Party chairman Chris Patten, with its emphasis on 'Labour's tax bombshell' – a sensational but effective way of castigating Labour for having the cheek to suggest that taxes had to go up to finance public spending. The sad thing for Labour was that they were trying to show fiscal responsibility by explaining how their manifesto pledges would be financed. Ironically, Patten, who had so successfully undermined Neil Kinnock's electoral hopes, became good friends with Kinnock when, later, they served as British commissioners in Brussels. Both were strongly pro-European. The other twist was that Patten himself, having masterminded the nationwide Tory victory, lost his own seat in Bath – hence his sojourn in Hong Kong as the last Governor, from 1992 to 1997.

But before we move on from the election of May 1992 to Black Wednesday that September, it is worth going back to aspects of the pre-Maastricht picture and the build-up to ERM entry in October 1990.

In the end, Mrs Thatcher's opposition to the ERM was worn down by a combination of events. One was that the Treasury had run out of options: monetarism, monetary targets, shadowing the D-Mark had all failed, and the Lawson boom had set inflation on a path that was encouraging some officials to urge even higher interest rates than the 15 per cent that Major inherited.

Major had very strong views on inflation. He had seen people's savings being eroded, and regarded inflation as a social scourge as well as an economic problem. He thought that even the Treasury, where he had worked for two years as Chief Secretary, negotiating spending limits with other departments, did not appreciate how affected he had been by childhood memories of hardship, which he associated with inflation. Indeed, in his memoirs he makes a wry comment about the Chancellor he succeeded and who had landed him with a legacy of accelerating inflation. He complains that Lawson was 'not always sensitive to the frailties or needs of others. He did not know what it was like to run out of money on a Thursday evening, whereas I did.' He also differed from Lawson in being concerned about the way the Thatcher government had been cavalier in its policies towards manufacturing, which was suffering from high interest rates.

Yet high interest rates were what he inherited, and they constituted what Sir Edward Heath had memorably described in a golfing metaphor as Lawson's 'one club' weapon to get himself out of the 'bunker' of inflation. So Major was a man with a mission, as the year-on-year increase in retail prices index rose from 7.7 per cent in January 1990 to 9.4 per cent in April and 10.9 per cent in September. He wanted inflation down but was saddled with the single club then so fashionable in Whitehall and Threadneedle Street.

As we shall see, the next panacea to be sought by the Conservatives was to be inflation targets, but they were not resorted to until the current panacea, ERM entry, had also proved a failure. The irony was that Major and his Treasury officials considered introducing inflation targets in his one and only Budget, in March 1990: the problem was that, to be realistic, the target would have had to be set at such a high level as to be embarrassing.

Major had two advantages over his predecessor in working on Mrs Thatcher. One was that she was in a Wildean situation, where to lose two Chancellors over the ERM would have qualified as carelessness. The other was that, in contrast to Lawson, he was not confrontational (the veteran financial journalist Christopher Fildes, who once worked for Lawson at *The Spectator*, memorably said that 'Nigel would cross the road to pick a fight').

Douglas Hurd, who had succeeded Howe at the Foreign Office, was not confrontational either. The two got on well and worked together to persuade Thatcher. Hurd was a Foreign Office man through and through; he did not pretend to be an economic expert – not that the so-called experts got the issue right themselves! – but espoused the ERM issue for political reasons, not least because he wished to repair relations with Germany after Mrs Thatcher's well-publicised opposition to German reunification.

The emollient approach of Chancellor and Foreign Secretary began to pay dividends in May, when Mrs Thatcher exposed a flank: reflecting some Treasury fine-tuning with what it called 'the underlying inflation rate', she maintained in a public speech that the Madrid conditions on the inflation rate were becoming achievable. 'If you compare like with like, we are not so far above Europe's average for inflation.'

Lower inflation had been one of the so-called Madrid terms for ERM membership – an agreement hammered out in fraught discussions between Mrs Thatcher and her increasingly desperate pro-European Cabinet colleagues, Geoffrey Howe and Douglas Hurd, aided and abetted by long-suffering officials. The word Madrid was attached because the compromise was reached as part of the business of an EU summit in Madrid in June 1989. However, instead of coming down in accordance with the object of the agreement, the inflation rate had accelerated between 1989 and 1990, from 7.8 per cent to 9.5 per cent (year on year) compared with a German inflation rate of 2.7 per cent in 1990. In effect, the goalposts were moved, largely because previous efforts at tackling inflation had failed. The rate was well above what had been implied by fulfilment of the Madrid terms.

Amid all the ups and downs and to-ing and fro-ing, as far as the Treasury was concerned the definitive decision to apply for membership was made in June 1990, although precise timing was still up for grabs. An inspired report in the *Financial Times* referred to September or October, stressing that Major wished to enter at a relatively high exchange rate to demonstrate his counter-inflation credentials. On 10 July, Major made the most definitive public statement yet. He said Britain *would* be joining the ERM, adding, 'That is not just my idiosyncratic view; that is the view of the British government. It is our agreed policy.'

Officials most closely involved say that the tipping point for the Prime Minister was when inflation reached 9.8 per cent in June and July. One senior official recalled that every time he saw Mrs Thatcher from then on, she excitedly asked him when they were going to take the plunge. Britain eventually joined in October 1990, when inflation was at 10.9 per cent. Some fifteen years later, Major told an audience at the London School of Economics that, in the end, Mrs Thatcher had been 'extremely keen' to join the ERM because of the seriousness of the economic situation and, in particular, the recrudescence of inflation.

* * *

The story of how the financier George Soros 'broke the Bank of England' on Black Wednesday has gone into folklore. David

Marsh of the Official Monetary and Financial Institutions Forum (OMFIF) think tank, the historian Richard Roberts and I covered the immediate run-up and aftermath in *Six Days in September*.

Shortly before Black Wednesday, my wife and I were staying with Ian Gilmour and his wife at their villa in Tuscany. One day, Ian came out onto the terrace rather excitedly to say, 'Bill, I've got a good story for you. The Treasury have just rung to ask whether Norman Lamont is staying here. There's a financial crisis brewing and they don't know where he is. This gives you a great column for your return from holiday: "Treasury loses Chancellor in Tuscany."'

I do not myself speculate in the foreign exchange market, but I well remember attending a press briefing at the Bank of England on the Tuesday afternoon 15 September, given by the overseas director of the Bank, Andrew Crockett. Andrew was always very frank and straightforward. Although the briefing was supposed to be about a forthcoming World Bank–IMF meeting in Washington, other matters were covered. As my colleague Anatole Kaletsky and I left the building, we looked at each other and agreed that it was all over. Without being specific, Crockett had given the impression that things were desperate.

Although John Major, Chancellor Norman Lamont and their inner Cabinet colleagues battled for most of the day in a vain effort to 'save the pound', a senior Treasury official told me, 'We knew it was all over at ten past eight in the morning.' The pound went on falling and all efforts to support it failed.

There was something extraordinary, and ironic, about the way the British 'stuck to the rules' and did not concede that the game was up until nearly all the reserves had been exhausted. One could not have imagined the French bothering to obey the rules in similar circumstances.

Black Wednesday was a political disaster for the Conservatives, who undoubtedly lost their reputation for economic competence. But, paradoxically, it was a kind of forced rescue operation for the British economy. The exchange rate at which we had joined the ERM had been excessively high from the point of view of industry's international competitiveness, and the high interest rates needed to 'protect' the pound's value prolonged the domestic recession.

I think Anatole Kaletsky was the first commentator to rename the day 'White Wednesday'. I myself, only half-jokingly, suggested in my *Observer* column that Helmut Schlesinger, the president of the Bundesbank, should be given a knighthood for his role in contributing to the crisis, when he gave an interview, on the eve of Black Wednesday, making it clear that he thought a currency realignment – i.e. a devaluation of the pound – was necessary.

Reports of that interview were the final straw.

On Black Wednesday itself I was lunching at the Garrick Club at the same time as Dominick Harrod, the BBC's economics editor. Dominick suddenly left the building in a hurry. He had reported on a 'shock' rise in the Bank of England's interest rate from 10 per cent to 12 per cent at 11.15 that morning and, believe it or not, he told a group of us at lunch, they have just announced another rise to 15 per cent.

In fact, that 3 per cent rise to 15 per cent never took place. There was widespread misunderstanding about this: it was in theory due to come into force the following day, but was rendered pointless after Norman Lamont announced at 7.30 that evening that our membership of the ERM had been temporarily suspended.

In this case 'temporarily' has meant 'permanently'. Afterwards

I met City figures who said that, if the government had been serious about the 15 per cent, they planned to drown their sorrows
on champagne before bankruptcy proceedings commenced.

The Bank, under instructions from the Treasury, had been
intervening all morning in a vain attempt to support sterling,
with the currency reserves draining away. The 2 per cent rise in
interest rates was part of the attempt to restore confidence in
the current value of the pound within the ERM but, like the
intervention, was doomed to failure.

The fact of the matter was that the game was up well before
Lamont's announcement. Indeed, the suspension took place at
4 p.m., after Major had wasted hours in a vain attempt to request help from our Continental partners. The hedge fund king
George Soros said he had made in excess of a million pounds in
a matter of days by selling – technically known as 'shorting the
pound'. It was not just George Soros who called it right. 'Short
selling' of sterling to the Bank of England was rife. There were
many less-publicised operators than Soros. Selling of sterling
was being conducted on a massive scale, not only by traders but
also by bank and corporate treasurers and asset managers generally. In a world of deregulated capital markets, where the annual
total of foreign exchange trading exceeds transactions to finance
ordinary business by a multiple of some hundreds, a central bank
is basically defenceless when the tide turns against it.

And turn it certainly did. It was a torrent of speculation. The
obvious question was: why did the government allow it to go on
all morning and into the afternoon, draining the reserves in a
public display of national humiliation? Way back in 1985, during
one of the many episodes when Lawson was trying to persuade
Mrs Thatcher that we should join the ERM, a Treasury official, Geoffrey Littler, theorised about the circumstances when,

at a time of crisis, the government might suspend intervention to prop up the pound. A former senior Treasury official, Lord Burns, is on record as saying, 'It was always anticipated that we would make use of this in an emergency.'

There has been many a post-mortem on this subject. My own view is that Prime Minister John Major had invested so much of his reputation on what he hoped would be the success of ERM membership that he just could not admit to himself that the writing was on the wall.

Basically the approach of the Major government to Black Wednesday was farcical. To plough on all morning and well into the afternoon when officials knew the game was up by 8.10 a.m. was pointless. One was reminded of the sketch in *Beyond the Fringe* when, in World War II, a superior officer tells a junior that the time has come to make a futile gesture and the latter had been chosen to be that gesture.

What it boiled down to was that, having been disappointed by what they regarded as the lack of understanding of our position on the part of our EU partners, John Major, encouraged by the Foreign Office – pro-EU to a fault on this occasion – stuck to the rules. Douglas Hurd, the Foreign Secretary, said, after it became clear that the 11 a.m. rise in interest rates from 10 per cent to 12 per cent had not staunched the outflow, that the FCO lawyers had advised that the UK was obliged to stay in the ERM and carry on intervening 'under a treaty obligation'.

This was at a gathering of senior ministers in Admiralty House, where the Prime Minister was based while No. 10's defences were being strengthened after a terrorist attack. The meeting had been called to discuss contingency plans should there be a French 'no' vote in a referendum on the Maastricht Treaty the following Sunday. In fact, proceedings were taken over by the currency crisis, whose outcome ensured that there would be no need for such contingency plans to protect the pound: its protection was being destroyed as they sat there.

With regard to the legal advice, Kenneth Clarke told my colleague David Marsh when, with Richard Roberts, we were writing our book *Six Days in September* that it was rather a pedantic point. 'Who was going to challenge us in the courts?' He then joked, 'The only person who could perhaps have claimed later that he was damaged would have been George Soros.'

Why were other, non-economic ministers kept there all morning? Kenneth Clarke later suggested, 'We were there to put our hands in the blood.' It was a case of spreading the blame and providing cover for the Prime Minister.

But it was not just the Foreign Office. Major himself was concerned that sudden withdrawal would damage the hard-fought Maastricht Treaty of earlier in the year. At least one senior Treasury official who was used to dealing with fellow Europeans was also anxious to obey the letter of the law, when it is doubtful that, for example, the French would have done so in similar circumstances.

Kenneth Clarke duly succeeded Lamont and is generally considered to have enjoyed a reasonably successful chancellorship from 1993 to 1997. I recall an incident when Major and Clarke flew to Tokyo for a G7 summit. I was on the plane and, on the way back, was amused to see Ken come to the rear of the plane to talk to the press. I cannot remember what he said, but I do recall that he looked rather eccentric in a kind of jumpsuit provided by the airline and that I did not have much time to listen to him because along came Gus O'Donnell, then John Major's press officer.

He said, 'The Prime Minister would like a relaxed word with you.'

So I went up to the front of the plane, but rather over-interpreted the word 'relaxed'. Knowing that he had gone to Rutlish School, not far from my own grammar school, Wimbledon College, I opened the bowling with a reference to our shared background. It soon became clear that he was not at all interested. He launched into a bitter criticism of his former Chancellor, Norman Lamont, saying that if he, Major, had been presiding at the Bath meeting of finance ministers that took place shortly before Black Wednesday, the outcome might have been very different.

The Bath meeting had been fractious, with Lamont chairing it and pressing the Bundesbank president Helmut Schlesinger for interest rate cuts that he (Lamont) subsequently admitted he knew Schlesinger was in no position to deliver. Schlesinger had to be restrained from walking out.

A week after Black Wednesday, there was an IMF meeting in Washington, where Lamont was asked why he was looking so cheerful. 'Well,' he replied, 'it is a very beautiful morning, but it is funny you should say that. My wife said she heard me singing in the bath this morning.' I referred to this episode in a subsequent book, and could not resist saying that 'he had certainly not sung in Bath' – a line that, I was delighted to hear, went down well in the Bundesbank.

Now, I have indicated that I grew up with the Bretton Woods system. I sympathise with efforts to avoid wild fluctuations in exchange rates and was not viscerally opposed to the thinking behind the ERM. But, as noted earlier (and as John Major generously recorded in his memoirs), at the time of our entry to the system I wrote that we were joining at the wrong time, for the wrong reason and at the wrong exchange rate.

We tied our currency to the D-Mark at just the time when Germany's reputation for low inflation was bound to be threatened by the costs of reunification of East and West Germany. So it proved. Moreover, we went in at a relatively high rate, which looked to some of us to be unsustainable, and indeed was. And the reason for doing so was more to do with trying to make up for previous failures of policy to control inflation than with considerations of our medium- and long-term competitiveness.

The amazing thing is that the implications of German monetary union (between West and East) for the German inflation rate were already apparent. But joining the ERM had become such a British establishment obsession that the point was overlooked. Shadowing the D-Mark and hence the low West German inflation rate had been Lawson's post-monetarism economic panacea, which led to the Lawson/Major desire to join the ERM. But the event took place at just the time when the unified German economy's inflation rate was 'taking off', requiring tighter monetary policy – i.e. higher interest rates – than was needed for a UK economy in recession.

The need to keep interest rates high to hold the exchange rate within the agreed bands most certainly prolonged what had turned out to be the second worst recession, lasting from 1990 to 1992, since the Second World War. Some officials, such as the Treasury's chief economic adviser Alan Budd, rationalised this as giving the government a better chance of eradicating inflation – or most of it – from the system.

One of the many ironies of the Black Wednesday experience was that the Chancellor, Norman Lamont, who had succeeded Major in 1990 – a Eurosceptic to boot – was himself against the whole idea of joining the ERM. He once told me that he had asked his officials, 'Why are we doing this?' – to which the answer was that the Treasury had lost one Chancellor and could not afford to lose another.

But, of course, they did. Immediately after Black Wednesday, Lamont offered to resign but Major would have none of it. A widespread view was that Lamont was being used as a human shield to protect the position of the real political author of the policy, the Prime Minister himself. However, the time came for the human sacrifice, and Lamont was duly sacked from the Cabinet in spring 1993, after a series of unfortunate gaffes reported in the press.

The Black Wednesday episode was an embarrassment not only for the Conservative Party, but also for the Treasury and the Bank of England. It also aroused the interest of the security services. Shortly afterwards, I was invited to lunch at the Poule au Pot restaurant in Chelsea by an old acquaintance from my Cambridge college, who worked for MI6.

It was November, and he was sitting in a dark recess, in candlelight. He looked as though he was trying to create an air of mystery. The main object of his enquiries seemed to be to find out more about what had happened on Black Wednesday, why, and was there some secret explanation lying behind it all. I tried to give the whole story, but, frankly, nothing I said could not have been obtained from what I myself or others had written in the newspapers.

CRISIS 7

2007–09:
FINANCIAL CRASH

When I was on secondment to the Bank of England in 1976–77, the morale of Bank staff was still recovering from the shock of two events in the financial markets, one of which had occurred only a few weeks before I joined. This latter, in March 1976, was what was widely considered its inept handling of an interest rate reduction that briefly gave rise to an impression that it did not care about a fall in pound. The other was the 'secondary banking crisis' of 1973–75.

The March 1976 episode figures in the chapter on the IMF crisis of that autumn. The secondary banking crisis, although it preceded the financial crisis of 2007–09 by several decades, nevertheless had a lasting impact on both the Treasury's and the Bank's attitudes towards financial supervision.

Under a monetary regime known as competition and credit control, the Heath government and the Bank had bowed to the burgeoning movement in favour of giving freer rein to market forces, allowing greater competition for borrowers by banks and building societies – in other words, breaking up what was seen as a cartel. The episode has been extensively covered in some excellent accounts, such as Margaret Reid's *The Secondary Banking*

Crisis. In a nutshell, the policy encouraged a proliferation of dubious and risky lending institutions, which ended in tears – almost including the collapse of the mighty NatWest bank – and required a major rescue operation by the Bank of England.

I found when I worked at the Bank that banking supervision was considered a dangerous career move. The feeling, encouraged by the fallout from the secondary banking crisis, was that banking supervisors were 'on a hiding to nothing'. This view was reinforced in the 1980s by the failure of Johnson Matthey Bankers (JMB) in 1984 and of the corrupt Bank of Credit and Commerce International (BCCI) in July 1991. As if these were not enough, we then witnessed the collapse of Barings in 1995.

Robin Leigh-Pemberton, who was Governor of the Bank from 1983 to 1993, once rather rashly remarked, 'It is not the task of regulators to prevent financial institutions from making lending mistakes.' Leigh-Pemberton was very much a 'gentleman banker'. He had been chairman of NatWest and was thought by several bank colleagues to have been chosen to be Governor by Mrs Thatcher because of her penchant for matinée idols. Another in that category was the politician Cecil Parkinson, who was wonderfully indiscreet and once told me, 'We are using the North Sea revenues to finance unemployment.' Leigh-Pemberton was a charming man, but his Bank colleagues soon observed that he regarded his gubernatorial duties as secondary in importance to his role as Lord Lieutenant of Kent. He seemed surprised by his appointment, as many others certainly were. He once told me he had only met Mrs Thatcher a few times before being appointed.

It was soon obvious that he needed serious experienced support at a high level, which was why the veteran Bank official Sir George Blunden was invited to emerge from retirement to become a powerful deputy governor. Sir George had a wicked sense of humour, once observing to me, 'They have brought me back from the dead. I can do anything I like.'

Bank failures provided great scope for recrimination and buck-passing. It was felt strongly within the Bank that a particular official was made to carry the can for the failure to anticipate trouble at JMB, with some of her colleagues believing that she had been victimised because she was a woman, and that her warnings had been ignored.

Plenty has been written about the failure to act in time over BCCI, when its problems were common currency in the City. Leigh-Pemberton, by this time Lord Kingsdown, told me well after his retirement that the Bank had been hesitant to act because it feared accusations of racism, given the 'developing country' structure and ownership of the bank, which had been founded by Agha Hasan Abedi, a Pakistani financier. Incidentally, the BCCI issue offered an example of the dangers of a widespread practice at the time: the inclination of retired politicians to take non-executive directorships in a deal whereby they received an emolument and the organisation could obtain kudos by adding their names to the head of the corporate writing paper. My wife, a commercial barrister and former Bank of England economist, still recounts her horror at seeing our former Prime Minister James Callaghan appear at a World Bank/IMF function in Berlin in 1988 sporting a BCCI badge.

In the words of Marjorie Dean and Robert Pringle, both expert observers of banks:

Supervision is a big yawn until things go wrong ... when the Bank of England closed the corrupt Bank of Credit and Commerce International in London in July 1991, indignant voices were to be heard asking for the regulatory and monetary functions in

Britain to be officially divided, the implication being that, because the central bank gives too much attention to the latter, to the detriment of the former, it had failed to spot irregularities at BCCI as soon as it should have done.

Lord Kingsdown's remark suggests that perhaps it had spotted them, but procrastinated. Nevertheless, the issue pinpointed by Dean and Pringle was important, and gave rise to much academic and political debate. The decision made by Gordon Brown and his economic adviser Ed Balls to separate the functions represented, at least in part, a desire to punish the Bank for its regulatory failures. But it was also a decision made in the belief – perhaps, in the light of subsequent experience, one should say 'hope' – that bank failures would not occur on their watch, under the new regulatory institution, the Financial Services Authority (FSA), they set up from 1997.

There was much debate not just about the division of attention between monetary policy and regulation, but also about whether the two responsibilities could be in conflict: for instance, there might be a desire not to tighten monetary policy when it might be wise, for fear of damaging a vulnerable financial institution.

Whereas Gordon Brown's premiership proved controversial, there has been widespread praise for his decision when Chancellor to make the Bank independent – more precisely, to give it operational independence in monetary policy, i.e. in the setting of interest rates. Although the warning signs were there in various speeches while Brown was shadow Chancellor, I confess that, in spite of knowing Brown and Balls well, I myself was surprised, not to say shocked, when the announcement of independence was made within days of Labour's landslide election victory in May 1997. It took some time for the news to sink in with some journalists when Brown made his dramatic announcement at a press conference in the Treasury. The news was accompanied by an announcement of a change in interest rates. In the question session, the new Chancellor was asked when the next change in interest rates might be. Such a question would have been a long shot at the best of times. But the questioner had not got the message. There were to be no more decisions about interest rates from the Chancellor: the ball was now firmly in the Bank of England's court (though not in its Court: the Bank's operations are overseen by its Court, but interest rate decisions were to be made by the new Monetary Policy Committee, chaired by the Governor and comprising a mix of Bank executives and external members).

After the announcement, I went across the road for coffee with Robert Chote, later to become director of the Office for Budget Responsibility under the Conservative government from 2010, but then economics editor of the *Financial Times*. We were both of the view that this was a very strange decision, given the Labour Party's long-nurtured criticism of the deflationary bias of the Bank of England under Governor Montagu Norman in the interwar years, and the Wilson government's travails with Governor Cromer in the 1960s. I had always been struck by the remark attributed to that great Fabian Sidney Webb, later Lord Passfield, to the effect that the Attlee government nationalised the Bank of England in 1946 in order to avoid a repetition of 1931, when the Labour government fell to be replaced by the National Government. The Labour government under Ramsay MacDonald from 1929 to 1931 was essentially on a rack as a result of the Conservatives' decision in 1925 to put the pound back on the gold standard. The considerably higher exchange rate placed a huge constraint on economic policy and contributed to the onset of the depression. The restoration of the gold standard was a decision taken by Winston Churchill when he was Chancellor and something he regretted for the rest of his life. He had been persuaded by ultra-orthodox Treasury officials and the similarly orthodox Bank of England and its Governor Montagu Norman. One of the saddest and very human aspects of the decision was that it was made after a dinner of relevant politicians and officials at 11 Downing Street and although Keynes, a fierce opponent of the move, was there, he was not very well and on bad form. When the National Government, which followed the collapse of the Labour government in the summer of 1931, went off the gold standard, Passfield also said, 'Nobody told us we could do this.' One suspects that Keynes had told them many times that they could.

Chote and I were worried about giving control of interest rates to unelected bankers. My opposition to the move, in my next *Observer* column, was quoted twenty years later in David Kynaston's monumental history of the Bank of England: 'I believe, with only modest reservations, that Labour has taken leave of its senses.' I was not alone. The commentator Anatole Kaletsky wrote in *The Times* that Brown was 'locking the pound in a golden casket and throwing away the key'. We were, however, in a minority.

Given the conventional view that independence has proved a great success, I have often been teased by Ed Balls about my initial verdict. I tend to say that it is too early to judge the success of independence. But it has to be admitted that, when it later became clear that the inflation target given to the MPC was symmetrical, one became less apprehensive. There was not a built-in deflationary bias. If inflation was likely to be lower than the target, then the MPC was obliged to take expansionary action. I was worried, and still am up to a point, about the democratic aspects of this – indeed, former deputy governor of the Bank of England Sir Paul Tucker has written a lengthy tome about the democratic legitimacy of central banks (*Unelected Power: The Quest for Legitimacy in Central Banking and the Regulatory State*). The reassuring aspect of the arrangement is that it is the Chancellor who sets the inflation target.

But, when it came to the separation of the regulatory and monetary functions of the Bank, this did not prove to be a happy divorce. First came the collapse of Northern Rock in late summer 2007; a year later, the crisis at the Royal Bank of Scotland (RBS) came to the fore after a long period when the absurdly overambitious chief executive Fred Goodwin embarked on the ill-advised takeover of the Dutch bank ABN Amro. There has been quite a blame game evident in the various post-mortems conducted ever since, and this has become apparent in the memoirs of the key policymakers, not least in writings by Brown, who had just become Prime Minister at the onset of the crisis, Alistair Darling, who received the 'hospital pass' of being made Chancellor on the eve of the deluge, and Governor Mervyn King himself.

In the end, it is the Treasury and ultimately the taxpayer that have to cough up when things go wrong and banks have to be rescued. Of course, they do not *have* to be rescued. The key point is whether there is what is known technically as a 'systemic rise', that is to say, whether taking action would have wider, ominous implications for the economy at large. Another factor that has to be taken into account is what became known as an obsession of Governor King in 2007 when the Northern Rock crisis occurred.

King was worried about 'moral hazard' – the fear that automatically rescuing a bank would encourage others to take excessive risks, knowing that they could expect to be bailed out by the government. Although the FSA was formally separated from the Bank – physically too, because it was located some miles downriver at Canary Wharf – there was in fact a tripartite system. The FSA was responsible for day-to-day supervision, the Bank was responsible for overall financial stability, and the Treasury was there at the other end of town with obvious responsibilities when the crisis arose.

When one thing led to another, and the failure of Northern Rock was followed by the much bigger disaster of the Royal Bank of Scotland, various chickens came home to roost. It was common knowledge in the City and Whitehall that Governor King was not really interested in the City in general and keeping in touch with bankers in particular. This was in sharp contrast to his predecessors going back many years. Lord Cromer in the 1960s and Gordon Richardson in the '70s and early '80s were both very much City grandees, with a firm background in merchant banking – the business that, after the Big Bang revolution in the 1980s, became known as 'investment banking'. Both Sir Leslie O'Brien (Governor 1966–73) and Eddie George (Governor 1993–2003) were lifelong Bank insiders, joined at the hip to City institutions. They believed in keeping in daily touch with what was going on in the banks and other money market institutions.

This was not the case with Governor King, who was considered by many to regard the Bank as a kind of academic institution for economic research. When he rose from being chief economic adviser to Deputy Governor and ultimately Governor, his initial view was that he did not wish to be disturbed in the mornings, which he regarded as 'thinking time'.

King had been an early champion of the move to inflation targeting, first under Chancellors Lamont and Clarke in reaction to the Black Wednesday collapse of the previous counter-inflation policy, and later under the stewardship of Brown and Balls. His main interest as Governor was macroeconomic policy, as the British economic ship of state sailed through what King christened the nice decade – signifying non-inflationary, consistently expansionary growth. In reality, of course, it was low-inflationary consistently expansionary growth.

For Brown and Balls – and, indeed, the official Treasury – the benefits of bank independence were appreciable. The Labour Party had lost its reputation for economic competence during the IMF crisis of 1976 and the 1978–79 Winter of Discontent. The Tories had lost theirs on Black Wednesday. Gordon Brown was determined to render Labour trustworthy with the economy – hence the repeated emphasis on 'prudence with a purpose'. Making the Bank independent was a remarkable devolution of power over monetary policy, enabling him and the Treasury to get on with other matters. The Chancellor is outnumbered in Cabinet by 'spending ministers'; Ed Balls became fond of pointing out that the Chancellor now possessed a useful weapon in the face of ministerial demands: 'If I give in to you, the markets will take fright about spending and the Bank will raise interest rates.'

Two other points made to me repeatedly by Treasury officials over the years were: first, that decisions about whether to change interest rates tended to take up an inordinate amount of time; and, secondly, that the pursuit of sound policies was frequently thwarted on Budget Day by seeing their Chancellors, often encouraged by their Prime Minister, give way to the temptation to announce a surprise cut in interest rates.

The trouble was that the wonders of Bank independence were eventually subject to Macmillan's famous obstacle of 'events'. Anxious to please the City, Brown and Balls were happy to go along with light-touch regulation, although Brown had for some years been calling for stronger global financial regulation – 'a proper monitoring of risk and an early warning system'. But, as he wrote after the deluge, 'I had to accept that I had lost the argument.'

However, Brown freely acknowledged in retrospect that it had been a mistake to subscribe to what had become an international consensus. This consensus, led by the then chairman of the Federal Reserve, Alan Greenspan, held that the sophistication of modern financial markets had reduced the dangers of a financial crisis via the diversification of risk, all those fancy new 'products' and what became known as 'financial engineering'.

During the summer of 2007, and the advent of the Northern Rock crisis, Brown had moved on to No. 10, and his long-time colleague and fellow Scot Alistair Darling was installed at the Treasury. Governor King may not have been over-interested in regulation, but Darling certainly was. Indeed, in his instant memoir of the crisis, Darling disarmingly admits that, as shadow minister for the City in the run-up to the 1997 election, he had been largely responsible for the architecture of the FSA.

There was a lot of bad blood between the Treasury and the Bank of England after the onset of the financial crisis. The Treasury itself was short of banking expertise but rapidly built it up. The Treasury was angry that the Governor made so much of what he saw as the dangers of 'moral hazard' – his concern being that rescuing one financial institution would be the thin end of the wedge for other miscreants. There was an amazing episode when the Treasury found that King was lying low in his country retreat and not answering calls, to the point where they had to despatch a messenger to deepest Kent to elicit a response. Darling discovered that he was not allowed, under the rules of the tripartite regulatory structure, to order the Governor to provide liquidity to the market.

Darling is vitriolic about the attitude of the Governor in his memoirs, describing him at one point as 'the Sun King', which has obvious echoes.

By now the crisis was international, and the Federal Reserve and the European Central Bank were providing liquidity to their markets. Indeed, the crisis had not begun with Northern Rock in August 2007. Although there were plenty of post-mortems and recriminations about the deficiencies of the British tripartite regulatory model, Brown, Darling and King were not responsible for the way that the US sub-prime crisis and the bursting of the US housing bubble led to the onset of the Bear Stearns collapse on 17 July 2007 and the ramifications in Europe. I myself first became aware of the international repercussions when on holiday at our annual retreat in Puyméras, the heart of Côtes du Rhône country, near Gigondas and Chateauneuf du Pape.

On 9 August, the French bank BNP Paribas froze three of its investment funds. As the crisis unfolded, it became evident that globalised financial engineering had certainly spread risk. But there were also the risks of 'irrational exuberance'. Way back in the late '90s, the then Governor of the US Federal Reserve, Alan Greenspan, had expressed concern about 'irrational exuberance' in the markets. But they had seen nothing yet. The spreading of risk had ensured that European financial institutions, not least supposedly staid German banks, were also severely affected by what had begun as the US sub-prime crisis. As the crisis unfolded, it became clear that the kind of German bank that had been considered cautious and staid was up to its neck in dubiously valued securities. This was the result of a combination of the closer international links between the banks, and the gambles they took as lending rose way out of proportion to their capital base.

Much has been written about the connections between all

those derivative financial products that proved worthless. But it is an open question whether they were the truest cause of the banking crisis that began in the United States and spread further afield – though not, interestingly, to nearby Canada. I recall the first time I met Mark Carney, who subsequently became Governor of the Bank of England. It was in January 2009. We were the only occupants of a funicular lift, bringing us down to the main street in Davos – from, it has to be admitted, rather a good drinks party hosted by Barclays Bank. 'Hi!' said the other occupant. 'I'm Mark Carney, Governor of the Bank of Canada.' After I had duly introduced myself, he said, 'We didn't have a banking crisis in Canada.'

Canada's experience was the exception to the rule that, in a globalised financial world, with sub-prime 'paper' turning up on bank balance sheets all over Europe, it was difficult to avoid being tainted by the crisis. For a time, it was fashionable to blame financial engineering for the banking crisis but in Thucydidean terms the truest cause could well have been a recrudescence of the historical pattern of greed and excessive risk-taking – parallels with the Dutch tulip mania and South Sea Bubble – to relieve so many people of their senses. But the assumed sophistication of the global financial system was the proximate cause and was to magnify the effects. The general atmosphere was epitomised by the slogan 'This time it's different' – an indication of the human propensity not to learn from history. My great hero J. K. Galbraith was particularly good on this subject. In my last interview with him, he had some wonderfully irreverent remarks to make about the faith that the world was putting in Alan Greenspan. Of all the quotes I have waded through in thousands of pages on the crisis, the one that seemed to capture it most was by the Conservative MP for Hereford, Jesse Norman: 'I can tell you precisely what was responsible for the crash. It was because bank leverage, which was twenty times capital in 2000, went up to fifty times in seven years.'

The big development after Bear Stearns was that the financial markets seized up. Nobody trusted anybody: if those in charge of one vulnerable organisation knew about their problem, they naturally assumed – unfortunately, with good reason – that others were in the same boat.

The culture of risk-taking at RBS was astonishing. So too was the level of arrogance and ignorance. The period between the collapse of Northern Rock in late summer 2007 and the injection of masses of capital into banks such as RBS in the autumn of 2008 proved what is known in the trade as 'a learning curve' for most of the participants, whether bankers or politicians and officials trying to cope with the biggest financial crisis in living memory. The financial journalist Christopher Fildes was fond of saying, 'Things usually go wrong in financial institutions when there is nobody left in the firm who remembers the last crisis.' But this time it was different in scale. After RBS had doubled its debt in just over a year from mid-2007, its chairman telephoned Gordon Brown saying the bank had a cash-flow problem but all it needed was 'overnight finance'. As Brown notes in his memoirs:

> A few days later his bank collapsed with the biggest losses in banking history. RBS's problems were not simply about liquidity, and additional cash flow could not have helped for more than a day or two. The problems were structural. The bank owned assets of unimaginable toxicity and had too little capital to cover their losses.

Although many people involved have been critical of Mervyn King's lack of interest in the run-up to the crisis and slowness to react afterwards, his critics acknowledge that early in 2008 he did grasp the importance of the burgeoning insolvency problems at the Bank. As every economics student soon learns, banking is at heart a kind of confidence trick. If depositors rush to withdraw their funds, the bank is soon in trouble. Borrowing 'short' and lending 'long' is all very well in good times, but not when there is a collapse of confidence. The building society Northern Rock was over-dependent on extremely short-term funds, offering 100 per cent plus mortgages, which they funded by borrowing very short-term funds. It was perfectly rational for members of the public to rush to withdraw what might otherwise be considered longer-term savings when it was reported that the institution was in trouble, and, at that stage, government guarantees of the safety of deposits had not been confirmed. Those guarantees were soon announced, but not before memorable scenes of queues outside Northern Rock branches were flashed around the world. It did not help that, unlike some other building societies, Northern Rock had very few branches, so that the impression of panic was magnified enormously.

The other memorable television image of the time was the sight of employees of Lehman Brothers in Canary Wharf emerging hurriedly from their building with packing cases as, a week after the nationalisation of the troubled US mortgage firms Fannie Mae and Freddie Mac, Lehman Brothers filed for bankruptcy on 15 September.

That Lehman Brothers was allowed to go under shook financial confidence so much that it certainly added to the momentum for a large-scale recapitalisation and rescue of the banking system. Concerned about the historical association between Old Labour and nationalisation, Gordon Brown had resisted calls for immediate nationalisation of Northern Rock, even when Governor King was saying this was the obvious answer. Finally, on 17 February 2008, Chancellor Darling announced that Northern Rock would 'temporarily' be taken into public ownership. Several years later, the Treasury's most senior official, Sir Nicholas Macpherson, acknowledged, 'With the benefit of hindsight the Treasury was slow off the mark in addressing the problem. There was a five-month period of drift.' The episode, he said, was a 'monumental collective failure, of which the Treasury was a part'.

Eventually Gordon Brown 'saved the world' with his powerful advocacy of the need to recapitalise the banking system and administer a massive fiscal and trade credit boost to counter what IMF managing director Dominique Strauss-Kahn had memorably termed 'The Great Recession'. Brown's 'saving the world' remark came in a speech to the House of Commons after the American economist Paul Krugman had praised him with a similar phrase in his regular column in the *New York Times*. Brown corrected himself to say 'saved the banks', but it was too late. Nevertheless, there was a lot in it. Brown had a determining influence on the way the US and the Eurozone went about recapitalising their banks. We must not be too insular, however: the US Federal Reserve was vital in assisting the banking system of the rest of the world in the rescue operation.

In his memoirs, Brown is candid about the weakness of his own reforms:

Although the crisis exploded out of America, British regulation was deficient too. We had created what I still believe is the right framework – a tripartite group of Bank, regulator and government as our early warning system – but from the start the FSA had been in a territorial war with the Bank of England and, as

I look back on their minutes, none of the three partners gave the tripartite system the time, input and commitment that was needed.

As for regulation, Brown adds, 'The assessments of the FSA depended less on in-depth examination by investigators than on bland assurances from the investigated.' He puts a historical finger on it when concluding that all this was 'a product of the neoliberal culture of the time that talked about better regulation but in fact favoured even more deregulation'.

Although I have referred above to proximate causes and the Thucydidean 'truest cause', there were indeed historical factors contributing to this neoliberal culture. In the UK, these began with the way that Bank officials noticed after the removal of foreign exchange controls in 1979 that most of the subsequent trade was being conducted by foreign banks. They thought, in what turned out to be their naivety, that opening up the City and exposing it to greater competition from overseas financial institutions would somehow strengthen the City's traditional institutions. Instead, these were swamped, and US, German and Japanese banks moved in, with many City figures taking the money and running.

I recall that in my early days on the *Financial Times*, banks were required to maintain strict liquidity and capital ratios. Such 'fuddy-duddy' conservative practices went out of fashion under the Thatcher market reforms of the 1980s. Then came the fall of the Berlin Wall in 1989, the collapse of the Soviet Union in 1991, and the unleashing of an extreme free market approach, which I like to think I warned about in my book *The Spectre of Capitalism*.

The banking crisis was the apotheosis of this trend.

The invasion of the City of London by American investment banks had imported a new culture – harder working, longer hours, bigger risks and absurdly high rewards for what was deemed to be successful trading. The raison d'être of the financial district had once been to serve the interests of business, industry and ordinary people. Unfortunately, a large gulf had emerged between banks and their customers – not all banks, I hasten to add, but there was sufficient corrosion of traditional values for the more flamboyant banker to lose touch with reality. Gordon Brown recalls a conversation with a leading banker in 2008: 'I questioned the justification for continuing to pay bankers large bonuses even as the consequences of their poor judgements were coming to light. "But they'll leave the country," he responded. I refrained from giving him the response that ordinary members of the public would have given him.'

This reminded me of the time I was attending a high-powered seminar in Washington in the aftermath of the banking crisis and Paul Volcker, an outstanding chairman of the US Federal Reserve in the early 1980s, made a comment on the following lines: 'People tell me here in Washington that bankers' bonuses are justified because otherwise bankers will move from New York to London. But I read in the *Financial Times* this morning that high bonuses are being justified in London on the grounds that otherwise bankers will move to New York.'

Volcker also spoke very much to the point when he stated in the wake of the banking crisis – in my opinion only half-jokingly – that, for all the development of 'new financial products', the only worthwhile financial innovation in recent decades had been the cash machine, otherwise known as the ATM.

Volcker was also very critical of modern investment banking practices and their contribution to the crisis. I was lucky enough to be in the audience on several occasions at seminars of bankers in Washington when Volcker, a firm believer in old-fashioned values, made sardonically perceptive criticisms of modern financial practices in which his successor, Alan Greenspan, styled 'Maestro' by his biographer, had placed so much faith.

Although the Queen herself posed that famous question as to why nobody warned about the banking crisis, there was no shortage of officials and economists who were uneasy before the crash – a famous example being when Raghuram Rajan, then chief economist at the IMF, was in effect shouted down when he voiced his concerns at the annual Jackson Hole central bankers' conference in August 2005. Bill White, then chief economist at the Bank for International Settlements in Basle, issued many a warning, reported by, among others, Martin Wolf of the *Financial Times* and, indeed, by me in *The Observer*.

Unfortunately, the supposed wonders of deregulation were all the rage, and the consensus and herd instinct ruled. There was a notorious remark by Chuck Prince of Citibank that, even if problems were on the horizon, participants just had to 'keep dancing'.

At which point, I should like to pay a tribute to the late Margaret Reid, who was a colleague of mine on the *FT* in the 1970s, and whose book on the 1986 Big Bang, *All Change in the City*, published in 1988, was remarkably perceptive about the likely deleterious consequences of rampant deregulation. She was especially concerned about the fact that 'the money washing through the currency markets is now thirty or more times the scale of underlying trade and invisibles business'. Similarly, she highlighted that 'another uncomfortable recent feature of the City has been evidence that, here and there, the enterprise spirit was going over the top and resulting in practices pushing up against, or over, what the law allows'.

At all events, one way or another, all these factors contributed to the banking crisis that politicians, central bankers and officials had to cope with in 2007–09. Gordon Brown may not have been the only one, and he kicked himself for having boasted in Parliament that he had 'saved the world' – an observation that, as noted, was first made in regard to him by the economist Paul Krugman. Nevertheless, he played a crucial role in the bank recapitalisation movement of late 2008 and the trillion-dollar stimulus to the world economy agreed at the G20 meeting in London at the beginning of April 2009. Brown hosted that meeting, and was praised for his vital role by Barack Obama, then US President.

Despite the manifold criticisms made of Brown for his domestic handling of the premiership he had long coveted, when it came to the biggest economic crisis to hit the advanced economies since the Second World War, he was the right man, in the right place, with the right contacts, having spent eight years when Chancellor as chairman of the IMF's key political committee.

It happened as follows. I was seated next to a European finance ministry official at an Anglo-German dinner in London. It was October 1999, and Gordon Brown had been Chancellor of the Exchequer for just over two years. 'I am surprised', said the official, 'that your Chancellor should want to leave and take the IMF job.' So was I! It was the first I had heard of it. 'It is surprising, isn't it?' I replied. He then proceeded to say how amazed his minister had been to receive a phone call from Brown asking whether he would support his candidature for the managing directorship of the IMF.

I drew on this conversation in the opening paragraphs of my column the following Sunday. Without quoting my serendipitous source, I raised the possibility of such a move in the form of a question. That weekend I was at a conference in Ditchley Park, Oxfordshire. My brother Victor was duty editor at *The Guardian*, whose editor, Alan Rusbridger, was now also editor-in-chief of *The Observer*.

Victor rang me to say that Alan had rung him to ask whether my suggestion was true, and, if so, why wasn't it a front-page news story. My loyal brother replied that he was sure it was true, and he was equally sure that there was a good reason why the information had appeared in that form. (Although Victor and I are in frequent touch, we had not spoken about the story before it was published.)

The fact of the matter is that it was obvious to me that, as a news story, my information could easily have been denied. Gordon Brown is famous in Labour Party circles for keeping options open, and examining any proposal that interests him in the minutest detail. He had spent many years preparing for the chancellorship, and had a list of many things he wanted to achieve. The managing directorship of the IMF is a prestigious post, but, in my experience, the politicians who have held that job have usually had their eyes on returning to domestic politics. (A subsequent example, of course, was Dominique Strauss-Kahn, who was prevented from returning to French politics by events that ought to have been within his control.)

It would have been quite extraordinary for Brown to jump ship within two years of gaining the chancellorship. On the other hand, flirting with the idea could easily have been a bargaining counter in his endless discussions with Tony Blair about the 'succession' to the premiership. If anything, the incredulity of the said European finance minister's reaction to Brown's enquiry was enough to convince me of the need to handle the issue cautiously. Nobody denied what I had written in my column.

Sadly, many years later Gordon Brown would have loved the IMF job. After the global financial crisis, during which, as we have seen, he played a major role, he was rightly exercised about the way so many countries moved to policies of austerity when it was far from clear that the prospect of sustainable growth had been restored.

The enforced resignation of Dominique Strauss-Khan in 2011 was, in theory, the perfect opportunity for Brown to go to the IMF. Unfortunately, from another point of view the timing could hardly have been worse. George Osborne, champion of austerity policies, was now Chancellor.

Although Britain had been one of the most important architects of the Bretton Woods Agreement of 1944, which led to the formation of the IMF, we had never fielded a candidate for the top job there. In Gordon Brown we had a pre-eminent potential candidate in 2011: not only did Brown have ten years as finance minister to his credit, but for most of that time he had also been chairman of the IMF's key political policy-making committee, the International Monetary and Financial Committee (IMFC), during which time he had greatly impressed his opposite numbers and IMF officials.

But, having 'saved the world' with his key role in the G20 fiscal and monetary stimulus of 2008–09, Brown was vehemently opposed to Chancellor Osborne's approach. Osborne did not care for him anyway, and there was no way that the British government would champion his cause. We were therefore subjected to the sight of a British Chancellor backing a French candidate, Mme Christine Lagarde, for the post. Any idea that the French would have proposed anyone other than a French candidate has only to be aired to be laughed out of court.

CRISIS 8

2010–16: OSBORNE'S AUSTERITY

I referred earlier to the way that, when I had the original interview that led to my job at the *Financial Times*, one of the great *FT* commentators of the time, Michael Shanks, came into the room. It was immediately clear to me that the editor, Gordon Newton, quite enjoyed treating the celebrated author of the bestselling *The Stagnant Society* as just a typical member of his staff.

While I was working on this book, another former *FT* colleague told me he had been re-reading Shanks's book and found himself amazed at the complacency of the tone. The title may have suggested that there were lots of things wrong with the state of the nation in the late 1950s and early 1960s, but for Shanks, the kind of Keynesian economics I learned at Cambridge had completely changed the world. Recessions, let alone depressions, were a thing of the past in the US and UK. Thus:

> Twenty years have not been long enough to accustom the British working class to the idea that full employment and prosperity are here to stay. Thus every temporary downturn of trade is treated like the coming of Armageddon, the return of the soup kitchen

and the labour queue … It is easy to see how unrealistically gloomy this attitude is – and how self-defeating.

Yet if Shanks had still been with us in the England of 2010 onwards, he would have seen the modern equivalent of soup kitchens all over London and in provincial towns. We had indeed experienced what Dominique Strauss-Kahn had termed 'The Great Recession', and some economists and commentators, including myself, had made no bones about calling it a depression.

The recessions of 1979–81 and 1990–92 were bad enough. But the banking crisis referred to in the previous chapter led to the biggest setback to the economy since the Second World War. A combination of monetary and fiscal stimulus stopped the rot – world trade was collapsing at an annual rate of 20 per cent in the second half of 2008 and the early months of 2009 – and the London meeting of the Group of 20 leading industrial nations on 1 and 2 April 2009 marked the historic moment when policymakers, with Gordon Brown exercising impressive leadership, saved the day.

Unfortunately, relief was short-lived. Gordon Brown's government was summarily dismissed by the electorate in May 2010, and in came the Cameron government with a Chancellor, George Osborne, who immediately embarked on a policy of austerity. Moreover, at the 2010 meeting of the G20 which took place in Toronto shortly after that election, Osborne sided with the German representatives in an all too successful bid to reverse the stimulus agreed by the G20 just over a year earlier.

I have known many Chancellors, and always, until Osborne arrived on the scene, got on well with politicians from both major parties. One can have policy or ideological disagreements and still respect the other side. But there was something about the cynical way that Osborne introduced his austerity programme which, frankly, got beneath my skin. He and his Prime Minister, David Cameron, started by blaming the financial crisis on 'Labour's mess'. It mattered not that in opposition Cameron and Osborne had supported Labour's public spending programme. With blatant disingenuousness, the new Chancellor and his colleagues now blamed the crisis on Labour's 'excessive' public spending.

Alas, it was a brilliant propaganda coup, which went down all too well with a British public that seemed, deep down, to suffer from a masochistic streak. Time and time again economists and commentators such as myself tried to point out that Labour had not been responsible for the recessions in the US and Continental Europe. The fact that the national debt had shot up and the budget deficit had reached wartime proportions was the result of a crisis that had hit most of the Western world. My friend Sir Nicholas (later Lord) Macpherson, then the most senior Treasury official, went along with the broad thrust of the austerity programme. Traditionally, it is the Treasury's natural inclination to seize almost any excuse to cut public spending. And Sir Nicholas delighted in being not a Keynesian but an admirer of that austere pre-war Chancellor Philip Snowden – anathema to Labour on account of his budget orthodoxy at a time of depression. But Macpherson believed in civil service neutrality, and could not subscribe to misleading propaganda. In a review of my book on the crisis, Macpherson – I believe to his Chancellor's annoyance – emphasised that 'it was a banking crisis, pure and simple'.

At this stage, I should point out that Gordon Brown's chancellorship had certainly encouraged the Treasury to let down its guard on the public spending front. After establishing his credentials for 'prudence' with an initial two-year freeze on public spending in 1997–99, Brown had, when it came to his attempts to help the poor, made the Treasury into something of a spending department itself. But the extent to which he relaxed his prudence was much exaggerated by his critics, and the principal beneficiaries were education and the health service.

In fact, the key ratio of net debt to gross domestic product during and at the end of Brown's chancellorship – 1997–2007 – compared favourably with the figures for Kenneth Clarke's chancellorship – 1993–97 – under the Major government. The big rise in the ratio came with the onset of the financial crisis in 2007–09. Despite all the successful propaganda about 'Labour's mess', the fact of the matter was that the share of government net debt to GDP in 2007 was lower than in any G7 country except Canada. The subsequent rise – from 35.9 per cent in 2006/07 to 52.5 per cent in 2009/10 – reflected the impact of the recession on demand for goods and services, and therefore on tax receipts, as well as extra spending on social security as unemployment rose by 800,000 between 2007 and 2010.

I fear that there was an unholy alliance between George Osborne and Mervyn King, the Governor of the Bank of England at the time. At the Bank it was a case of 'panic stations'. Absurd comparisons were made with the plight of the Greek economy, which was in a much more serious position and, unlike the UK, decidedly uncreditworthy. But King encouraged both Osborne and his coalition partner, the Liberal leader Nick Clegg, to embark on premature restrictive policies at just the point when the economy was on the mend.

Not to put too fine a point upon it, a burgeoning recovery was knocked on the head. Public spending plans were cut back, not least for investment, and taxes were increased. But in a snub to the general public and the poor who would experience the most hardship, a temporary increase in the top rate of tax under Labour was partly reversed.

Osborne made great play with the putative need for austerity. This conjured up comparisons with the immediate post-war period and the austerity under the Attlee governments of 1945–51. But that was an entirely different crisis. Britain ended the war in an almost bankrupt state. It took years for the country to adapt from a wartime to a peacetime economy. As troops returned to the labour force and civilians working in armament factories became redundant, they were redeployed to peacetime occupations. But there were severe shortages of goods, and imports were restricted through lack of funds. Taxes had to be levied to keep a lid on consumer demand until the economy recovered. For a long time there was 'too much money chasing too few goods'.

When, a few years ago, my book *Mr Osborne's Economic Experiment* was launched by the Strand Group of King's College, London, I could tell that the younger members of the audience were really struck by two family stories I told about that post-war austerity. One was that rationing was so severe that my brother and I had to share a boiled egg. The other – related – story was that when our mother told my brother that another child might be on the way, his comment was, 'I should rather have a hen that laid eggs.'

I was continually lost in admiration for the way that Cameron and Osborne got away with their cynically misleading claims that Labour's allegedly rash public spending had precipitated the financial crisis and therefore led to the need for austerity. I had no hesitation from that first Budget of Osborne's in June 2010 in attacking his austerity policy in my *Observer* columns. His predictions of a continuing recovery were wide of the mark, for two basic reasons. The first was that he was openly taking measures to restrict the speed of recovery with his fiscal policy, raising taxes and reducing the growth of public spending; the second was that, insofar as he was relying on monetary policy

to offset the deflationary impact of fiscal policy, this was largely futile because, as most would-be borrowers in business and
industry soon became aware to their cost, the banks were now
going from one extreme to the other. Having been bailed out
by the state for their risky lending in the run-up to the financial
crisis, they were now not only being grudging in their response
to requests for loans: they were often being disgracefully punitive
in their attitude towards hard-pressed businesses that were in
what should have been temporary trouble, but which, thanks to
the banks, sometimes became permanent.

Osborne's basic offence was not only to ignore but actually to
laugh at Denis Healey's law about not digging deeper when you
are in a hole. The British economy *was* in a hole, on the mend
from the worst recession since the war, having recorded a sharp
drop in GDP of 4.2 per cent between 2008 and 2009.

This was the biggest recession – indeed, depression – since
the 1930s.

In years gone by, recessions – minor by comparison with this
one – were usually followed by periods of above-average growth
as the economy recovered, and moved back to what economists
call 'trend growth' – traditionally some 2.5 per cent a year. Thus,
there had often been periods of 3 or 4 per cent growth for several
years after a slowdown – the 6 per cent jump recorded during the
dash for growth under Chancellor Maudling in 1964 (referred to
earlier) being very exceptional. The art is supposed to be to keep
a recovery under control so that it does not get out of hand and
result in an increase or even an acceleration in inflation.

It soon became evident that Osborne was using the pretext of
a budgetary 'crisis' to aim at shrinking the state. Traditionally, the
Treasury would use a 50/50 mix of increases in taxation and cuts
in public spending when administering deflationary medicine.

But Osborne made it a case of four fifths reductions in public expenditure and a mere one fifth in tax increases. Moreover, the cuts were concentrated on public investment and the social services, with the blame for much of the hardship being conveniently shifted to local authorities.

There was a 40 per cent reduction in grants from central government to local authorities – a guarantee of hardship for those working in or dependent on locally provided services. Queues for doctors' surgeries and admission to hospitals got bigger; the housing shortage developed into a major crisis, with many more homeless sleeping in the streets; and basic services such as libraries and road repairs were neglected. With a few notable exceptions in some of the big cities, such as the development of St Pancras and King's Cross stations in London, Britain became a shabbier place. The macroeconomic implications for infrastructure were epitomised in a startling statistic: public sector net investment fell from £60 billion in 2010 to £35 billion in 2016.

For several years, it looked as though the nation was experiencing the worst of both worlds: slow growth, aggravated by the restrictive economic policy, but also slow progress in reducing the budget deficit. From the Keynesian perspective, this was no surprise: an economy needs deficit financing to emerge from recession and a decent rate of growth in order to boost tax revenues and – guess what! – reduce the deficit. Rather late in the day, Osborne's successor, Philip Hammond, while continuing with prominent elements of the austerity policy, began to talk in the autumn of 2018 of the connection between economic growth and automatic reductions in the deficit – a Keynesian conversion that seemed to have escaped George Osborne.

We saw in the post-2010 government propaganda a return to the era of 'household economics' much favoured by Mrs Thatcher in the early 1980s. Under this doctrine, the nation is seen as a household. What does a household do when its finances are in trouble? It cuts back. But if everyone cuts back in accordance with household economics – if most households cut back – there is a gaping hole in the demand for goods and services, and unemployment goes up. Unemployment did in fact rise during the 2008–09 recession, from 5.3 per cent in 2007 to 8.1 per cent in 2011. After that it came down slowly, and certainly not as rapidly as in traditional economic recoveries. This was attributable to the impact of the austerity policies.

It is generally agreed by historians of the period that during the austerity that accompanied both the 1939–45 war and the transition to peacetime, the burden was shared by all sections of the population. Under Mr Osborne's regime at the Treasury, the load fell disproportionately on the weak and the poor. I recall a discussion with David Cornwell (aka John Le Carré) at the outdoor cafe at Kenwood in London when he suddenly declared, 'It is planned penury!'

'Wow!' I said. 'May I quote you?'

Many charities and research institutions, as well as local newspapers, provided chapter and verse on the damaging impact of 'planned penury'.

The terrible thing is that not only did it cause widespread poverty and social distress, it was also economically unnecessary, indeed destructive.

Professor Robert Neild – the very same Robert Neild who was chief economic adviser to the Treasury in the mid-1960s, referred to earlier – captured the economic absurdity of the policy in an article for the Royal Economic Society. He was writing shortly after the 2010 Budget which inaugurated the Osborne regime:

> Confidence, or lack of it, is at the core of the economic crisis. Mr
> Osborne justified his harsh and urgent budget tightening by the

need to maintain confidence and avoid a threat to our sovereign debt. But that budget policy, together with the uncertainty of the business outlook abroad, has undermined the confidence of our businessmen and has led us into depression.

As he pointed out, businessmen (and women!) need to have confidence in the future demand for their products if they are to invest in new buildings and machinery, thus generating more employment. But as a result of Osborne's deflationary Budget, 'that confidence has been drained out of them'. The putative reason for this was to boost foreign confidence, yet the threat to foreign confidence in the British economy was wildly exaggerated. Indeed, by making such an issue of this, Osborne and Co. were, if anything, lowering foreign as well as domestic confidence in the UK. One would not have thought, from the new government's scare stories in 2010, that gross government debt, as a percentage of GDP, was at 80 per cent, lower than in France and Germany. All three countries had been affected by the financial crisis, which was the biggest calamity to hit them since the Second World War.

The reader may have gathered that, in these years covering British economic policy, I have occasionally felt isolated as a commentator – for example, opposing Thatcherism and monetarism in the early 1980s, when so many people supported what I regarded as her overreaction to the power of the unions and the Winter of Discontent.

Again, when almost the entire establishment was in favour of putting the pound into the European exchange rate mechanism in 1990, it was not a popular approach for me to argue that the government was doing so at the wrong time, for the wrong reasons, and at the wrong exchange rate.

But what was very odd, in later years, was to be at odds with the policy of my own newspaper.

The first half of the decade that ushered in the new millennium – the decade known by that ghastly catchword 'the noughties' – was relatively quiet on the economic front – all part of what the then Governor of the Bank of England, Mervyn King, had christened 'the nice decade'.

My column took a strange turn with the onset of the Iraq War in 2003. I had begun reading *The Observer* as a sixth-former at the time of Suez, and admired the stand it had taken against Sir Anthony Eden, the Prime Minister, and the ill-fated invasion of Suez, which ended in disaster. In the run-up to the Bush–Blair invasion of Iraq, it became clear, to my horror, that the paper I had admired since Suez, and worked for since 1977, was going to support the invasion.

I was horrified, and wrote a brief, ten-paragraph, private note to the editor, Roger Alton, explaining why I thought it would be wrong for Britain to get involved, and that the newspaper that had been right about Suez would be making a disastrous mistake if it backed the war. Roger circulated my note among the staff, and I received quite a lot of support. But not from the editor, who threw the weight of *The Observer* behind Tony Blair's fatal decision to 'hug George Bush close'.

To cut a long story short, during a quiet time for economic policy my *Observer* column proceeded to dwell on the folly of the invasion and to be completely out of keeping with the paper's editorial line. To be fair to the editor, while well aware of what I was up to, he never once objected to my 'resistance' column – at least not to my face.

During that period, I met many people who were disgusted with the paper, and some who stopped taking it. They were shocked, puzzled and sorry. The feeling lingered on. About ten years later, I bumped into the BBC's great foreign correspondent Martin Bell in the ticket queue at Waterloo Station and he said immediately, 'Why did *The Observer* support the Iraq War?'

When it came to the austerity crisis, I soon realised that I was once again out on a limb in that the coalition's propaganda, led by Mr Osborne, was remarkably successful, not only in blaming it all on 'Labour's mess' but also in exaggerating the danger posed by the size of the budget deficit that was successfully counteracting the pernicious effects of the Great Recession.

Their argument seemed to me to be accepted by far too many people: some, not trained in economics, could perhaps be forgiven for being susceptible to the 'household economics' approach, but others ought to have known better.

I don't wish to exaggerate the 'out on a limb' point. There were some sturdy Keynesians who also challenged the Osborne orthodoxy. Among them were the redoubtable US economist and Nobel Laureate Paul Krugman, and Professor Simon Wren-Lewis of Oxford University. I have already mentioned my old friend Robert Neild. Then there were continual efforts by the *Financial Times* commentator Martin Wolf, as well as Jonathan Portes at the National Institute of Economic and Social Research. When one felt a little isolated in the face of all too successful government propaganda, and wondered whether one was indeed missing something, it was always a relief to turn to the latest writings of the above, and others, for reassurance.

There can, as we used to say, be safety in numbers.

In this context, I should emphasise that there was nothing like the Iraq episode in my relations with *The Observer* over my opposition to the austerity programme. The paper's leading articles, as well as my colleague Will Hutton's pieces, were all opposed to the coalition's policies and covered the social impact extensively, as did Polly Toynbee and her colleagues on *The Guardian*.

During that early period, 2010–13, the economy was, in Ed Balls's metaphor, flat-lining. Balls had delivered a powerful critique of Osborne's policy in his Bloomberg speech of August 2010 when, bizarrely, in view of his economic qualifications, he had not yet been appointed shadow Chancellor.

Insofar as there was a macroeconomic justification for the austerity policy, it was that the fiscal squeeze would be counterbalanced by monetary policy – low interest rates, quantitative easing (a silly euphemism for expanding the money supply). But the confidence was not there, and the banks were not lending. Indeed, the official figures for credit growth were going backwards. As Wolf pointed out in the 2013 Wincott Lecture, 'Monetary policy clearly and decisively failed to promote recovery. Animal spirits were completely destroyed. Demand fell. It was a machine designed to fail.'

It was at about this time that a phrase was coined in an effort to justify the austerity policy: 'expansionary fiscal contraction'. This was, of course, a contradiction in terms, for which the fashionable modern word is oxymoron.

Those Treasury and Bank of England officials who went along with – indeed, actively supported – the strategy tended to obsess about the way that, until the financial crisis, the Treasury had been heavily dependent on revenue from the banks and other financial institutions, which had accounted for a quarter of corporation tax receipts – a sector which had now been bailed out by the taxpayer. But the loss of such revenue was no excuse for clamping down on the rest of the economy, which ought to have been stimulated, among other things, in order to provide substitute revenue.

Those who supported austerity used to argue that Osborne's bark was worse than his bite and that, after all, the economy was growing. But the point was that it took a long time to get back to pre-crisis levels, and by the end of the coalition government, output was as much as 20 per cent below what would have been expected from historic trends.

By 2018, Theresa May's government was boasting that the current budget deficit was in balance, giving the impression that somehow the austerity had been worthwhile – had paid off. Indeed, David Cameron and George Osborne, the main political culprits of the austerity programme – and now both out of government – were to be heard making this very claim. It is all very well to claim that one had 'balanced the books'. But, in macroeconomic terms, the key question is: at what level? What matters is not the balance of the budget but the balance of the entire economy.

We shall move on to the referendum in the next chapter, but at this point I feel I should emphasise my strong belief that the accumulated impact of the austerity programme played a significant role in the outcome of the referendum. It must surely have contributed to what was widely regarded as a protest vote.

Another important point is that, as I write in autumn 2018, the modern age of austerity is far from over. People may have been misled for a time when Theresa May assumed the reins of office and appeared to want to distance herself from the popular view of the Conservatives as 'the nasty party'. Indeed, there were early indications that the vicar's daughter was only too aware of the social problems she had inherited and genuinely wished to address them. In one dramatic move, she showed what she thought of the architect of austerity by unceremoniously sacking George Osborne.

That was before it became obvious that the approach to Brexit was going to absorb most of her political energy. Meanwhile, both the reports from the Office for Budget Responsibility and the warnings from the Institute for Fiscal Studies made it crystal clear that austerity was going to continue – indeed, the squeeze on the social services would become even more intense.

The macroeconomic background was that the economy's underlying growth rate had slowed down. Although there were no doubt other historical forces at work, there can be little doubt that the depressing impact of austerity on investment in both the public and private sectors has taken its toll on the nation's productivity. Indeed, the question of how to raise the nation's productivity performance has become a preoccupation of government and many economic institutes, as well as forming a running debate in the increasingly interesting letters page of the *Financial Times*.

On top of which has been the blow to further investment plans from the uncertainty caused by the government's handling of Brexit.

In the midst of the frantic, and to my mind absurd, negotiations on Brexit in October 2018, Mrs May managed to claim that the age of austerity was now over. However, for all the political rhetoric, the underlying arithmetic of the Treasury's, the OBR's and various think tanks' analyses showed that it was going to continue. Indeed, the OBR brought out figures showing that there had already been significant damage to the economy since the referendum, and there would be worse to come on any of the various scenarios for so-called hard or soft Brexits.

CRISIS 9

2016: REFERENDUM AND THREAT OF BREXIT

It was 8.15 p.m. on Wednesday 13 July 2016, some three weeks after the electors of the United Kingdom had voted by 51.9 per cent to 48.1 per cent to leave the European Union.

I had been to a drinks reception at the Foreign and Commonwealth Office, where all the talk was of the shock, horror and possible implications of the result of the referendum. Among the people I spoke to were former Treasury Permanent Secretaries, former Cabinet Secretaries and assorted Foreign Office officials. Of all British institutions, the Foreign Office, or FCO, had been the most passionately pro-European. But as I was departing along the august corridors of the FCO's palatial building – still very much a reminder of the days of the British Empire – a passing attendant broke the news that the new Prime Minister, Theresa May, had just made Alexander 'Boris' Johnson, one of the leading advocates of departure from the European Union, Foreign Secretary. Foreign Secretary! A leading Brexiter. What an insult to a hallowed institution!

I was leaving the building with two students, one of whom was doing a course at King's College, London, where I had been made a visiting professor. As we crossed Whitehall, one of them pointed down the street to a group of people drinking outside the Red Lion pub.

'That looks like David Davis,' he said.

'That *is* David Davis,' I said.

'Would you like to meet him?'

'Yes please.'

We walked the 100 yards or so, and before I could say anything myself, Mr Davis said, 'They have made me Mr Brexit!'

It was at the Red Lion that my friend Sir Kenneth Berrill heard some know-alls pontificating about the economy during the 1973–74 oil crisis. He interrupted and said, 'It's not quite like that.'

'And what do *you* know?'

'Well, I *am* the chief economic adviser to the Treasury.'

'And I'm the Queen of Sheba.'

It was also at the Red Lion that Charlie Whelan, a prominent member of Gordon Brown's entourage when the latter was Chancellor, took a phone call from Prime Minister Tony Blair in 1997, and broke the news to him that the question of Britain's possible entry into the single currency arrangements had been kicked into touch by his Chancellor.

At this point it is worth emphasising that, while being credited with keeping the pound out of the Eurozone, Gordon Brown himself is a passionate pro-European. It has been one of the absurdities of the Brexiters' position that they have (rightly) been accused by spokesmen and negotiators for our fellow Europeans of wanting to have their cake and eat it; yet, by securing exemption from the Eurozone during our EU membership, we have indeed been able to have our cake and eat it. As George Soros has observed, as long as we do not go ahead with Brexit, we enjoy the best of both worlds – the economic advantages of membership of the customs union and the single market, without the constraints on economic policy – most notably in respect of exchange rate rigidity – required by membership of the Eurozone.

I don't know of any Brexiters who, however critical of Gordon Brown for other reasons, do not praise him for the way he got the Treasury to conduct those five tests to assess the pros and cons of joining the single currency and came up with the decision to remain outside. This was a classic example of how, for all the Eurosceptical propaganda, we are not 'run by Brussels' and have not sacrificed our sovereignty.

First let me stress that, despite the way so many commentators talk, Brexit has not happened yet, and I am one of those who still hope it can be prevented. Yet, in a depressingly defeatist way, for much of 2018 BBC interviewers, while no doubt bending over backwards to be 'balanced', seemed to assume, from their questions, that Brexit was inevitable.

What has happened is a referendum in which just under 52 per cent of those who voted opted to leave the EU and just over 48 per cent to remain. This was, by any standards, an exiguous majority to determine such a major national decision, and the picture looks even more absurd when it is realised that only 37 per cent of the entire electorate voted to leave. Many of those eligible to vote were in the 18 to 25 age group. An irony of the outcome was that, before the previous general election, David Cameron's Conservative Party had changed the rules for voter registration, so that when teenagers became eighteen they were required to apply to go on the electoral register, whereas before there had been an automatic enrolment procedure. On the assumption that more of the younger generation tend to be Labour or Liberal rather than Conservative, this suited the Cameron government for party political purposes. But when it came to the referendum, called by David Cameron, many younger people, who tend to be pro-European, were too disorganised and not yet enfranchised to vote.

Thus, when one hears the repeated refrain 'the people have spoken' and is told that the outcome of the referendum must be honoured, one should, in my opinion, take this view with a pinch of salt.

If Brexit goes ahead, it will be a tragedy for the United Kingdom and bad news for the rest of Europe. We spent most of the 1960s trying to join what was then the European Economic Community; our application was turned down twice by President de Gaulle. And it was a triumph for Prime Minister Edward Heath when his good relationship with President Pompidou helped us to be accepted in 1973.

Decades later, it was the British government under Mrs Thatcher that pressed strongly for the formation of the single market, and it was Britain that championed the extension of the EU to embrace Eastern European former members of the Soviet bloc.

Quite apart from the economic threat to the UK from leaving the customs union and the single market, it seems unforgivably short-sighted for us to leave a co-operative alliance designed to further international security at a time when Europe has to cope with Putin to the east and Trump to the west.

The tragedy is that the majority of Members of Parliament are firm Remainers and regard the idea of Brexit as economic, diplomatic and cultural folly. Yet they seem obsessed by the referendum result, and at the time of writing it was an open question whether Parliament would have the guts to challenge the referendum decision when Prime Minister May presented it with the outcome of the current negotiations.

I regard the referendum result as potentially the biggest

economic crisis I have had to cover during half a century of economic journalism. As we have seen, the 1967 devaluation was considered a big crisis at the time, and for long after. However, in the end it was more of a political crisis for Labour than an economic crisis. Indeed, it was a necessary adjustment to the exchange rate from the point of view of international competitiveness, although the 'pound in your pocket' episode rather soured things.

The other crises covered in this book also had great political and economic significance: the three-day week, directly linked with the first oil crisis of 1973–74, and the 1976 IMF crisis had successive political repercussions for the Conservatives, under Edward Heath, and Labour, under Jim Callaghan. The sadomonetarism episode of 1979–81, which was part and parcel of early Thatcherism, certainly merited the term crisis, as I hope I have demonstrated in an earlier chapter.

The Black Wednesday 1992 crisis was the mirror image of the 1967 devaluation crisis, in that it constituted a necessary adjustment to the exchange rate, but political humiliation for John Major's ruling Conservative administration. The world financial crisis of 2007–09 was certainly the biggest economic crisis of the post-war years, the consequences of which are still with us in 2018 – as are the consequences of the austerity crisis of 2010 onwards, which, in Britain, aggravated the damage inflicted by the banking crisis.

The difference between all of these crises and the threat of Brexit is simple: although their impact may have been exacerbated by errors of economic policy, none of these crises was the result of a voluntary choice by the British people.

I say this while being well aware that previous crises were handled by governments elected by the British people. Thus sadomonetarism in 1979–81 was the result of the electorate's disillusionment with the previous Callaghan government, but it is doubtful whether there were many economic policy sadists among the 1979 electorate, or that they consciously voted for what was then the biggest recession since the 1930s.

But for all the flaws in claims by ministers such as David Davis that the British people voted by a 'resounding' majority to leave the European Union (as we have seen, it was 37 per cent of the electorate, which amounts to 27 per cent of the population), nevertheless they voted to leave – in many cases, without understanding the implications. The decision was not thrust upon them – although all manner of misleading information and downright lies (£350 million a week for the National Health Service) were.

It should never be forgotten that the second most popular search term the day after the referendum was 'What is the EU?' Moreover, astonishingly, after the referendum, Sir Ivan Rogers, Britain's former ambassador to the EU, had to explain to the three leading Brexiters in the Cabinet what the customs union and the single market actually were. Indeed, to this day I come across highly intelligent people who have no idea either. And, even as I write this in one of my local coffee bars, someone enquiring what I am up to says, 'I haven't a f— clue either.'

How did this come about? In 1975, when I was economics correspondent of the *Financial Times*, a number of us were diverted from our normal duties in order to cover the referendum campaign. I myself was allocated east London as far as Dagenham. The atmosphere was much less febrile than in 2016. My memory was that there was little doubt about the result, although, checking my old scrapbook, I see that I was more cautious in writing.

But the result, unlike more recently, was a resounding vote in favour of the status quo. In his official history of the negotiations that preceded entry in 1973 and the run-up to the 1975 referendum, the former senior civil servant Sir Stephen Wall captured the essence of Prime Minister Harold Wilson's approach:

> Wilson said more than once to Donoughue [Bernard, later Lord Donoughue, head of the No. 10 Policy Unit] that a victory in the referendum for the 'Nos' would empower 'the wrong kind of people in Britain: the Benn left and the Powell right, who were often extreme nationalists, protectionist, xenophobic and backward-looking'.

Do such descriptions not ring a bell with regard to some of the more prominent modern Brexiters? I think they do, although I do not for a moment wish to tar all Brexiters with the same brush.

Wilson is quoted as having told his Principal Private Secretary Ken Stowe, the morning after the referendum, when the outcome was clear, 'People say I have no strategy, cannot think strategically.' 'The unspoken implication', Wall notes, 'was that he had held fundamentally to the same view since he had first decided in 1965 that membership of the European Community was in the interests of the United Kingdom.'

Of course, just as Harold Macmillan's application had been rebuffed by President de Gaulle in 1963, so Wilson had also come up against de Gaulle's intransigence in 1967.

Edward Heath, who got on well with de Gaulle's successor, Georges Pompidou, succeeded in what was Britain's 'third time lucky' application in 1972, and we joined in January 1973. But in the February 1974 general election, which Wilson – to his surprise – won, Labour was committed in its manifesto to re-negotiating the terms Heath had secured. As Wall concluded, Wilson 'had seen that the only way to win a decisive victory over the anti-Marketeers in the Labour Party was to go beyond the party to the country at large. And it had taken ten years to achieve it.'

As Donoughue observed, his boss 'kept Britain in the Community as he always wished; he achieved the terms which his manifesto demanded [helped by Foreign Secretary James Callaghan and the young junior minister Roy Hattersley, who did the spade work], and he held together by Wilsonian elastic bands his Cabinet and his party'.

The irony is that, whether or not he was aware of the parallel, David Cameron was, in effect, trying 'to do a Wilson' and appeal to the people in order to keep his party together. However, unlike Wilson, he failed lamentably. If anything, despite the result of the referendum, the civil war within the Conservative Party has intensified since 23 June 2016. Indeed, it has become a cliché in political commentary that, but for fear of a Corbyn government, the Conservative Party during 2018 has sometimes looked as though it could be on the verge of splitting.

Before we go on, however, it must be conceded that even Wilson, for all his consummate political skill, had only scotched the snake of Euroscepticism in the Labour Party, not killed it. Wilson had long since retired from office when the Labour left, under Tony Benn, exercised such a baneful influence on the party's 1983 election manifesto. That manifesto, famously scorned by the Labour MP Gerald Kaufman as 'the longest suicide note in history' included a straight commitment – not a hint of a referendum! – to withdraw from the European Union.

Michael Foot had been the leader who led Labour to that

spectacular 1983 electoral defeat. Foot was on what might be called the soft left of the party, with far more liberal views than the dirigiste Tony Benn. I lunched regularly with Michael in his latter days – along with Ian Gilmour, the most left-wing Tory since Harold Macmillan, and the *Guardian* political journalist Ian Aitken. These lunches took place in the Gay Hussar restaurant in Soho, long a haunt of politicians of left and right, with caricatures of many of the regular diners on the walls.

On one such occasion, one of us, perhaps tactlessly, made a passing reference to Kaufman's 'suicide note' remark. Quick as a flash, Michael quipped, 'He got elected on it though.'

In fact, the former leader had long since repudiated his 1983 stance and become a passionate European, along with his successors Neil Kinnock, Tony Blair and Gordon Brown (although it has to be admitted that Gordon went out of his way as Chancellor, when fighting his corner in Brussels, to disguise his pro-Europeanism).

Yet, once again, when Cameron called the referendum that did not bring peace and quiet to the Tory ranks, a strain of Euroscepticism resurfaced in the Labour Party. And, unfortunately for the pro-European cause, the Labour leader Jeremy Corbyn's support for Remain was lukewarm at best, with many long-time students of his career maintaining that he was and remained a Eurosceptic. Certainly, unlike Labour politicians in 1975, Corbyn declined to share a Remain platform with Conservative pro-Remainers. And according to one well-informed report, shadow Chancellor John McDonnell has explained that he and Corbyn found it impossible to throw their hearts into the 2016 Remain campaign, not because they saw the EU as a capitalist club but because they did not want to be seen as an 'establishment cabal'.

How did it come to this? A Conservative Prime Minister

risking the future of the country on a referendum that, given the importance of the occasion, was presented with precious little explanation of what was at stake, and without a stipulation that the issue was too important to be decided by a narrow majority? And how come that Parliament, the essence of the sovereignty so theoretically precious to the Brexiters, should be so slow to pull its weight afterwards, when it is an established principle, stretching back to the writings of Edmund Burke, that MPs are representatives, not delegates?

Long experience has taught me to be wary of making forecasts in public, although attempting to predict the outcome of general elections, and many other events, is a well-established practice among my friends. Until shortly before the fatal day, 23 June 2016, when asked, I tended to say that the British are a naturally conservative people and would probably opt for the status quo, as they – we – had in 1975.

I was rash enough to put this into a review, for the OMFIF monthly bulletin, of what might turn out to have been the prophetic book *Brexit: How Britain Will Leave Europe* by Denis MacShane.

I say 'might' because at the time of writing I am still hoping that, somehow or other, the government can stop heading for the Brexit cliff. (Writing about this has become the major concern of my fortnightly *Observer* column.) But MacShane was certainly prophetic with regard to the result of the referendum. As he pointed out a good year before the vote, 'The political direction of travel of the Conservative Party over the last twenty years has been firmly against the EU. Labour has been silent and not made a pro-European case with vigour and impact.' It is by now widely accepted that the Eurosceptic press and pretty dubious campaign promises, not to say outright lies, on the part of the Leave campaign had a huge impact on the outcome of the referendum.

But MacShane made another forceful point: 'One of the major reasons why Britain may leave the EU is not so much the hostility of anti-EU editors as the indifference of editors who think they are pro-European but will not give space to fight Europhobe arguments and distortions.'

MacShane focused on the way the United Kingdom Independence Party (UKIP), whose main raison d'être was to take Britain 'out of Europe', was gaining ground: 'The votes UKIP candidates won in the European and local elections in 2014 as well as in parliamentary by-elections point the direction of travel of British public opinion and voting intentions.'

Of course, the objective of Mr Nigel Farage and his cronies was not, literally, to take us out of Europe, but out of the EU. But the way some of the more evangelical Brexiters talk – not least Michael Gove with his nauseating early 'exclusive' interview with Donald Trump, accompanied by Rupert Murdoch – they give the impression they would be happy to see these islands towed across the Atlantic and joined umbilically with the US.

Incidentally, use of the word Brexit – sometimes pronounced *Bregsit*, but I prefer Brexit with an 'x' – has been increasingly common currency for six years. I asked MacShane whether he had coined it. He said he thought so, but a good friend of his, called Peter Wilding, also lays claim. At all events, MacShane told me that an entry in his diary for 2012 states: 'A personal confession. I coined, or was one of the first to use, the name Brexit.' Using it subsequently in the *FT*, the columnist Philip Stephens noted that the term was derived from the word Grexit, much used by the economist Vicky Pryce, to describe the threat of Greek exit from the single currency – a possibility that was fought off at great expense to the Greek domestic economy and Greek living standards.

So far so good for Greece's membership of the Eurozone. Greece may have been tormented by the strictures of the Eurozone, but at the time of writing it is still a member and Grexit hasn't happened. Brexit, however, is now in prospect unless our nation comes to its senses. There have been endless post-mortems about the contributions to the outcome of the referendum, from fear of immigration to a collective protest against the accumulation of discontent arising from the impact of globalisation and the prolonged squeeze on living standards which began even before the 2007–09 banking crisis and was compounded by what I regarded as an ill-judged austerity programme.

These factors affected the outcome of David Cameron's decision to hold the referendum in the first place. We must now consider the confluence of factors which led him to make the strategic mistake of his premiership – which ranks politically with Tony Blair's catastrophic decision to back the US invasion of Iraq (and be economical with the truth about the existence of weapons of mass destruction).

As I wrote in an early chapter, before switching to the study of economics I had been a classicist. One of my favourite books was Thucydides's *History of the Peloponnesian War*, in which he set out to answer the question 'What was the truest cause of the war?'

What was the truest cause of the decision to hold the referendum? We have seen that Cameron, consciously or subconsciously, was trying to 'do a Wilson' by appealing to the country over a divided party. The two forces that led him into this corner were undoubtedly the rise of UKIP and the sheer determination of the Eurosceptic wing of the Conservative Party in Parliament.

What galvanised those Eurosceptics? Here, again, we have the confluence of two key developments. The first was Mrs Thatcher's reaction to a speech made by the then President of the European Commission Jacques Delors to the TUC annual conference in September 1988. This was the occasion when Delors expatiated passionately about 'Social Europe' and workers' rights, a vision which was anathema to Mrs Thatcher, and his speech came on top of his championship of moves towards the single currency. There followed a fortnight later the famous, or infamous, Bruges speech, and the declaration by Mrs Thatcher: 'We have not successfully rolled back the frontiers of the state in Britain only to see them reimposed at a European level with a European superstate exercising a new dominance from Brussels.'

Mrs Thatcher's hostile feelings towards Europe were not exactly assuaged around this time by Chancellor Nigel Lawson's persistent efforts to make her agree to sign up for membership of the European exchange rate mechanism (ERM). Nor, as noted in Chapter 6, was she too pleased at the unfortunate (for her) result of her advice to the Governor of the Bank of England Robin Leigh-Pemberton (whose appointment had been very much within her gift) to be guided by the approach of the Bundesbank president Karl Otto Pöhl in discussions at the Delors Committee (that man again!) on the pros and cons of moving towards a single currency. To her surprise, Pöhl gave his backing to the project – while insisting on rigorous, Bundesbank-style conditions – and Leigh-Pemberton 'went native'.

The single market, of course, was a quite different kettle of fish, and much championed by her, with the formidable application to the task of the British European Commissioner Lord Cockfield. Indeed, in his memoirs Kenneth Clarke describes the single market as Mrs Thatcher's 'finest achievement'.

This makes her subsequent behaviour in urging on the

Eurosceptics in the Conservative Party look pretty strange: with odd exceptions, the Eurosceptics have been cavalier in their desire to abandon the advantages of her 'finest achievement'.

Basically, Mrs Thatcher, after being forced out of office principally by pro-European colleagues, became very bitter, and focused her bile on her successor John Major and his attempts to 'put Britain at the very heart of Europe' (his words) while walking a tightrope in the effort to keep the party together.

From a diplomatic perspective, Major was successful in his objective of seeking an opt-out from the move towards a single currency at Maastricht in December 1991. He also negotiated an opt-out from the Social Chapter – which ought to have pleased Mrs Thatcher, given her concerns about Social Europe. (Personally, I was against this latter move, and delighted when the Blair government reversed it in 1997.)

However, there was by now too much of a head of steam behind the Eurosceptic movement in the party. To my mind, the crucial point of no return for Mrs Thatcher and the Eurosceptics – memorably described by Major as 'the bastards' – was Black Wednesday.

Although a necessary condition for recovery from the 1990–92 recession – via a dramatic easing of monetary policy made possible by the lower exchange rate – Black Wednesday was a political disaster from which the Major government was never likely to recover, and indeed did not. For Mrs Thatcher and her merry band of Eurosceptics, it proved that she had been right all along to resist Chancellor Lawson's campaign to join. Moreover, as we have seen in the previous chapter on Black Wednesday, joining occurred under Major's chancellorship, and the humiliating exit under his premiership. Black Wednesday imparted new vigour into the parliamentary Eurosceptic movement. They nagged away and nagged away and, with the help of UKIP, got the referendum they desired. Whether they achieve their ultimate aims – and they seem confused, not to say delusional, about what these are – is another story.

The militant Brexiters see themselves as heirs of Mrs Thatcher and completing the work of her often passionate struggles with Europe. Indeed, Lord Lawson has gone on record as claiming that 'Brexit gives us a chance to finish the Thatcher revolution'. I find this deeply ironic, not least because one of the factors contributing to the discontent that lay behind the referendum result was almost certainly the Thatcher-style attack on public services that formed an integral aspect of George Osborne's austerity programme.

But it also ignores the judgement of (Lord) Charles Powell, who was the civil servant closest to Mrs Thatcher for most of her time in office. In a lecture at Hertford College, Oxford, reprinted in *Half In, Half Out: Prime Ministers on Europe* edited by Andrew Adonis, Powell said Mrs Thatcher 'fought for a better Europe that would be more in tune with the requirements of economic prosperity and international security. Her battle was not to emasculate it, let alone abandon it.'

To *soi disant* Thatcherite diehards, who cite Mrs Thatcher's Bruges speech of 1988 as evidence that she would have approved of Brexit, Powell replied, 'There were limits to how far she was prepared to be influenced by Eurosceptics. The Bruges speech was not a surrender to them but a manifesto for a new direction for Europe that would make the European Community more successful, not undermine and weaken British membership.'

Another important contribution to this story came from Sir Ivan Rogers, our former ambassador to the European Union, who worked closely both with Tony Blair and David Cameron.

In a lecture in Oxford in 2017, Sir Ivan revealed that the crucial decision to place no limit on immigration from Eastern Europe after the 2004 expansion of the EU was made by Blair on the advice of Mervyn King, who was then Governor of the Bank of England. The idea was that the extra labour from Eastern Europe would keep pressure on wages down and help the Bank to achieve its inflation targets, which seemed at the time to have become the be all and end all of macroeconomic policy.

Later, when working with Cameron, Sir Ivan was able to observe the evolution of the Prime Minister's thinking about Europe:

> Cameron's core judgement, after many years in office being faced with the daily reality of EU negotiations, was that the optimal place for the country was inside the outer perimeter fence of single market and customs union. This was not passionate Europhilia: far from it. But a cold calculation – Angela Merkel once accused him of making no other sort about EU issues – of economic self-interest.

The more Cameron looked at the question of how the UK could secure its vital interests by opting for Brexit, Rogers said, 'the more obvious the conclusion that being even "just outside" was radically different from being "just inside" the fence'.

In other words, for all his frustrations about dealing with Brussels, Cameron knew full well that our existing position – within the customs union and single market, but outside the Eurozone and the Schengen passport agreement, with a 'get out of jail free' card with regard to participating in closer union – was indeed a case of having our cake and eating it – in Soros's neat phrase, the best of both worlds.

Not that Soros, or, for that matter, this writer, is at all happy with many aspects of the EU. Even as I write, there are signs in Italy that the existential crisis of the Eurozone – long predicted by such eminent economists as Nobel Laureates Joseph Stiglitz and Paul Krugman – may finally be on the brink of manifesting itself. I myself, with these and other commentators, have long been a critic of the austerity policy followed by the coalition government in Britain since 2010; the same applies to the Eurozone, where needless and economically and socially damaging policies of austerity have been imposed.

Yet, under pressure from the unrepresentative but all too vocal Brexiters in his parliamentary party, and the relentless and all too effective propaganda from UKIP, Cameron bowed to calls for a referendum, finally making a commitment in his Bloomberg speech of 23 January 2013. (One cannot resist noting at this point that his host, Michael Bloomberg, has joined those of us who are calling for the government and people to think again. After a forensic analysis of the advantages the UK already has, and the worrying implications of a departure for the rest of Europe, and indeed the world, Bloomberg pithily described the prospect of Brexit as 'a mistake'.)

There has been speculation that Cameron privately hoped that, notwithstanding their own commitment 'in principle' to a referendum at some point, the Liberals might let him off the hook. But the 2015 election result broke up the coalition and gave Cameron a working majority – which was to be squandered by Theresa May in a foolhardy decision to go to the country in the hope of a vote of confidence for her 'Brexit means Brexit' strategy. It was easy to mock this statement as meaningless, but she went on time and time again saying that, with her famous 'red lines', she was committed to leaving the customs union and single market. As I write in autumn 2018, we have witnessed a farcical series of exchanges with Brussels, in intervals from exchanges within the Conservative Party, which amount to trying to replicate the deliberately foregone advantages from a weak bargaining position outside!

There has been no shortage of examples over the years of politicians having second thoughts about rash commitments. Why, why, why did Cameron not go back on his commitment to a referendum?

I think the answer may lie in that familiar British aristocratic or upper-middle-class assumption – mainly among the male of the species – of 'effortless superiority'. So far in his life, David Cameron had had an easy ride. He had risen almost effortlessly to the top, and there was much talk among those who knew him well of 'that Etonian self-confidence'.

Moreover, the Scottish referendum, after a few nervous moments, had gone well for a Prime Minister who was leader of the Conservative and Unionist Party. During his mission to extract concessions from Brussels and the rest of the EU, he gave the impression to his counterparts of being overconfident that he could pull it off.

At this point I wish to pay tribute to a Dutch journalist, Titia Ketelaar, then based in London, whom I used to meet at our local coffee bar, Pistachio and Pickle. She may have been based in London, but she travelled the length and breadth of the country, and was the first person to alert me to the way opinion was turning against 'the metropolitan elite' in the Midlands and the north. She frightened me sufficiently to the point where I decided to place a small bet with bookmakers William Hill, whose political betting expert Graham Sharpe was keeping us all up to date with the mood of the punters. I am not a big gambler

– normally betting in fivers – but I placed £20 on a Leave vote, at 3 to 1 against – i.e. £20 to win £60, as a consolation if the vote should go the wrong way – which I still didn't believe it would.

Shortly after that, I met Sir Ivan Rogers in Brussels for the first time. He was still our ambassador to the EU, having had a lot of experience of trade negotiations over the years. He knew, and still does, more about the intricacies of the EU than any Englishman I have met before or since, and was absolutely firm about the folly of calling the referendum and the difficulties that lay in store – as he has demonstrated in lectures and appearances at seminars and before parliamentary committees since. When I told him I had placed £20 on Leave at 3 to 1, he said, quick as a flash, 'Only twenty quid?'

My regular contact with Graham Sharpe meant I was receiving almost daily bulletins about how the betting was going. It was a fascinating example of how people not so close to the betting industry can be misled. Most of the media and most of the people I encountered were impressed by the weight of money that was being placed on Remain. What I learned from Sharpe's bulletins was that far more bets were being placed on Leave. This seemed to indicate the way the 'non-elite' were thinking, and it turned out they were right.

Towards the end of the referendum campaign, there was panic in the ranks. I recall being telephoned by someone close to Cameron requesting the telephone number of Seumas Milne, Jeremy Corbyn's powerful press chief and close adviser – a former colleague at the *Guardian/Observer*. Cameron needed help. But it has to be said that there did not seem to be much coming from the Labour side.

Cameron's luck had run out. Back to the Greek classics of my youth: arrogance followed by hubris. And, unfortunately, the rest of us were landed with the result.

Now, one interesting aspect of this was the position of the Chancellor, George Osborne. Since the result, Osborne has said that he was against the decision to call a referendum. To my mind, it was a bad enough service to the nation that he embarked on a policy of austerity. But if ever a Chancellor should have stood up to a Prime Minister with whom – unlike in the case of Blair and Brown – he got on well, it was Osborne.

*   *   *

Of all the crises I have referred to in this book, the prospect of Brexit is by far the greatest and most worrying. Indeed, since 23 June 2016 I have devoted most of my regular columns to one aspect or another of the consequences, if it is not reversed, of the referendum result. Although I gather that from time to time abusive comments appear on the *Guardian/Observer* website, I never look at these. Most of the comments from people who trouble to write, as opposed to sound off on a Saturday night, have been favourable and supportive. Often I am stopped in the street and people make nice remarks and encourage me to carry on.

There is little doubt that the implications of the referendum were not widely understood. Both the Remain and Leave camps overdid their propaganda, with Leave producing a pack of lies, and the Remain campaign exaggerating the short-term consequences. Nevertheless there was one short-term consequence – the collapse in the pound – which has already had a marked effect on real incomes. Also, as we saw in the chapter on the 1967 devaluation, it takes time for an improvement in competitiveness to come through – hence 'making devaluation work'. In this instance, however, so much uncertainty has been created by the referendum that businesses have been holding back on investment plans and even the post-referendum devaluation has not improved the country's overseas trade position.

There are two overriding reasons for my concern. One is geopolitical rather than economic: it seems unwise, to put it mildly, to try to unhook ourselves from the rest of Europe when the United States, under Donald Trump, has declared a trade war on the rest of the world and Europe is very concerned about a threat from President Putin's Russia. The second concern is obviously economic: we have spent forty-five years being integrated into the wider European economy and in effect we have become an economic region of the EU. So much industrial production is geared to intricate supply lines and what is known as 'just in time' delivery systems. I suspect that a lot of the people who voted for Brexit do not realise that many of the things they take for granted, like the ability to buy fruit and vegetables delivered to their supermarkets overnight from France, Spain and other European countries, would be put at risk by the kind of customs restrictions that would be imposed by Brexit. One personal example: we needed at home a replacement part for a washing machine. 'No problem,' said our engineer. 'We will get it from Hamburg by Wednesday.' The production of cars in Britain, usually by foreign-owned manufacturers, is heavily dependent on the criss-crossing of the Channel for the delivery of components.

The combination of the customs union and the single market means that there is a free flow of goods with virtually no problems at ports and airports. As I write, it is becoming increasingly obvious that if the UK were to experience a hard Brexit there would be widespread chaos which would affect all of our lives, including people in mainland Europe.

There has been much confusion, indeed ignorance, in discussion within the UK about the customs union and the single market. Membership of the customs union removed physical barriers to trade within the EU, and the single market – let me emphasise again that this was Mrs Thatcher's proud achievement – removed many non-tariff barriers.

There seems to have been negligible progress since Mrs May committed the country to leaving the EU, with or without a deal, at the end of March 2019.

It is obvious that the country is bitterly divided on this issue. I was particularly struck in September 2017 when I attended a conference held by the Ambrosetti Foundation in Italy and listened to a speech by Michel Barnier, the EU's chief negotiator. This speech was widely misreported in the UK, the media's message being that Barnier had said that Britain would have to be punished for leaving the EU. This was not what he said, either in his public speech or in a private conversation we had at his request. The whole tone of his speech was one of sorrow, rather than anger, and he made the point that if Brexit went ahead there would be consequences for the UK and EU. This was an eminently reasonable point and it appears that belatedly people are waking up to this.

I fervently hope that, one way or another, this movement to what I regard as a cliff-edge can be stopped.

PART III

OBSERVER INTERVIEWS WITH CHANCELLORS OF THE EXCHEQUER, 2006–07

I thought it was worth reproducing some interviews with Chancellors I have had the privilege to know, written some years ago. They were first published in *The Observer* in 2006–07 and are reproduced here with the permission of the editor, Paul Webster.

1. DENIS HEALEY, DECEMBER 2006

There have been only two Labour Chancellors in the past thirty-five years. This is partly because Labour was out of office for so long during the Thatcher/Major period, and partly because the recent pattern has been for Chancellors not to be reshuffled, whatever – or possibly because of – the status of their relationship with the Prime Minister.

It is a sobering thought that everybody in this country aged twenty-six or under was born after the chancellorship of Denis Healey. From 1974 to 1979, Healey was seldom off the TV screens, even though the filming of Parliament had not yet begun.

Healey, like Gordon Brown in more recent years, was a forceful intellectual and physical presence in the Labour Party. Like Brown, also, he aspired to be Prime Minister, but not quite so much or so obviously. He never quite made it, but the wound did not fester. Indeed, he has continued to enjoy such an interesting life outside politics – with occasional sorties in House of Lords debates – that there is a widespread impression that in the end he did not mind missing the top job, although he would certainly have liked to have been Foreign Secretary.

But this is not quite the case, as I discovered when I went to see him recently on a beautiful autumn day at his country home in East Sussex, overlooking the South Downs.

I have known Denis Healey since he became Chancellor in 1974, and had been slightly concerned to hear that he was seen having trouble with a cash machine somewhere in Sussex, and heard to mutter, 'I shouldn't be allowed out at my age.'

Well, I can report from my enjoyable morning with the old bruiser that this was just a classic Healey joke. At eighty-nine he is in fine fettle, slimmer than one remembers, but in full grasp of the conversation, suffering no more lapses of memory than people half his age.

Which reminds me: when I told a prominent London figure that I was going to see Healey, he replied, 'I shouldn't bother. He's lost it.' But from the tone of the interview the only thing Healey had lost was any belief in Tony Blair.

We began gently with an attempt, at my suggestion, to establish once and for all that Healey never came out with the quote that the Conservatives are still fond of digging up, namely that he wished 'to squeeze the rich until the pips squeak'.

'I never used it. I quoted something from the 1920s. That can happen. Jim Callaghan never said, "Crisis, what crisis?"' What the then shadow Chancellor in fact said, at Labour's 1973 conference, was, 'There are going to be howls of anguish from the 80,000 people who are rich enough to pay over 75 per cent on the last slice of their income.' The 'pips squeak' was originally used by First World War leader Lloyd George; Healey did quote fellow Labour Cabinet minister Tony Crosland, requoting it 'in reference to property speculators, not to the rich in general'.

Such tax levels seem and were a long time ago, much favoured by the Hungarian economists Tommy Balogh and Nicholas Kaldor, who used to advise Labour. 'Nicky was very good. Tommy was no good. I used to call them Buda and Pest,' says Healey.

He explained that he could not attend the launch of the new book *The Chancellors' Tales* later that week (containing the text of a lecture by him) because he was being given an award by the government of Hungary, a country he knows well. In his LSE lecture he had contrasted his time at the Treasury with his earlier period, under the first Wilson government (of 1964–70), as Secretary for Defence, where 'any decision you took was implemented by people you controlled wherever they were, even if they were in Borneo or Aden. In the Treasury, the decisions you take are implemented by people over whom you have absolutely no control: employers, workers all over the country, and of course consumers, not only all over your own country but all over the world.'

The most uncontrollable were the unions, the Labour Party's main financial backers at the time. 'My biggest problem, frankly,' he told me, 'was trying to get the unions to be sensible about pay.' Younger listeners might have fallen out of their comfortable chair in Healey's sun lounge as he recalled, 'In my first year the overall increase in pay was 26 per cent.' I remembered it well. I recalled Sir Kenneth Berrill, then head of the Whitehall think tank, telling me, 'At this rate of inflation the miners will be earning a million pounds a year in no time.'

The unions were subsequently battered. It is all so much easier for Gordon Brown, whose decisions on the Bank of England and the Eurozone Healey greatly admires. Does Brown consult him? Only when they bump into one another. 'As Chancellor he's been very good indeed – but very lucky. He's had no serious challenge from the unions, or the left, either from personalities or policies – no Nye Bevan, no Tony Benn.'

Not only did Healey have problems with the unions over pay, the barons also helped to thwart his leadership ambitions. In 1976, after Wilson's resignation, and in 1981, when Tony Benn challenged him for the deputy leadership (which he had gained, literally as second prize, when he lost to Michael Foot in the post-Callaghan leadership race) he faced tough union opposition.

'That problem totally disappeared with one man, one vote under John Smith,' he reflected. He had beaten off Benn's challenge, as he says in his memoirs, 'by a hair of an eyebrow'. He feels strongly to this day that polls showed he would have had a majority of 2.5 million over Benn if it had been one man, one vote, but he was almost beaten by the block vote of the Transport and General Workers' Union.

In his magisterial work *The Chancellors*, Edmund Dell, a junior minister in Healey's Treasury, says there were 'three Healeys' in 1974–79. First, the 'political' Chancellor, who had inherited a disastrous situation but postponed the medicine until after the second general election of 1974; then the 'orthodox' Chancellor, who had to resort to the International Monetary Fund during the 'annus horribilis' of 1976 to save the pound, and then let it rise too high when the markets discovered the North Sea in 1977; finally, the 'resurrected' political Chancellor, 'with his eyes on an election victory and on the succession to No. 10'.

It was a gruelling time, and it needed someone as tough as Healey to cope. There were differences with his Prime Minister over the IMF, but in the end Callaghan backed him. In his address at Callaghan's memorial service in Westminster Abbey last year, and with Lady Thatcher sitting in the front pew, Healey claimed that Callaghan was the best Prime Minister since Attlee. This is the kind of controversial statement Healey has always loved making.

He also insists that if the statistics had been correct (the public borrowing figures were subsequently revised downwards), resorting to the IMF would have been unnecessary – arguable, and we shall never know. But it is at least possible that history would have looked very different.

'If we had had the right figures, we would never have needed to go for the loan. It was the most difficult period of my life getting the Cabinet to go for it. The PSBR [public sector borrowing requirement] estimate was horrific. In the end Jim Callaghan was on-side. He was a very good PM at a very difficult time.'

Yet the Callaghan he so admired fatally postponed the election expected in October 1978 – an expectation on which Healey's 'political' Budget of 1978 was based. In his memoirs, Healey says, 'I do not regret the political price I may have paid for my work as Defence Secretary and Chancellor; I have always been in politics in order to do something rather than to be something.'

He insisted to me that, whatever Dell and others might have

thought, his main reason for standing for the leadership was 'not for me, but to keep the wrong people out – like Tony Benn'.

Unlike the next Labour Chancellor, Gordon Brown, 'I never wanted to be leader of the party…' Then came what was for me a remarkable admission: '…though now I wish I had been. And I could have been if I had wanted. At the time I said I would prefer to do anything rather than be leader.'

What had changed? 'In fact, the Prime Minister can do anything if he wants to, as Tony Blair has shown.'

Then came the rub. 'Unfortunately it was nearly all wrong: the Iraq War, foundation hospitals, university top-up fees – and now cash for peerages.'

Were there no saving graces? 'He did quite well in his first year. Since the invasion of Iraq everything he's done has been wrong. And, almost certainly, he agreed at Granita [the restaurant where he and Gordon Brown are believed to have struck a deal] to go after two years [of the second term]. But he's still hanging on, and no one can be certain he'll go. Yet the sooner he goes the better.'

This was strong stuff from one of Labour's most respected elder statesmen. Several times during the conversation he returned to the subject of Iraq.

'Tony Blair had no reason to go with Bush. He had insisted on the UN, but still did. He could have made that [the UN] the reason. He has no understanding of foreign affairs or defence. My generation had been in two world wars.' Again: 'I know more than Tony Blair. My main interest is Iraq and it's been an absolute bloody disaster.' I had noticed on the coffee table that current or recent Healey reading included books on Iraq and Suez. When I said that Harold Wilson had not sent troops to Vietnam, Healey gave me the impression it had been a close thing but said, 'I'd have resigned [as Defence Secretary] if he'd sent troops.'

Healey's grasp of foreign affairs has always been formidable, and most writers about him have tended to say his only real regret was not having been Foreign Secretary. His honest admission about the lost leadership throws this into a different light. But the outstanding impression one has is that he loses little, if any, sleep over the way his career turned out, only about the way a Labour government with such a huge majority has squandered its assets in a foreign policy that he is on record as having warned against well in advance.

Though he admires Gordon Brown, he notes that Brown 'has no experience' of foreign policy. Nevertheless, was he a Brown man? What about the possible threat from John Reid? 'He's quite a possibility. John Reid is quite a serious candidate. But I much prefer Gordon. I think he'll get it myself.'

But the former defence policy hawk and champion of nuclear deterrence thinks the world has moved on, and worries about Brown's Mansion House speech in which he went a long way to commit to the renewal of Trident.

'I'm doubtful about the wisdom of going on with Trident. The only nuclear threat is the terrorist one – [for example] nuclear weapons on cargo boats on the Thames, or in New York harbour or San Francisco. Most of the important countries are very, very vulnerable, and the only answer is better intelligence.' He is concerned about 'the very cavalier way in which the Russians look after their nuclear materials'.

Listening to Healey, you can't help reflecting on the high calibre of the politicians of his generation, even if, in his case, he had a mischievous habit of reminding you of it. But on this occasion I have to concede that I led him to it: 'The quality of politicians in the past was exceptionally high. They tended to go into the profession much later than now, after a lot of experience of the real world.'

And here comes the controversial but considered opinion of an elected politician from a previous generation, who has been in the Lords since he retired from Parliament in 1992: 'It would be sensible not to have an all-elected Lords. It would lead to US-style gridlock. You would not have sensible people.'

Lord Healey would like 'at least half of new peers chosen by a very carefully selected committee who are not party politicians'. For Healey, the value of the Lords is that 'there are so many people who don't give a bugger, including ex-politicians who are not worried about the whips'.

But we could not keep off foreign affairs, his great speciality, and Iraq in particular. 'I don't blame Robin [Cook] for going, or Clare [Short]. I agreed with them. Gordon Brown bears no direct responsibility, but he made a big mistake in supporting Tony. Iraq is going to be his biggest single problem.'

2. LORD HOWE, JANUARY 2007

Lord Howe of Aberavon was Margaret Thatcher's longest-serving minister. As, one by one – sometimes two by two – they fell out with the Iron Lady, Howe was the great survivor – until he had finally had enough, and in a stunning resignation speech on 13 November 1990 precipitated the events that led to her own resignation.

Just before Christmas last year, Howe celebrated his 80th birthday, and Baroness Thatcher attended a party at the Foreign Office. The location was appropriate: Howe is still much involved in a Foreign Office advisory group. Two months before his birthday, he spoke in Cardiff about the need for a recreation of British foreign policy after 'the serious damage done to most of its components as a consequence of the profoundly ill-judged Anglo-American invasion of Iraq and subsequent response to the onslaught in Lebanon'.

The party was an occasion for peace feelers of a different kind. One of the guests told me that Howe said the events of 1990 'could not wipe out fifteen years of close comradeship'.

Older readers will remember Howe as a quiet, unassuming but loyal and persistent servant of Thatcher. He had the air more of a country solicitor than of a high-flying Cabinet minister. Courteous, mild-mannered and kind, he appeared to have an incongruous relationship with the seemingly uncaring economic and social doctrines that became known as Thatcherism. Even critics of his chancellorship, such as your correspondent, couldn't possibly dislike him.

Yet when it came to economic policy, Howe was as hard as nails. Not long ago he gave a reflective speech on his 1979–83 chancellorship at the London School of Economics. He told his audience that in the 1960s he had written two tracts for the Bow Group (a Tory think tank) on the welfare state, which, many years later, were to be described by Nicholas Timmins, the commentator on social affairs for the *Financial Times*, as having 'summed up much of what was to be the radical right's agenda during the 1980s'.

Howe's tough approach to the economy evolved during the 1970s. As Solicitor-General in the early part of Edward Heath's 1970–74 government, he worked hard on the Industrial Relations Act of 1971 and seethed when many of its provisions were repealed by Michael Foot in 1974. Steel entered his soul as, during the 1974–79 Labour governments, Britain became known as 'the sick man of Europe', with the annualised monthly inflation rate rising in 1975 to more than 25 per cent, and public spending and borrowing scaling un-Conservative heights. The final straw was the 1978–79 Winter of Discontent.

It was in those opposition years that new Conservative think tanks were added to old, and Thatcher and Sir Keith Joseph – the biggest departmental spenders under Heath – became proselytising converts to monetarism. But it was Howe, as Chancellor, who was the toughest of the lot.

The theme of his LSE talk was: 'Can 364 economists all be wrong?' This was a reference to his 1981 Budget, which was designed to remove several billion pounds from the economy when the UK was in the depths of recession. The 364 economists had written to *The Times*: 'There is no basis in economic theory or supporting evidence for the government's present policies ... The time has come to reject monetarist policies.'

Sir Geoffrey, as those of us who knew him then still refer to him, has argued for two decades that the 364 were wrong and that his apparently deflationary Budget in fact sowed the seeds of economic recovery. But the recovery was tenuous at best. Unemployment kept rising, to more than 3 million by the mid-1980s. And, insofar as the Budget marked a turning point, this was because of something the 364 economists could not have known: namely that, under the influence of Thatcher's economic adviser Sir Alan Walters, monetary policy was being relaxed, with the object – eventually successfully – of bringing the pound down from dizzy heights where the atmosphere was threatening to suffocate even the best of British industry.

In fact, the Thatcher government itself was forced to reject monetarism policies, and today Howe is derisive about the confused message given to him by monetary economists at the time. But when I met him recently at the House of Lords, he displayed not a shadow of doubt that the shock therapy of his chancellorship had been justified.

'Everyone knew we were in the last chance saloon,' he said. And to those of us who say he and his colleagues did not make matters any easier by promising in 1979 to honour vast public sector wage claims (a blatantly electioneering move), he answers that this commitment was given 'against my strong advice'.

This is important because inflation was around 10 per cent when the Thatcher government entered the last chance saloon, and the Clegg Commission pay awards aggravated the trend of inflation. On the rather important other hand, Howe revealed to me that in his first Budget of 1979, when he slashed income tax rates, it was he who insisted on almost doubling the main rate of VAT from 8 to 15 per cent, when Thatcher herself wanted a ceiling of 12.5. This fed into the retail price index, also affecting wage claims and subsequent inflation.

Similarly, he was much more hawkish than Thatcher over the 1981 Budget. He is rather proud of the fact that the public image is of the Iron Lady and the hesitant Chancellor, whereas the truth was rather different. At a crucial pre-Budget meeting, Howe concluded, 'I'm going to listen to the Jeremiahs, not the voices of comfort.'

It is well known that Howe held strong pro-European views at the Foreign Office that set him on a collision course with Thatcher. But before we got on to Europe and foreign affairs, he wanted to reminisce about the 1970s and events leading up to that last chance saloon. 'Had we won [in 1974] and had the Industrial Relations Act survived, we would have saved a whole decade.' But he added, 'In retrospect, what happened enabled us to do really tough things in 1979.' (This reminded me of Geoffrey

Goodman's impression from discussions at the time with Howe and others – recorded in *From Bevan to Blair* – that they were 'quite content to let the Wilson government grapple with an "impossible" economic climate, inflation, pressure from the IMF and cuts in social spending'.)

Interestingly, Howe recalls trying to dissuade Joseph – John the Baptist to Thatcher's Messiah – from making the controversial speech in Preston in 1974 that actually advocated higher unemployment. 'I first went to the Centre for Policy Studies [the Thatcher–Joseph think tank] to try to persuade Keith Joseph to soften his speech.'

He insists that the tough approach of the Heath government in 1970–72 – before the U-turn as unemployment hit 1 million – was right. 'Selsdon Man was not a myth. We were persuaded against our will. Perhaps we needed ten years of a learning curve, which enabled us to rethink the strategy.'

One aspect of his tough approach as Chancellor of which Howe is most proud is the abolition of exchange controls in October 1979 – as dramatic as Gordon Brown's granting of independence to the Bank of England eighteen years later. It was something he had wanted to do since, as he says in his memoirs, 'several courtroom encounters in 1969 [in his barrister days] had convinced me of the totalitarian nature of this regime'. He found support from the Bank of England, which hoped in that way to moderate the rise in the pound. Thatcher was hesitant and said, 'On your own head be it, Geoffrey, if anything goes wrong.'

Yet the pound kept rising and unemployment went on up after the tough 1981 Budget. The state of the economy played a large part in making Thatcher the most unpopular Prime Minister since records began, but the Conservatives were saved in the 1983 election by the political boost from the 1982 Falklands

War and the reaction to the left-wing, anti-European Labour manifesto of 1983.

Yet it was the anti-Europeanism of Thatcher that was to rile Howe and prove her undoing. From the Foreign Office, the increasingly frustrated and spurned Howe was to prepare his own Exocet. In 1983, he had wanted to stay at the Treasury, and was half expecting the Home Office. The prospect of dealing with prisons did not appeal. He recently told a friend, 'I have every reason to be grateful to Cecil [Parkinson]' – because it was the exposure of his affair with Sara Keays that prevented Mrs Thatcher from making Parkinson, her preferred choice, Foreign Secretary.

In his memoirs, Douglas Hurd, who became Home Secretary in 1985, dates the problem between Thatcher and Howe from the Westland affair in 1986, when she was almost forced to resign, and Howe and Hurd pressed for a return to Cabinet government. 'But nothing happened, except that Mrs Thatcher recovered her poise. The Prime Minister became increasingly overbearing towards Geoffrey Howe, who had been her close political companion in the early years of her government.' Sir Robin Day once asked Howe at a dinner party, 'What would have happened if Westland had gone the other way?' An eyewitness says Howe replied, 'I would have been Prime Minister.'

He was sacked from the Foreign Office and made Deputy Prime Minister in July 1989, after Thatcher had finally had enough of the efforts of Howe and Chancellor Nigel Lawson to persuade her to put the pound into the European exchange rate mechanism. Howe certainly wanted to be Prime Minister. It still might have happened in 1989, if Thatcher had retired on her 10th anniversary. I asked whether there was a sudden moment when it all went wrong with Thatcher, but he sees it as a process of erosion, dating from 1986, and the abortive discussions about the

ERM and Europe – a relationship 'eroded by the divergence of our positions on the European Union'. There were also 'tensions over South Africa'. (Howe was much more liberal than Thatcher, to put it mildly.) But when he gently said that Thatcher's Bruges speech (in 1988, when she went out on a limb to oppose further European integration) was 'a demonstration' of his problems with her, I think I was meant to deduce that it was also pretty close to the final straw.

But things dragged on. It was common gossip that they were both at their wits' end in what had become an incompatible political marriage. Edmund Dell in *The Chancellors* concluded, 'Even differences on Europe might not have led to the final breach, had any mutual sympathy survived between these two pillars of the Thatcher revolution.' Talking to Howe, I was not so sure. The differences on Europe were central to the erosion of mutual sympathy.

The big issue was ERM – membership as a discipline when monetarism had failed – and, of course, the prospect of the single currency. I asked whether, in the light of Black Wednesday and the UK economy's subsequent perceived success outside the ERM, he might regret that the EU had become a resigning issue. 'I regret that anything became a resigning issue,' was his firm reply.

The irony was that he resigned after Thatcher had bowed to pressure from almost the whole establishment, and from new Chancellor John Major, to join the ERM. The final straw was her report back to the Commons after an EU summit in Rome at the end of October 1990. Thatcher had not only dismissed the idea of a single currency but also alternative proposals her own ministers were making. Then she boasted at the Guildhall that 'the [EU] bowling's going to get hit all round the ground. That's my style.'

That prompted Howe's memorable line in his resignation speech the next day about the difficulties faced by the Cabinet: 'It's rather like sending your opening batsmen to the crease only for them to find, the moment the first balls are bowled, that their bats have been broken before the game by the team captain.'

Recalling this, Howe chuckled and told me that years later a passer-by in Banbury had turned to his companion and said, 'Isn't that the chap who attacked Mrs Thatcher with a cricket bat?'

Metaphorically, he did, and the peroration was devastating: 'The time has come for others to consider their own response to the tragic conflict of loyalties with which I have myself wrestled for perhaps too long.'

That speech was an almost historic rejoinder to those who still recall Chancellor Denis Healey saying an attack from Howe, then shadow Chancellor, was 'rather like being savaged by a dead sheep'. Healey has since admitted that this was a deliberate diversion from 'some telling points' Howe had made. Howe told me that, years later, someone came up to Healey and him at the theatre in Stratford and said, 'We didn't know you two were friends.' In fact, Howe describes them as very good friends. Indeed, the Healeys were staying with the Howes when the two former Chancellors were spotted at Stratford.

The memory prompted Howe to lament the 'non-clubbability' of certain modern politicians. Talking of which, or whom, he complained about the complexity of Brown's tax and benefit system. A stickler for detail, with all his legal background, he says, 'It is completely beyond me to give any advice to anyone [about claiming benefits].'

He has advice for shadow Chancellor George Osborne, who is, he says, 'intelligent but not courageous enough' about attacking what Howe regards as 'the relentless growth of public spending as a percentage of gross domestic product'. Yes, just as in 1979, Howe wants 'a reduction in the tax burden'.

The point that really made me sit up came towards the end of our conversation, when Howe said he had often asked himself whether the Tory Party was better or worse off for Thatcher's disappearance. Could it have been better for her to lose an election? His answer to his own question was emphatically no. He concluded, 'John Major was too young to become Prime Minister, but deserves huge credit for consolidating Thatcherism. If Neil Kinnock had won [and he insisted he likes Lord Kinnock personally], Thatcherism would have been swept away – the prize was delivered by her resigning and not being defeated [at the polls].'

And whose resignation led to the resignation that saved Thatcherism...?

3. NIGEL LAWSON, MAY 2007

Nigel Lawson may be in idyllic semi-retirement in France, but he still has the stomach for a battle over climate change that could keep him in the headlines alongside his celebrity offspring.

The industrialist Sir Derek Hornby once related the following exchange: he was having a drink with Lord Lawson when his friend asked, 'Derek, you've got famous children, haven't you?' Hornby replied, 'Yes, I suppose I have – and a famous son-in-law.' (Sir Derek is the father of novelist Nick Hornby and father-in-law to novelist Robert Harris.)

Lawson pondered this, then asked, 'Do you find that people are more interested in your children than you?' (Lawson is the father of celebrity cook Nigella and journalist Dominic.)

Hornby considered. 'Yes, I suppose I do. It's rather nice, really.'

'So do I – and I was Chancellor of the Exchequer,' replied Lawson senior, with a twinkle in his eye.

Time moves on. Lord Lawson of Blaby, Chancellor of the Exchequer from 1983 to 1989, and before that a distinguished journalist on the *Financial Times*, the *Sunday Telegraph* and *The Spectator* (which he edited), is back in the news.

Lawson's contrarian stand on global warming has attracted much attention. His position is also more subtle than sometimes made out: he is quite happy to have fun by pointing out how often the scientific consensus of previous centuries was overturned by subsequent events and discoveries. But the gravamen of his attack is not so much his questioning of the science – Lawson is not in the George W. Bush denial camp – as his scepticism about the conventional view as to what the response should be.

When I told Lawson about this occasional series of interviews with former Chancellors, he quipped, 'You'll be on to Gordon Brown before long.' Having agreed to meet, he suggested that we do the interview in France, where he spends part of the year in what is, given his latest campaign, semi-retirement at most. The attractions of a trip to deepest Gascony spoke for themselves. And when I consulted about hotels, he and his wife Thérèse generously recommended Chateau Lawson.

No, it is not called that, but their converted eighteenth-century house – remote and peaceful at the end of an avenue of cedars near a deserted mill – used to be an Armagnac domain. When he is out there, the former Tory statesman relishes the old-fashioned, courteous way of life in the local towns and villages – a refreshing contrast to a Britain whose loss of much of that sense of repose may not be unconnected with certain aspects of the Thatcherite reforms behind which Lawson was such a driving force. If Nicolas Sarkozy has his way, that way of life could come under threat in France as well.

As it happened, the French were voting for a new President on the weekend when our rendezvous took place. Lawson was supporting Sarkozy, while his wife and I were on the losing side – not for the first time in political battles with Chancellor Lawson. He was a strong Chancellor with a first-class intellect, the sort of boss the Treasury admires.

One of the purposes of this series is to allow for reflection after contemporary controversies have died down. And there were plenty of those during Lawson's tenure – well and honestly documented in his brilliant memoir, *The View from No. 11*.

One of the many attractive things about Lawson – and I write as a commentator who was continually critical of his policies, while getting on well with him personally – is his directness. He did not wish to talk about his difficult relationship with Margaret Thatcher – 'I have said enough about that in my memoirs' – but he was at pains to set the record straight about the issue that eventually led to his resignation: the 'shadowing' of the Deutschmark, his advocacy of membership of the exchange rate mechanism, and the associated difficult relationship with Thatcher's economic adviser, Sir Alan Walters.

'People are puzzled that I proposed ERM membership and opposed European economic and monetary union. But EMU is not in Europe's interest and certainly not in Britain's interest. EMU is essentially a political step – a means of intensifying European political integration. In my view, there are some advantages, but there is no net economic advantage – indeed, there is a net disadvantage. But joining ERM was something I saw as a purely economic step.'

When the pound eventually entered the ERM, a year after

Lawson's resignation, the adventure lasted only two years and ended in political disaster. But Lawson now reveals that he intended it as a temporary measure: 'Membership only needed to last until we'd achieved a sufficient record in lowering inflationary expectations and overcoming our inflationary psychology.'

In which context he praised Mervyn King, the current Governor of the Bank of England, for attaching great weight to inflation expectations, and was especially interesting in commenting on the criticism he had received in the '80s for describing inflation as 'a blip' (when it turned out not to be) and as the 'judge and jury' (of monetary policy).

The Chancellor who did so much to promote monetarism in the early days reflected, 'Counter to the extreme monetarist view that you just control the money supply and that's what it's all about – even if you know what the money supply is – a lot of the remarks one makes as Chancellor are attempts to generate expectations in a favourable way. They are operational, not prediction.'

This struck me as a fair point, and of some interest to those who criticised him at the time. But the fact of the matter was that, on the inflation front, Chancellor Lawson ran into trouble. His failure to control inflation expectations, along with the 'Lawson boom' and the troubles with Thatcher and Walters, became the first draft of the history of his chancellorship.

When I had first asked him about 'regrets', he had insisted that he did not like to dwell on the past. He naturally regrets the events that led to his resignation, 'but I really don't believe in brooding, because you can't do anything about it. Indeed, for the same reason I don't even spend time thinking about things that went right. I believe in moving on – which is one reason why I am so involved in the climate change issue.'

Nevertheless, he courteously allowed me to return to the Walters issue and summed it up thus: 'Walters was extremely useful when he was at the Treasury full-time in the early '80s. He was outspoken as an adviser and rightly so [the Treasury had made sure that, although at No. 10, Walters was given all the relevant papers]. But when he returned as a part-time adviser he had become a minor public figure, making public statements that were incompatible with the status of an adviser.'

The focus of Walters's criticisms was the former Chancellor's obsession with the ERM, but it sounds as though, if Walters had been more aware of Lawson's real strategy – temporary ERM membership to cure inflation – things might have turned out differently. But, as Lawson says, no point in brooding.

Nevertheless, he believes that too little attention is paid in this country to economic history. 'If you look at past cycles, you understand a great deal more, not least about inflation.' This brought him to think aloud. 'Curiously enough, I missed out on the fact that we were embarking on globalisation. I was not aware how far it was going to develop. It's been extremely beneficial, and the emergence of China means that global inflationary pressures have abated to an immense extent.

'Of course, Gordon Brown claims the credit. I didn't see globalisation coming, but am glad it has. Perhaps I was excessively concerned with the problems of inflation at the expense of doing more on the supply side.'

But, let's face it, he did quite a lot on that front. Asked what he was most proud of in his chancellorship, he had no reservations: 'Playing a significant part in what I thought was the transformation of the British economy in a way that to a considerable extent has endured.

'What motivated me was that it seemed to me things needed

to change. It was a lot of hard work, but unrewarding work if things were to be undone by the next government. Therefore it was important to remain in office long enough so that what we did was not overturned. Broadly and to a considerable extent – not totally – that happened.'

In other words, New Labour, after all those years of opposition, broadly accepted the Thatcher/Howe/Lawson settlement.

This gave me the opportunity to make the point that all the familiar tales about Walters, the ERM and the problems with the Lawson boom have diverted attention from the fact that, like it or not – and some of us don't – Labour has not dared to reverse Lawson's amazing 1988 Budget strategy, when he brought the top rate of income tax down to 40 per cent and the basic rate to 25 per cent. Quick as a flash, he replied, 'Not yet they haven't.'

We were conversing on the terrace, with an idyllic view of the Gascon countryside. Things became even more idyllic when my host – it was now midday – gently suggested, 'Do you think we have done enough of this interview to treat ourselves to a drink before we go on?'

Your correspondent batted for England and gamely concurred. We had a glass of floc, a Gascon aperitif of white wine laced with Armagnac – apparently invented when overproduction of the local spirit threatened to drive the price down and new uses were required. But before the first sip, Lawson excitedly said, 'I've just remembered a Big Regret.' He repeated, 'A big, big regret.'

I put down my undrunk glass and took up my pen. 'I very much regret that Margaret prevented me from giving the Bank of England independence. I'd proposed it in 1988. It was fully worked out. It would have been much better for the Conservative Party if it had been implemented.'

As we sipped our floc, I reminded Lord Lawson – still not

yet fully retired – that he had once expressed a desire to retire to Greece. 'It was Mycenae,' he recalled. 'This is a compromise – halfway to Greece. I can speak the language – I can't speak Greek – and when we are here I can leave in the morning with the benefit of the hour's difference, fly from Toulouse and be in the House of Lords by lunchtime.'

Which brings us back to current preoccupations: Lawson's active membership of the high-powered House of Lords Economic Affairs Committee, which has already reflected his sceptical view on global warming. I got the impression that he would have liked at least half of our interview to be about global warming, but trust that he appreciates that there is still a lot of interest in the chancellorial history of the father of Nigella.

At any rate, he expatiated enthusiastically on the way he was attracted by the 'multi-dimensional' aspects of global warming – the science, the economics and the politics. Whatever the mounting scientific evidence, he believes the economic implications – the choices, the complications, the alternatives – are not fully understood.

'It has always seemed to me that the economic dimension is very important, but also very neglected. People thought that once the science was straightened out – and it is true that there is not a lot of scope for differences in the science – all would follow. But it doesn't. It is not at all clear what makes economic sense – or what is politically feasible.'

Lawson insists that the conventional view – urgent action now to help future generations – is unfair. 'How big a sacrifice is it reasonable to ask people today to bear, in order to benefit generations 100 years hence who'll be substantially better off than we are today?' he asks.

He is fully in sympathy with the Chinese for resisting the Kyoto-type approach. 'I understand their view entirely. I've no time for the Chinese regime, but they have a huge population, most of whom are extremely poor, and the most important thing is to lift them out of poverty because otherwise they'll die in large numbers. They need the fastest possible rate of growth, and that means the cheapest energy. The point is that the Chinese are not prepared to sacrifice the present generation for the generation 100 years hence, and that is absolutely understandable.'

The old Chancellor with a new cause is insistent: 'The idea that the European Union should take the lead [over global warming] and that the UK should lead within the EU only means we suffer, because we lead and others don't follow.'

He is quite determined, and fully aware of the risks to his reputation in the face of what has become a formidable and fashionable consensus. With that familiar twinkle in his eye, he added, 'As a superannuated has-been, I've got involved because political correctness makes it damaging for anyone in politics to speak out. I don't need to worry.'

Indeed, my host went on to say that he has had a big response from the public. 'My postbag, or should I say my email bag, has been overwhelmingly favourable.'

So there you are. Watch out, Nigella, Dad's back in town, and clearly only semi-retired in Gascony. And by the way, the Chancellor who surprised everybody by slimming drastically, and producing a related book on the subject, seems to his weekend guest to be in very good shape. Despite my age advantage on a man who recently celebrated his 75th birthday, I could not beat him at ping-pong.

4. JOHN MAJOR, JUNE 2007

Sir John Major, Chancellor of the Exchequer (1989–90) and Prime Minister (1990–97), has been back in the news recently – not so much for political reasons as for his widely acclaimed book on cricket, *More Than a Game: The Story of Cricket's Early Years*. He has also been prominently sighted at Test matches.

In the preface to his book, he takes a nice swipe at New Labour when he recalls the arrangement by which he and Kenneth Clarke would be kept up to date on the Test score at Cabinet meetings: 'When I was Prime Minister, Cabinet met on Thursday mornings at the same time as Test matches began. *In those days, Cabinet debated policy and took decisions so the meeting stretched on to lunchtime.*' (My italics.)

When he passed the note of the score to the Cabinet Secretary, Sir Robin Butler, and Chancellor Clarke, the Deputy Prime Minister, Michael Heseltine, would be driven 'to distraction'. As he says, Heseltine would see notes going to 'Prime Minister, Cabinet Secretary, Chancellor... was sterling crashing? Was there a crisis? A ministerial resignation? No, they were the Test scores: disbelievingly, Michael filched the notes from my blotter for the Heseltine Papers.'

Well, there might not have been sterling crises and dramatic ministerial resignations during the Clarke chancellorship (1993–97), but it was in the aftermath of one dramatic ministerial resignation (Nigel Lawson's from the Treasury in 1989) that Major became Chancellor, and another, that of Sir Geoffrey Howe from the Cabinet in 1990, that propelled Major to No. 10. And it was the crash in sterling, on Black Wednesday, that became one of the main folk memories of Major's premiership.

It is now ten years since Major left office and almost fifteen years since Black Wednesday, and one can detect a certain amount of frustration at the way the history of that period has been quietly rewritten. It was under Major's chancellorship that the pound entered the exchange rate mechanism (ERM) in October 1990 and it was under his premiership that the ignominious exit took place almost two years later.

One of the myths is that Margaret Thatcher was against entry. But, as *The Independent*'s political columnist Steve Richards recently reported, Major, in a rare public (non-cricket-related) appearance, told an audience at the London School of Economics in April that Thatcher had been 'extremely keen' to join the ERM because of the seriousness of the economic situation and, in particular, the recrudescence of inflation.

It is true that Thatcher had ruled out ERM entry many times during the 1980s. But, by 1990, the Cabinet felt it had run out of options. Ministers had tried everything else – assorted monetary targets, shadowing the Deutschmark – and failed. The recession of the early 1980s brought the inflation rate down from more than 20 per cent to around 3.5 per cent, but it took off again with a vengeance during what became known as the Lawson boom.

Major himself felt passionately about inflation. He thought that even the Treasury, where he had worked for two years as Chief Secretary – then a powerful job negotiating annual public spending limits with departments – did not understand how affected he was by childhood memories of hardship, which he associated with inflation.

In his memoirs, he complains that Lawson 'was not always sensitive to the frailties or needs of others. He did not know what it was like to run out of money on a Thursday evening, whereas I did.' The memory is still there in his new book. He refers to his regrets that his aged parents never saw him play cricket at school, with 'the struggle to make modest ends meet when the week outran the money'. For Major in his childhood, those who had no savings and did not own their own homes were the ones whose living standards suffered from inflation.

With inflation rising in the spring and summer of 1990 – the year-on-year increase in the retail prices index was 7.7 per cent in January, 9.4 per cent in April and 10.9 per cent in September – the discipline of the ERM had become the latest panacea. Those most closely involved recall that, when inflation reached 9.8 per cent in June and July, Thatcher changed her view. Indeed, one senior official recalls that, every time he saw the Prime Minister, she excitedly asked him when they were going to take the plunge.

It is difficult these days to meet anyone who does not claim that we entered the ERM 'at the wrong rate, at the wrong time and for the wrong reasons'. Yet polls showed a huge surge of opinion in favour at the time and Major's recollection is that Thatcher wanted an even higher rate than the DM2.95 chosen. Also, that John Smith, the shadow Chancellor, was twitting him week after week for not joining and that one Gordon Brown was also firmly in favour.

Perhaps what irks Major most is the widely held view (including in the modern Conservative Party) that membership of the ERM caused the high level of interest rates associated with the 1990–92 recession. Interest rates were already at 15 per cent before entry and had been at that level for a year. In his memoirs, Major cites the verdict of the highly respected former Bank of England economist Christopher Dow that the recession was the result not of the ERM, but of 'the rebound from the previous boom psychology … Collective, manic euphoria which pushed up prices and encouraged many to go into debt left the economy exhausted.'

Major likes to draw attention to the fact that interest rates actually came down during most of the period of ERM membership, from 14 per cent (entry had been accompanied by a 1 percentage point cut at Thatcher's insistence) to 10 per cent. On Black Wednesday itself, they were raised to 12 per cent, but the much-quoted increase to 15 per cent never actually took place. It was scheduled for the following day, but, of course, by that time, the reserves had been exhausted and the white flag hoisted.

In Major's view, previous governments' periodic successes in curbing inflation had collapsed in the face of political cowardice or, more politely, political reality. He has written, 'We entered the ERM to general applause and left it to general abuse. Yet membership turned Britain into a low-inflation economy...' He acknowledges that 'high interest rates and a weakening economy played a part in the fall of inflation and would have done so had we been in or out of the system. But the ERM gave credibility that our policy would otherwise have lacked.'

In effect, while believing the ERM has been wrongly blamed for the recession, he concedes that membership prolonged and deepened that recession and that this helped to contain inflationary pressures. But at what social costs! It was early in his chancellorship that Major said, 'If it isn't hurting, it isn't working,' and the anger with the way the Conservatives managed to preside over not one but two major (no pun intended) recessions between 1980 and 1992 understandably and justifiably lingers on, even if the years, selective memory and self-justification have clouded the circumstances.

Perhaps Major, in common with Lawson, always saw membership as a temporary affair? What seems clear is that he did not see it as Britain's route to the Eurozone. Indeed, he fought long and hard in incredibly difficult circumstances to obtain Britain's opt-out at the Maastricht meeting of December 1991. He saw and bargained with every other European leader in advance. It was probably only because the other leaders feared he would block the treaty that he secured an opt-out that has proved very useful indeed to Gordon Brown.

My impression is that Major never really wished to join the Eurozone, whatever the Eurosceptics thought, but he did not rule out the possibility that, if the financial markets had really taken against sterling, circumstances might have changed.

Black Wednesday was never forgotten or forgiven. My own view back in 1990 was the minority one that entry was a mistake. German unification and the associated problems with German inflation meant that it was just the wrong time to subject this country to the whims of the Bundesbank. Major himself is reputedly still very sore about the German central bank's disruptive tactics during the run-up to Black Wednesday. And many other things went wrong around the same time, such as the uncertainty about the outcome of the French referendum, which made the markets very jittery.

But Major remains just as sore about having been, in effect, in charge of a minority government – so great was the disruption from the old Thatcherites, led by the lady herself as a back-seat driver, opposing policies of which she had once approved, and the new Eurosceptical intake who had no folk memory of the Second World War and did their damnedest to wreck his efforts to be as close to 'the very heart of Europe' as British economic interests permitted.

In retirement, Major remains extremely busy – he has banking and business interests and is quietly involved in many charities. He was always a compassionate Tory and regrets not having faced up more to his right wing. He has strong views on the way the country was taken to war on a false premise and worries that New Labour has lost its soul. Major believes that, whatever the embarrassment of Black Wednesday, Blair and Brown had a much better economic inheritance than they have acknowledged. But one doubts whether Labour has given up on reminding the Tories about that humiliating episode fifteen years ago.

5. NORMAN LAMONT, JULY 2007

Norman Lamont was the most obvious political casualty of Black Wednesday. As Chancellor of the Exchequer and Prime Minister, Lamont and John Major together presided over the fiasco of our membership of the European exchange rate mechanism being officially 'suspended'. Lamont offered to resign at the time – but 'not too insistently', according to a member of the Major camp. The following spring, the Chancellor was sacked from the Treasury.

Major offered him the post of Environment Secretary. There is a passage in Sir John's memoirs that made me sit up: on being offered Environment, plus continued use of the Chancellor's country residence, Dorneywood, Lamont declined. In Major's words, 'It was a stilted series of exchanges that illustrated the chill that had descended upon our relationship ... "Yes, Prime Minister." "No thank you, Prime Minister." "I wish to leave the Cabinet" were the only words he spoke. He turned and left. We have never spoken since.'

When I went to interview Lord Lamont at the Mayfair offices of Balli Group (of which more later), the first question I was bursting to ask him was, 'Major's memoirs were published in 1999. Is it still the case that you two are not on speaking terms?'

Lamont, once a candidate for the most loathed politician in the land, is a genial person. He grinned and said, 'No. Grass grows over the battlefield. We had to talk when the Black Wednesday papers were released [under the Freedom of Information Act in 2005].'

Why did they have to talk? 'We had to see if we could agree on what to say. Then we went to lunch. All was harmony. These things run out of steam. It was a long time ago. You can't go through life brooding about these things.'

There was a time when the Foreign Office was considered the second most important post in the Cabinet. No longer: the Treasury is the place. As for the Department of the Environment – well, certainly in 1993 it would have been such a demotion that for Lamont it was an insulting offer. Part of his resignation speech still lingers in the public memory: 'We give the impression of being in office but not in power.'

But the sacked Chancellor also said, 'I have been privileged to present three Budgets. All three achieved the objectives that I set for them. The first [1991] drew the sting of the poll tax; the second [1992], by introducing the 20p income tax band, helped us to win the election; the third [1993], unpopular though it undoubtedly was, made a significant step toward reducing our budget deficit.'

He was right. The poll tax had been hugely unpopular and contributed to the downfall of Margaret Thatcher. Labour, which was caught out by the clever way in which the Conservatives made hay of John Smith's 'shadow Budget' of 1991–92, were wrong-footed by Lamont's lower-rate band, which scuppered their own similar proposal. The 1993 Budget, whose fiscal rectitude was endorsed by Lamont's successor, Kenneth Clarke, not only reduced the budget deficit but, by so doing, gave Gordon Brown a happy fiscal inheritance in 1997.

There were wonderful echoes in Lamont's sacking of Nigel

Lawson's resignation. As he told *The Observer*, 'When Nigel Lawson was resigning, I wrote a letter to him saying he shouldn't resign over the ERM. Indeed, Giles Radice [now Lord Radice, then a Labour MP] asked me in the House why I was not resigning with Nigel. I said, "Because I don't agree with the ERM policy."'

So why did he accept a chancellorship whose main macro-economic aspect, apart from normal Treasury public spending duties, had become managing our membership of the ERM? 'I was agnostic – very mildly in opposition. After all, the ERM had existed since the 1970s and had been quite successful.'

It is an intriguing story. Lamont told a London School of Economics audience a few years ago, 'My own attitude was ambivalent. I was not involved in the decision to join.' (He was Chief Secretary to the Treasury at the time, concentrating on the control of public spending.) 'There was a very peremptory announcement at the Cabinet ... The day we joined the ERM, I met a senior civil servant in the Treasury and said to him, "What have we done this for?" And he replied, "Oh, for political reasons." I replied, "Well, I don't think I would like to have given up the flexibility of the exchange rate." I never imagined at that time that this decision was going to be one that would have such consequences.'

Although for many people Lamont's appointment as Chancellor was a bolt from the blue, he had in fact been Financial Secretary to the Treasury from 1986 to 1989 and Chief Secretary from 1989 to 1990. Indeed, he is the only person ever to have been Financial Secretary, Chief Secretary and Chancellor.

As Chancellor, Lawson had championed Lamont for promotion to Chief Secretary, although, as he says in his memoirs:

Margaret did her best to talk me out of it ... Thus it was that, little more than a year later, Norman was in a position to run

John Major's leadership campaign following Margaret's enforced departure, and to succeed John as Chancellor. If politics does nothing else, it develops an appreciation of irony.

Many observers concluded that Lamont became Chancellor as a reward for running Major's leadership campaign in 1990, but Lamont says, 'While I was hoping I might be Chancellor, that was not why I supported John Major or ran his campaign. We never talked about it.'

For Major, it was simple: of four possibilities, neither Chris Patten nor Ken Clarke had any Treasury experience. John MacGregor and Lamont were 'both credible candidates' (each having worked at the Treasury), but Lamont was still there 'and so was more familiar with current policy ... The case for a familiar face known to the markets and the City was very strong.'

That policy was essentially using the discipline of ERM membership to get inflation down. Lamont became increasingly unhappy with this approach as the recession took its toll, not least towards the end, in 1991–92. He would ask senior officials, 'Why are we conducting this policy?' As he recalled the other day, 'I remember saying we should suspend our membership to a senior civil servant, and he said: "This was in your manifesto in 1979, decided by the previous Prime Minister, the present Prime Minister, [and] the man who was Foreign Secretary then and now. We've been in for a year and a half – what makes you think you've got the right to abandon it?"'

Having accepted the poisoned chalice of the ERM, Lamont did not resign. I asked a senior Treasury official at the time, 'If he is so unhappy with your policy, shouldn't the Chancellor go?' To which the reply was, 'We can't afford to lose another Chancellor.'

Lamont's view is that if he had resigned immediately after

Black Wednesday, Major's position would itself have been shaky. It was Major's and the Cabinet's policy that had collapsed. Major told him, 'You are a lightning conductor for me.'

For Lamont, Black Wednesday enabled economic policy to be rebuilt 'out of the ashes'. He did not 'sing in the bath' on Black Wednesday itself, but, asked at a press conference in Washington a fortnight later why he was so cheerful, replied, 'Well, it is a very beautiful morning, but it is funny you should say that. My wife said she heard me singing in the bath this morning.'

This remark did not go down well with the British public. Nor did 'Je ne regrette rien,' which was a reply the following spring, during a by-election campaign at Newbury, to the question, 'Chancellor, which do you regret most, seeing green shoots or singing in the bath?'

To be fair to him, the context was the first signs of economic recovery, assisted by the lower exchange rate and lower interest rates that went with freedom from the ERM straitjacket. He had claimed to catch sight of 'green shoots' prematurely, and unseasonably, the previous autumn.

He had set in place, after Black Wednesday, the new monetary policy for which the independence of the Bank of England would eventually be the icing on the cake. As he says, 'It consisted of an inflation target, the institution of regular monthly meetings with the Governor, and regular inflation reports.'

But it was no good to him personally. He was intimately associated with the second-worst recession since World War II (and the worst to hit the south). 'I remember,' he told the LSE audience, 'several years later, after I had stopped being Chancellor, I got in a taxi and the driver said, "Mr Lamont, I saved your life! I was driving up St James's Street one day and you were crossing the street and a man in the back said, 'Five hundred quid if you run the bastard down.'"'

Lamont may have sung in his bath, but he certainly did not sing in Bath, where he chaired a meeting for European finance ministers and central bank governors shortly before Black Wednesday and failed to secure interest rate cuts from the Bundesbank that might have eased sterling's position with the ERM.

'This was a last resort,' he says. 'I knew what the constitutional position of the Bundesbank was and that they were not likely to yield to our demands.' (Which, he insists, were made on behalf of many other ERM members affected by high German rates, not just the UK.)

The ERM debacle was, he accepts, 'undoubtedly politically very damaging to the government. On the other hand, there is an economically strong argument that we did get the best of both worlds – very rapid deceleration in inflation – from 10.6 per cent in November 1990 to below 2 per cent four or five months after I left office. We did that with the ERM, and, when the mechanism had fulfilled its task, it then disintegrated.' Before I could raise objections to this rather Panglossian view (shared by the Treasury's chief economic adviser at the time, Sir Alan Budd), Lamont anticipated me, saying that a more gradualist approach would have run up against political hurdles. In effect, the ERM policy about which he had such reservations, and for which he suffered personally, got inflation out of the system in a way British politicians, without the straitjacket, would not have done.

I reminded him of his terrible remark that unemployment was 'a price well worth paying', to which he replied, 'The *Financial Times*, which condemned it, had said practically the same thing a few weeks before.' The fall in inflation 'could not have been achieved without an impact on output and jobs'.

As Chancellor of the Exchequer, of course Lamont was

closely involved with Major in the Maastricht negotiations of 1991, which led to the birth of the euro, from which the Major government obtained its famous opt-out. I suggested that until the eleventh hour the British government had hoped the single currency would be delayed indefinitely. Lamont is a diehard Eurosceptic, but he said, 'John Major, who had talked about being "at the very heart of Europe", sometimes believed it wouldn't happen. I was more strongly opposed to the euro, but was convinced that it would.'

Why his certainty about Continental intentions? Lamont recalled his first meeting with other European finance ministers: suddenly he was 'face to face with all these people who believed in Europe and believed in the political unification of Europe'. French finance minister Pierre Bérégovoy told him his children would live in 'a United States of Europe'. Does Lamont think this is still the plan, after the French and Dutch referendums that rejected the EU constitution? 'There is a huge political engine there. Look at the way they are pushing ahead.'

More trouble here for Cameron's divided Conservative Party, I thought, while the former Chancellor continued, 'The sad thing is that the single market [always the main British project] is not much of a reality.'

Lamont is very close to David Cameron, who worked for him during the dark days of Black Wednesday and hails from a very Eurosceptical background. Having earlier sung the praises of the economic policy that resulted from what some have since called 'White Wednesday', Lamont startled me again by saying, 'The other consequence was that it [the ERM affair] solidified British opposition to the euro. That, historically, may be seen as one of the major consequences.'

One of Lamont's genuine regrets is that, in common with so

many others in and around the Treasury, he had finally come to the conclusion that the Bank of England should be granted independence, but had been unable to persuade Major of the need for reform.

For some reason, this reminded me that someone very close to Gordon Brown had recently told me that Brown and Lamont had always got on well. 'Yes, I think I always had good relations with Gordon Brown. I've never seen him throw computers across the room or bite his nails. He's always been very straightforward with me.'

Then came an interesting elucidation of something he had alluded to in his memoirs: 'I did go and see Tony Blair and Gordon Brown about making the Bank of England independent. I said, "It is not my job to help the Labour Party, but I think the country needs it and I have failed to persuade the Conservative Party." Tony Blair said, "You don't understand the Labour Party."'

And then, with an old-fashioned gleam in his eye, Lamont said, 'The day before the announcement, Gordon Brown rang me up and said, "We've decided to take your advice."'

The former Chancellor had more advice for another former Chancellor: 'Gordon shouldn't underestimate Cameron.' Lamont said of his former speechwriter and political adviser, 'He is remarkably quick and clever.' (We were talking the day before Cameron caught Brown out at his very first Prime Minister's Questions.)

In addition to his membership (with Lord Lawson and others) of the House of Lords Economic Affairs Committee, Lamont has a dozen or so directorships or consultancies that occupy him – including his work for Balli, a private Anglo-Iranian industrial and trading company, which has led to his being chairman of the British Iranian Chamber of Commerce.

The West's relations with Iran are potentially a somewhat

hotter issue than Black Wednesday. Some final advice from Lamont: 'I'm not pro the Iranian government – not pro-theocracy – but war with Iran would be a disaster.'

Over a subsequent lunch, he gave me his strong views about how badly the US has handled dealing with Iran.

He seems fully recovered from the horrors of his final months as Chancellor in 1993, when, as Major says in his memoirs, 'Norman's credibility plummeted … His position was becoming untenable … I had no choice but to make a change.'

But the public may not, even now, have had a similar recovery. As I left the restaurant, the former Chancellor hailed a taxi for me. I said to the taxi driver, 'That was Norman Lamont.'

'I know,' came the reply, in rather menacing tones. I could not help wondering whether it was entirely fair that Norman Lamont had become the scapegoat for an entire government.

6. KEN CLARKE, OCTOBER 2007

Late in January 1994, a group of economic journalists were on their way into the Schweizerhof Hotel in Davos for a 'British dinner'. The principal guest was the Right Honourable Kenneth Clarke QC MP, Chancellor of the Exchequer.

Clarke had been Chancellor since May 1993, when he succeeded Norman Lamont, who took the (delayed) rap for Black Wednesday, and who for various other reasons had become accident-prone. Although Clarke had been around a long time – Paymaster-General in 1985–87, Chancellor of the Duchy of Lancaster in 1987–88, then successively Secretary of State at Health (1988–90), Education (1990–92) and Home Secretary in 1992–93 – he was a relatively unknown quantity to economic journalists.

'Has he agreed to see you?' asked one. 'No,' said another. 'I've made several requests for interviews, but they've been turned down,' said a third. 'I think he's too scared to see us,' opined another.

Now, it is an important part of this tale that Clarke did not know who else was going to be at the dinner. The arrangement in Davos is that people sign up for whichever dinner they like. At any rate, the relatively new Chancellor gave a dazzling performance, displaying a lot more flair for economic matters than he had been given credit for, and expatiating knowledgeably on a wide range of subjects, including Kemal Atatürk, founder of the Turkish Republic. At the end of the evening, those very same journalists could be heard saying, 'Amazing, what a performer. We've just been talking to the next Prime Minister.'

It was not to be. The Conservatives lost the next three elections (1997, 2001 and 2005). Furthermore, they consistently refused to elect as leader the one man who might have given them a fighting chance against Tony Blair and Gordon Brown, and all because of internal division over Europe, which could yet tear the party apart.

However, Clarke is bloodied but unbowed. When I saw him during the week that the Northern Rock crisis had temporarily panicked the government into seeming to give a blanket guarantee to all bank deposits, Clarke had been commenting all over the airwaves, and I kept thinking that the Conservatives fully deserved John Stuart Mill's jibe 'the stupidest party' for having tried to consign him to the wilderness.

He had been on the edge of the wilderness before. He was a Heath man – indeed, government whip for Europe in 1974 – more of a 'one nation' Tory than a natural Thatcherite. But Margaret Thatcher had regarded Clarke and Peter Walker as examples of 'people that it is better to bring in because they would cause more trouble outside'. Thatcher liked the fact that such characters 'fought their corner hard', and admitted that 'the left' (of her party) were better at presentation.

After Clarke had held various junior jobs, Thatcher decided by 1987 that 'he should be given a higher billing'. By 1988, he was at Health, where, from the left of the party or not, she found him 'extremely effective ... tough in dealing with vested interests and trade unions, direct and persuasive in his exposition of government policy'. But when he got to Education, Clarke disappointed his political mistress with his firm belief in state provision and his public dismissal of her advocacy of a pet proposal of the right's – education vouchers.

In those previous departments Clarke was in many ways blazing the trail for New Labour's policy of trying to make public services more efficient and more responsive to public demand. He was an active reformer and maintains in *The Chancellors' Tales* that the offer of the chancellorship by John Major was 'a bit of a surprise to me'. He also notes, 'I am sure the police service, the prison service and various other parts of the Home Office were happy to be spared the rather turbulent process of reform on which I thought we were due to embark.'

Having been noted by Thatcher as a possible successor – some time before his part, as the 'candid friend', in her downfall – and thought of by Major as a possible Chancellor in 1990, but ruled out partly because Major thought that Norman Lamont's previous Treasury experience would be important, Clarke arrived at the Treasury at the end of May 1993.

There were early, and rather engaging, gaffes. There was a reference to a nappy factory in the north that turned out not to exist. There were also suggestions that, by comparison with, say, Nigel

Lawson (Chancellor 1983–89), he was somewhat laid-back. But he was less relaxed than he appeared, and after all that activity by Lawson, and the unfortunate episode with the exchange rate mechanism under Major and Lamont, perhaps a more laid-back approach was no bad thing.

Clarke's chancellorship is rightly considered to have been a highly successful one from the growth point of view – indeed, Labour has a devious practice of including the years 1993 to 1997 in boasts about an unparalleled period of growth, as if Brown had been there in the Treasury with Clarke.

Perhaps less widely appreciated is the emphasis he put from the start on sorting out the public sector's finances. The emphasis on 'stability' predated Brown's arrival in 1997. Clarke once told me he soon lost interest in that chronic obsession of Chancellors, tax reform, 'when I discovered there would be losers as well as winners'.

But he was well experienced in the subject of control of public spending – indeed, he had been singled out by Lawson as one of the most effective members of what was then known as the Star Chamber. This was the ministerial tribunal that resolved differences between the Treasury's public spending supremo (the Chief Secretary) and spending ministers – described by Lawson as being 'as near to a coherent system as any government has achieved'.

In a characteristically cheeky way, Clarke has recalled, 'I knew that one way I might get more money out of the Treasury [for his own department] was if they thought that my fiscal conservatism could be turned to their advantage as long as they settled with me.' This experience stood him in good stead from the moment he became Chancellor. 'I had the advantage of becoming Chancellor in the aftermath of a great crisis,' Clarke recalled. 'We had not encountered one quite so bad, and the great advantage was that the Prime Minister could not sack two Chancellors.'

Although Clarke arrived at the Treasury some eight months after Black Wednesday, he maintains that things were still pretty black when he got there. 'My objective was to try to win back our reputation for economic competence and try for the Holy Grail of growth and low inflation.' He sat back, a picture of contentment in his office overlooking the Thames in the relatively new parliamentary extension opposite Big Ben, and said, 'I succeeded on both fronts.'

The veteran of the Star Chamber added, 'It sounds easy. The difficulty was that I had to concentrate almost daily on reducing the pressure on the public finances … Life was one long public spending round with my colleagues getting ever more distressed.'

Clarke recalled feeling quite embattled (a situation his personality is not averse to) with colleagues wanting to reintroduce tax relief for housing. The background was the period of negative equity and the collapse of housing prices in the denouement of the Lawson boom. 'Most of my colleagues wanted to pump up mortgage interest relief but I was determined to get rid of the subsidies that had contributed to the boom.'

In those early days, before the economy had returned to 'sustainable growth', he felt he was concentrating on the inflation target (inherited from Lamont) and his fiscal rules, whereas colleagues, opposition and press were demanding instant results. People forget how long it took for Clarke's chancellorship to be praised for the growth.

I asked whether he had ever thought what it might have been like if he, and not Lamont, had been Chancellor during the ERM period. Fascinatingly, he said, 'One day the full story of Black Wednesday will be revealed. Everything that ran up to it could have been avoided – [at least] there was a sporting chance that it could.'

Wow! Could he reveal all now? 'No. It's too soon. It would make people too neurotic.' In Clarke's view, the ERM disaster was caused by 'Lawson's mistakes in monetary policy' and 'loose fiscal policy. In the ERM we only reduced interest rates. The pressure on the exchange rate was because of loose fiscal policy and ever-mounting levels of public debt. This made it impossible to resist an exchange rate decline.'

He recalled wryly, 'Some thought we were protected by a Bundesbank guarantee. It should have been obvious we weren't. We should have taken advantage of the rules to have a modest devaluation. But there was a collective decision to do that only if the French did it too, and the French were not inclined to.'

We both recalled that the conventional view was that devaluation would lead to inflation, yet there was a sizeable devaluation in the markets during the early part of his chancellorship which boosted growth but not inflation.

'I gained the sense that inflationary pressure in the real economy was weakening all the time,' Clarke says. 'I did not believe that the devaluation would lead to wage inflation. I argued [with the official Treasury] that globalisation and the supply-side reforms must have done something to change the conditions of the 1980s. People in China were going to keep inflation down.'

Clarke is not so dismissive of economic forecasts as, say, Denis Healey: 'You need to have forecasts, but you must not believe either yours or anyone else's – and certainly not accept those based on ideology or the last economic downturn.' His 'feel' was right. As Major has pointed out, under the chancellorships of Lamont and Clarke, earnings – the main element in inflationary surges of the past – 'never rose by more than half the lowest rate of increase in the 1980s'.

Clarke was ahead of Brown in telling everyone that they must avoid 'boom and bust'. Sensible economics were sensible politics. He claims that his first 'unified' Budget in November 1993 set a record for the largest increase in taxation delivered by any Chancellor since the war.

He wanted to make the Bank of England independent in matters of monetary policy, but was prevented by Major. However, he prepared the way by making the Bank 'as open as possible'. In spring 1994, he began publishing the minutes of the monthly meetings of Chancellor and Governor. 'But I couldn't persuade anyone that they were genuine until they recorded that Eddie and I disagreed, by a quarter of a per cent [on the appropriate level of interest rates].'

He also put an end to Treasury censorship of the Bank's quarterly inflation report and the Governor's speeches. He wanted the Governor to become a public personality – but also that the openness should be taken more seriously than 'being "The Ken and Eddie Show"'.

It seemed a topical moment to ask him if he would have done what Brown did and hived off banking supervision. He was vehement: 'It never occurred to me to hive off banking supervision. This tripartite system [the Treasury, the Bank and the Financial Services Authority all having a role] does not work. The Bank of England's ability to have informal relations, the Governor's ability to get people into the Bank, was quite useful. With the FSA as regulator and the Bank responsible for "financial stability" we do not have a happy division. They all disagree with one another.'

There was a bank failure early in his chancellorship – that of Barings. He recalled that he was surrounded in Downing Street that weekend 'by minions trying to sell it [Barings] to banks in the Far East who were too sensible to buy it'. So, while the world was gripped by the way the oh-so-reputable Barings had been brought down by a rogue trader, the Chancellor went off to see Nottingham Forest play Queens Park Rangers. As he has put it, 'I got fed up after a time so I suggested to Sir Terence Burns [the most senior Treasury official], who was a very keen supporter of Queens Park Rangers … that we would be just as well employed if we went along to the ground and watched the game.'

Clarke said Mervyn King had been right to say a banking crisis was only a matter for the Bank if there was an impact on the real economy. As far as Northern Rock was concerned, 'Is this systemic risk? Yes, with a run on a bank this size.' He insisted that it was essentially a political judgement: 'The Chancellor is the leader.' According to Clarke, Alistair Darling should not have waited for two or three days of queues. The question was: 'Can we allow this panic to continue? The answer is "No".'

We got back to his own chancellorship, and to his belief that good economics was good politics. Did he think his Budget of 1997 had been too cautious – rather like the folklore surrounding Roy Jenkins's Budget of 1970, shortly before Labour unexpectedly lost the 1970 election?

'I had the same problem as Roy Jenkins – half the party didn't realise we were going to lose the election anyway … it was assumed I'd give money out on a grand scale – buy votes!' He claimed that neither he nor Jenkins fomented an already damaging political situation.

'The 1997 election wasn't fought on the economy. It was obvious that we were going to be massacred. We ran the worst election campaign that I've fought in since 1966. Conservative HQ was in a bunker. We were destroyed by internal war over Europe plus sleaze.' And another thing: 'The sleaze was exaggerated, but the civil war wasn't.'

That wasn't all. Clarke added something that your correspondent has certainly never heard before. 'I am not sure that John [Major] would have been able to form a government if we had won – because of the civil war.'

The Conservatives have had a succession of leaders since – but never Clarke, who is unashamedly on the 'wrong' side of the party's divisions on Europe.

In his memoirs, Major says that, despite Clarke's 'more enthusiastic pro-Europeanism, we rarely disagreed. If I had fallen under a political bus I expected Ken to succeed me, and had told him so.'

It was not to be, although personally I take a Churchillian view of Clarke, and still hope something will turn up for him. I wondered whether internal party opposition had caused him regrets?

'If I started losing sleep, I'd give the job up. I've only carried on because I've enjoyed it and still do. Unless my constituents decide they've had enough, I certainly intend to carry on. I'm enjoying the maverick stage of my career. I'm not talking about the leadership – I must have broken the record for standing for the leadership.'

AFTERWORD AND ACKNOWLEDGEMENTS

This book has been some time in the making, to put it mildly. It was first suggested to me at least fifteen years ago by two good economist friends, Meghnad (Lord) Desai and Robert Chote. Meghnad is a Labour life peer, and Robert was then an economic journalist, before he moved on to be director of first the Institute for Fiscal Studies and, later, the Office for Budget Responsibility.

Robert suggested a book on Chancellors, and Meghnad a book based on my old *Observer* columns. The problem was that Roy Jenkins had got there first with the early history of Chancellors, and the former Labour Cabinet minister Edmund Dell had written close to the definitive work on post-war Chancellors right up to John Major, who was Chancellor from 1989 to 1990 before becoming Prime Minister. As for recycling the columns, I felt, rightly or wrongly, that I should prefer to reflect in tranquillity on things that stood out in my memory, with occasional consultation of the files.

Then there were those, such as the Cambridge economist Bill Martin, whom I first met when he was working in the City, who were interested in memories of Fleet Street and the background to my journalistic career. Simon Holberton, whom I met when he was on the *Financial Times*, was in this camp, and both encouraged me to continue, having seen earlier versions.

My thanks are due to all the above, and to Alastair Macdonald, an old friend and former journalist and civil servant, for valuable comments at early stages. Peter Hennessy and Andrew Adonis, both former journalists, distinguished academics and now in the House of Lords, also read and commented on work in progress, as did Alun Evans, chief executive of the British Academy. Ed Balls also read early chapters, as did former Treasury Permanent Secretary Lord Macpherson. I was also encouraged to carry on by Richard Brown, the former IMF and Bank of England economist, who introduced me all those years ago to my wife.

However, several events intervened. First I was diverted by writing *The Prudence of Mr Gordon Brown* (2003); then by *Saving the World? Gordon Brown Reconsidered* (2012), followed by *Mr Osborne's Economic Experiment* (2014) and (jointly with David Marsh and Richard Roberts) *Six Days in September: Black Wednesday, Brexit and the Making of Europe* (2017). There was also what is known as 'the day job'.

My friend Helen Fry, one of the group of fellow coffee drinkers I meet regularly at Kenwood, suggested I get in touch with Mick Smith of Biteback, and that led to a meeting with my wonderful editor Olivia Beattie and colleagues at Biteback. They read what I had written so far and said, 'Nobody will be interested in your journalistic memoirs as they stand. They need a structure.'

When I told Ed Balls about this, he suggested that the memoirs should be rejigged under the title *The Nine Lives of the British Economy*. This went down like a lead balloon with Biteback, but it inspired them to call it *Nine Crises* etc.

I found it a daunting task to meet this brief, and in the modern world, where computers are essential, could not have married the memoirs with the crises without the invaluable help of my part-time secretary, Linda Knights, and my two older daughters, Clemency and Benedicta, who have been wonderfully helpful. Clemency, who took on the lion's share of the help in the latter stages, said encouraging her father to complete the task was like getting her son Nick to do his homework.

INDEX

22/3/19.